The Serpent and the Nightingale

The Serpent and the Nightingale

CECIL PARROTT

FABER AND FABER
3 Queen Square London

First published in 1977
by Faber and Faber Limited
3 Queen Square London WC1
Printed in Great Britain by
Latimer Trend & Company Ltd Plymouth

British Library Cataloguing in Publication Data

Parrott, *Sir* Cecil
   The serpent and the nightingale.
   1. Parrott, *Sir* Cecil 2. Diplomats—Great Britain
  —Biography
   I. Title
   327'.2'0924   DA585.P37

   ISBN 0-571-10869-5

To Hansi, Michael and Jasper

Contents

Illustrations

11

19 The pride of Prague Cathedral, the Wenceslas Chapel.

20 The pride of Prague, the Charles Bridge.

21 Draining the historic Bohemian fish-ponds.

22 *Yakee dar!* Peter Thomas arrives in Prague.

23 1968: Russian tanks in Wenceslas Square, Prague, under the statue of the saint. (*Associated Press*)

24 1968: Goodbye to culture! Russian tanks in the Old Town Square. (*Associated Press*)

FIGURES

BOOK I

Czechoslovakia 1945-1948

In the first volume of my autobiography, *The Tightrope*, I began by describing the five years I spent at the court of King Peter of Yugoslavia, and ended with my experiences during the war in Stockholm, where I eked out a precarious existence as head of the British Press Reading Bureau, my own invention. The Bureau's function was to provide a comprehensive coverage of the press and propaganda of the German and German-occupied countries. In 1945, at the end of the war, I was appointed Information Officer and First Secretary in the British Embassy in Prague.

1. Golden Prague 1945–1946

During my stay in Stockholm, I had begun to take an interest in another Slav country and its culture—Czechoslovakia. Whatever else the war might have brought me, this 'extra-mural' course in 'Bohemica' was to have a lasting influence on my future. With a knowledge of two Slav languages—Russian and Serbo-Croat—I had been rash enough to embark upon learning a third. Czech was a 'hard' language in more than one sense of the word, but I grew to love it—and to have a special affection for the people who spoke it, too.

I needed a Czech reader when I was building up my Press Reading Bureau and I applied for help to Dr Vladimír Kučera, the former Czechoslovak Minister in Stockholm, who had resigned after Munich and was now in exile in Sweden. When he warmly recommended his ex-Cultural Counsellor, Dr Emil Walter, who needed a job, I was happy to be able to offer him employment. A specialist in the culture of the Scandinavian countries who had translated the *Edda* into Czech, he became not only a valued member of our Bureau but a close personal friend as well. He was the shyest and most modest of men. It would be difficult to find a man more sincere and yet at the same time so withdrawn. In spite of his gentle and self-effacing manner, however, he had a blazing patriotic flame in his heart, rather like the lion on the Communist Czechoslovak crest today, which has a partisan's beacon fire in its vitals. Woe betide you if you defended the Slovaks (on whom he blamed the break-up of his country), or had an indulgent word for Germans or Hungarians.

Many times he asked us to his home in Djursholm where he and his dear wife, Ani, introduced us to the music of their country. She was the perfect Slav beauty, and her likeness was to be found in many paintings in Bohemia. The Czech historian Palacký drew a romanticized picture of his Slav ancestors as peace-loving and good and living in a golden age. Ani might have stepped out of his pages.

She was an accomplished pianist and, with her deft hands guiding my clumsy ones, we glided together through the whole of Smetana's *My Country*, his quartet *From My Life*, and the operas, *The Bartered Bride* and *The Kiss*. As a boy of sixteen I had once heard *Vltava* played in the old Queen's Hall by a ladies' symphony orchestra. But until I came to Ani's drawing room and played this and other pieces in the cycle, I had never appreciated the magical qualities of Czech music to the full. With her I seemed to see the castles mirrored in the waters of the river and take part in the wedding dance on its shores. And in *From Bohemia's Meads and Groves*, I was in a dreamland along 'the rich, fertile Elbe valley', to use Smetana's own words.

I loved the plays of the brothers Čapek also, and performances of *The Insect Play* at the Stockholm theatre or of *Mother* on the Swedish radio will always mean more to me than any performance of the same plays in Czechoslovakia. But the pleasure I had from the productions of *The Bartered Bride* and *Jenufa* at the Stockholm opera, excellent as they were, could not equal the thrill of hearing them for the first time in Prague or Brno.

Kučera used to send reports to President Beneš and his Foreign Minister Jan Masaryk in London on what he had learnt about conditions in Czechoslovakia under the Germans. As he had to rely on our diplomatic bag for his courier service, he used to bring his letters to me, written in English and left open, so that I could read them before sending them on. This was the political part of my 'extramural'. Later, when I was recalled to Britain for a brief consultation, he put me in touch with Masaryk and Jaroslav Smutný, the President's Chancellor. When one day I saw in the hall of the Czechoslovak government building in London a big, fattish man sitting on a table, gaily swinging his legs, his large, sad eyes twinkling roguishly, I had to pinch myself to realize that it was Jan himself.

Returning officially to London to prepare to take up my post as Information Officer at our Embassy in Prague, I was lucky enough to have as tutor in Czech no less a person than the accomplished announcer of the Czech services of the BBC, Ota Ornest, who was later to become Director of the Prague Municipal Theatres. We were soon busy reading Čapek's *Adam the Creator* together, a very prophetic play. It told how Adam had received from God the gift of creation and formed from dust a succession of human creatures most of whom, contrary to his intention, turned out to be either Communists or Fascists. The play ended with a tug-of-war between Right and Left, the bitter reality of which I was to experience myself in Prague from 1945 to 1948.

The war was not yet over and, although the Soviet army had crossed the Czechoslovak frontier on 18 August 1944 and German resistance was breaking down, I had no idea how long I should have to wait in London before Prague was freed.

Those days of suspense were fateful not only for me but for the young Czechoslovak Republic itself—still only twenty-seven years old. In 1939, few Czechs had doubted that in the end the Allies would defeat Germany and that they would be liberated. It was only half way through that they began to realize liberation might come from the east rather than the west. There was a secret agreement between the US and Soviet high commands that Prague would be occupied by Soviet forces and that the Americans would not advance beyond the town of Pilsen in western Bohemia. In the event, the Russians were so slow that General Patton's forces arrived in Pilsen four days before they reached Prague. Meanwhile, the Czechs, impatient for liberation, rose prematurely against the German garrison in the capital, and escaped massacre thanks only to the anti-Soviet Russian troops serving under the defecting General Vlasov, who had up to then been fighting side by side with the Germans. Prague radio, now in the hands of Czech patriots, sent out anguished appeals to the British and American troops. 'Attention! Attention! Calling the American units of General Patton! The Nazis are murdering innocent citizens. We need your help! I repeat: we need your help!' Most people in Prague, not knowing of these military agreements, could not understand why the American forces did not come rushing in to save them, nor did they know that Churchill, grasping the crucial political importance of the situation, had tried in vain to persuade Roosevelt to allow Patton to march ahead. Alas, the Czechoslovakia which I was to come to was to be a country mainly occupied by Russian troops, with only a comparatively small strip to the west held by the Americans. The rivalry between Russia and America for the control of Central Europe was well under way.

I was hoping that I would be able to join a party of Czechoslovak officials and British and foreign diplomats who were leaving by boat for Constanza and going from there by road to liberated Slovakia. Just before midnight one March evening, I was waiting with my bags packed and on the point of taking a taxi to the station when suddenly the telephone rang and I was told that the Russians had refused to allow us in. It gave me my first warning that henceforth it would be they who would call the tune in Czechoslovakia.

It was not until June that the Russians allowed our party to set out for Prague. We arrived in a big convoy of cars, passed by the historic battlefields of the White Mountain and descended into Prague's great citadel, the Hradčany Square. From its commanding heights I could feast my eyes on the longed-for Golden City which lay spread beneath in a blaze of beauty. In that brief moment I fell in love with Prague.

But now to business. I had never run an Information or Press Department before and now I had to build one up from scratch. When I came, there was so little room in the old Embassy at Thunovská 14 that my assistant and I could be offered nothing better to work in than its coal-hole. So highly did our lords and masters value public relations! Eventually I was allowed to rent separate premises for our office. I found a convenient flat in a house in the same street, and soon set about engaging local staff and organizing my new activities.

The situation in the country was still highly abnormal. Whenever we crossed from the Soviet to the American zone or vice versa, or when we entered or left the larger cities, Soviet sentries advanced menacingly and threatened to shoot at our windscreen if we did not halt at once. My Czech chauffeur, who for some unexplained reason seemed elated to be driving the British 'Press Attaché', treated the Soviet guards with contempt and I had to beg him to show them a little more respect. Shattered windscreens and bloody noses were no rare sight at these Russian checkpoints.

The Russians had made the mistake of sending very poorly disciplined troops into Czechoslovakia, an error which they did not repeat when they invaded in 1968. The troops in 1945, although welcomed by many of the population as liberating allies, treated them as an occupied people and behaved as I have never seen Russians do in Russia or elsewhere. It was rumoured that they seized private cars and shot people if they resisted. I think that I may have experienced just such an attempted 'take-over'. I was driving along a road in the country outside Prague when a Soviet soldier with a flushed face, who looked as if he had been drinking, rushed at me from a wood and tried to force his way into my car. When I struggled to push him out, he wedged his foot in the door and fumbled for his revolver. I thought my last hour had come but all he produced was a safety-pin! After an exchange of words I managed to dislodge his foot, press mine on the accelerator and dash off. What for us was a rarity was by no means uncommon for the Czech population. When I went out in the evening with Czechs in Brno, the capital of Moravia, they all carried revolvers.

The troops were often drunk. I once saw a Russian officer emerging from the Ambassador Hotel with his tunic unbuttoned, a Russian prostitute on one arm and a bottle of champagne in the other. I also went round some of the most modern and luxurious flats in Prague and saw how the parquet flooring in one was like a balloon because Russian officers billeted there had left the water taps on for the whole weekend. Some of the best rooms in a villa I visited which had been commandeered and used as a Russian hospital, were indescribably filthy and drawing-room curtains had been cut off with bayonets and used as rags for cleaning boots. In spite of Stalin's boast about the great advances attained by the 'workers' state', the Russians at that time were far behind the Czechs in living standards and the appreciation of cultural values.

Those first days in 'liberated' Czechoslovakia were unforgettable. The occasion was a very joyful one in spite of the shortages of food and other necessities. The universities had been banned since 1939. Schoolteachers and sixth-formers had been driven into factories through total labour mobilization. The Prague National Theatre and other theatres had been closed down. In the concert programmes Wagner was an obligatory component, with some of the most treasured Czech music proscribed. Now it had all changed overnight.

Not long after my arrival, I went along to the reopened National Theatre. The opera to be performed that night was Smetana's *Libuše*. The theatre's motto was 'The Nation to Itself', and now once more it was able to resume the role for which it had been destined.*

The occupation and dismemberment of the country by Nazi Germany in March 1939 had aroused an upsurge of national feeling among Czechs, who stretched out defenceless arms in the desperate hope of preserving what still remained of their sacred national

---

* Soon after its original opening in 1881 it caught fire and had to be rebuilt. As the Austrian authorities would not pay for it, the money had to be raised—twice—by public subscription.

heritage. Thus in the early summer of that year, the 'Musical May', as the Prague Spring musical festival used to be called, was turned into a national 'manifestation'. Under the baton of Talich, the great Czech conductor, the performance of Smetana's tone poem *My Country* and his opera *Libuše* evoked a deep, heartfelt response. Never was a nation so much at one. From that moment Czech national music was inevitably suspect in Nazi eyes.

When the liberation came in May 1945 and the government and most of the exiles had returned from abroad, it was with thankfulness and emotion that the nation celebrated its newly won freedom by producing operas which had been forbidden under the Nazi occupation.

At the opera there was a very representative audience including President Beneš and members of his government and the Diplomatic Corps. This opera has one notable feature. In its closing scene Prague's founder, Libuše, who according to legend was chosen by the Czech people as their judge because she had the power of sooth-saying, prophesies a great future for her city. But she warns her people that they will have to go through many trials and tribulations. The climax of the opera is Libuše's unforgettable invocation, sung fortissimo: 'My dear Czech people shall never die. They shall gloriously overcome the horrors of hell.'

I did not know all this at the time and when we reached this passage I was rather startled to find that the whole audience, including the President, was suddenly standing up. At first I thought that the President had to leave early, although it struck me as curious that he should be doing so at this point in the performance. The truth was that it was an occasion of the greatest solemnity. *Libuše* was their most national opera, composed by their most national composer, and having so often in their history—and so very recently—faced the 'horrors of hell', they all rose instinctively in a prayer of thanksgiving for their deliverance.

Another of the operas which was revived soon after the liberation was Dvořák's *The Jacobin*, in which a young Czech nobleman, Bohuš, is forced to leave Bohemia for France towards the end of the eight-eenth century. After the outbreak of the French Revolution he is falsely accused of being a Jacobin. On returning to Bohemia he and his wife Julie sing a poignant duet: 'In foreign lands we have been roaming—for many, many years alas', followed by the refrain: 'Only in song, only in song could we find our sweet relief.'

Again I was struck by the audience's emotional reaction. There were few dry eyes around me. Many of those there had experienced the bitter fate of being exiled and slandered, something which I now feel I share with them.

If it was a jubilant time for Czechs in Prague, it was also exhilarating to be British in those early days. The Czechs were overjoyed to see us after having been separated from the west for so long, and soon there were many on the streets in British battle-dress who had come home after war service in Britain, and to whom we could turn if we lost our way or could not cope with the language. I think there must have been at least three Anglo-Czech clubs in Prague and we were always being asked to patronize them. Soviet influence, however, was also strong and pervasive.

By refashioning the political party system, suppressing some parties and encouraging others, Beneš and the Communists had shifted Czechoslovakia's political axis dangerously towards the extreme left and brought it within the range of Soviet influence. The sixteen parties in the pre-war Republic were reduced to only six, two of which were the Communist parties of Czechoslovakia and Slovakia. The Communists had agreed to forego the premiership because they knew they could rely on the future Prime Minister, Zdeněk Fierlinger, a left-wing Social Democrat. But they took over the Ministries of the Interior (police), Information and Education (propaganda), Agriculture (the peasant vote) and Social Welfare (the working-class vote). And some of the other ministers, although not nominally Communist, were obedient fellow-travellers.

The Communists owed their strong position not to voting strength but to the support of the Soviet Union, whose forces occupied most of the country for the first six months or more. Moreover, by design Communist-dominated 'national committees' had been set up in the wake of the advancing Soviet troops under the supervision of the Soviet forces and Moscow-trained Czechoslovak *politrucs*. Gottwald, the leader of the Czechoslovak Communist Party, had from the very beginning insisted that the national committees should be assigned an important role in the future constitution and saw to it that Communists were allotted key positions in them. They had of course been originally intended as 'Soviets' and were designed to replace the traditional Czechoslovak parliamentary institutions.

Thanks to its control over the Ministry of Information the Communist Party had all the media at its disposal—press, radio and film.

Establishing itself in the Ministry of the Interior it was also able to
control the internal 'security' of the country and dispossess all who
could conveniently be labelled Fascists, while its hold over the trade
unions gave it almost unlimited power in the factories. The Communist Minister of Agriculture had the task of carrying out the
break-up of the larger estates and the sequestration of property held
by Germans or collaborators. By favouring the lesser farmers in the
redistribution of land and feather-bedding them, the party considerably enhanced its voting strength in the country districts at a
time when the Agrarian party, the traditional peasant party, was
proscribed and powerless.

Communist prestige undoubtedly stood high in the country at the
time. Many Czechs had been bitterly disillusioned by the collapse
of the old regime. Some had suffered terribly in Nazi concentration
camps. The Germans were detested, as we have seen, and the west
was not altogether trusted. At difficult times under the Austro-
Hungarian monarchy the Czechs had looked with vague hopes
towards their 'Slav brother' Russia. Under the Nazi occupation
many turned to the Soviet Union for liberation. Some were so
deluded as to think that the First Republic had proved itself unequal
to the Munich crisis and that Communism offered a new and surer
approach. They were prepared to believe that the Soviet Union
would prove a more trustworthy ally than the western powers had
been. To many the Soviet Union was identified with progress and
the Communist Party appeared to offer a new approach in comparison with the traditional parties which seemed bent on putting
the clock back.

My Information Department rapidly expanded. I came with one
assistant and soon had three female secretaries and a language
expert who translated the newspapers for the Ambassador and the
senior staff. A good while later I acquired several higher-powered
helpers: an Assistant Information Officer and Press, Film and
Broadcasting Officers. I even did the British Council's work for
them at the beginning because they only sent out to represent them
a girl who had been working as a secretary for the Czechoslovak
government in London. One day, when I was entertaining one of
the Czech announcers in the BBC, the lady in question disengaged
herself from the bar and asked me who the gentleman was I had
been lunching with. I asked her why she wanted to know. She was

greatly confused. Some time later she defected to the Communists and was by no means the only member of the Council staff to do so. My eyes were opened at a very early stage to the operations of the Communist intelligence services.

We eventually rented a large reading room down in the town (the former Čedok building in Na Příkopě), exhibited a daily British news bulletin in the windows, built up a film library and issued a British magazine. Now that I had an adequate staff, I could do what I most enjoyed and drive around the country speaking or lecturing.

This kind of life, where I lived away from the main Embassy but was within a stone's throw of it, offered me the best of both worlds. Unlike the Secretaries in the Chancery I was not at the beck and call of the Ambassador. My chief, Sir Philip Nichols, after some initial doubts, came to regard me with a more tolerant eye. He did not want to be involved with press and publicity work and was chary of intervening in anything I did. We soon became good friends and he did a great deal to help me get started in the Foreign Service. But at this point I was not fully established and was working for the Ministry of Information, a wartime Ministry which would soon be wound up.

While the Ambassador and his chancery dealt with Beneš and those ministers who had been in England throughout the war, my work lay principally with the media and with the Communist-ruled ministries of Information and Education, whose leaders had spent the war years in Moscow. The Minister of Information, Václav Kopecký, was a hard-line Communist who held a high place in the party hierarchy. There had been a famous puppeteer called Kopecký, and the Minister not only prided himself on being his descendant but bore a strong resemblance to his marionettes. He was an irrepressible, bouncy little man, delighted in gossip and vulgarity, indiscreet and provocative in his public speeches and an inconsequential prattler in private. To me he was always friendly—indeed his face seemed to light up when I spoke Czech with him. Whenever we met during the interval of a play he would reel off a long list of British authors whom he loved and had allegedly read. Among them, of course, Dickens had pride of place. Sometimes the Minister's memory failed him and he quickly passed to another topic. But he loved to air the little knowledge he had.

At one time, by a curious coincidence, this little upstart and one of the oldest members of the Czech nobility were living in the same palace in Prague. The aristocrat was Countess Waldstein, who is said to have lived till she was about a hundred. As the Waldstein palace in Prague—which was among the finest early baroque buildings in the city—had been built by the great generalissimo himself (more commonly known as Wallenstein), she as the descendant of a collateral line was permitted to occupy a small flat in it, even though it had been requisitioned by the Minister of Information. Other members of this distinguished family had been host to Casanova when he wrote his diary and had inspired Beethoven's famous sonata. Kopecký had his moments of kindness and tolerance and made no attempt to evict the old lady, but found her a hard nut to crack, as he told me himself. 'When I met the old Countess one day,' he said, 'I asked her: "Why do you spend all your time shut up here, Countess? A fine lady like you should go on the streets of the Wenceslas Square and show yourself off a bit!" "I should like to, Mr Minister," was the quick retort, "I should indeed. But I'm afraid of those frightful Bolsheviks!"' The fact that Kopecký recounted it to me with enjoyment showed that he at least had a sense of humour.

The other Ministry with which I had many dealings was the Ministry of Education and Culture and was headed by a markedly different type of man, Professor Zdeněk Nejedlý. In contrast to Kopecký, who was only forty-eight and still virtually unknown to the Czech public, Nejedlý was sixty-seven and had made himself famous, if not notorious, in pre-war Bohemia. He was an eminent musicologist who had made a valuable contribution to musical scholarship with his researches into the Hussite chants and the composers Smetana and Fibich. But he must have held a record among authors for uncompleted works. He began a life of Smetana, but after four volumes the composer was still living in his father's brewery, the author having got stuck in the history of medieval Czech breweries! Then came immense biographies of Masaryk and Lenin, similarly uncompleted.

His worst vice was his highly partisan, not to say vindictive, approach, which impaired his reputation as a scholar. As a young man he had pushed his romantic adulation of Smetana so far that he began to acquire the reputation of being a monomaniac. But what he had been powerless to do as a private individual, he achieved as a Minister, when he forced Smetana's works down everybody's gullet whether they liked them or not.

He also made the mistake of elevating a little-known composer, Fibich, to an exaggerated position far above Dvořák and pronouncing him 'the greatest opera composer of world literature in the time of Wagner'. One might have given him credit for standing up for Fibich, who indeed wrote some lovely music, if his adulation of him had not been so grossly overdone and if in the process he had not started a hate campaign against Dvořák and the whole of Dvořák's school, including Suk, the composer's highly gifted son-in-law.

Nejedlý was indeed the field-marshal in the ridiculous Smetana-Dvořák war which racked Bohemia's musical and political life for so long. He fired the first shots as long ago as 1901 when he declared that Dvořák's music was 'simple', conservative and suitable only for dilettantes. Proof of this was the success Dvořák had enjoyed in England! After Dvořák's death in 1904 he redirected his fire against the great composer's pupils, Suk and Novák. Suk's music was damned with faint praise and the composer himself even accused of being Austrophile. This grotesque personal vendetta could hardly have survived the Second World War had not Nejedlý joined the Communist Party and been swept into the government as Minister of Culture in 1945, where he found plenty of scope for his dogmatism and prejudice. His last sortie was his assault on the great conductor Talich, known for his inspiring interpretations of Dvořák, whom he banished from Czech musical life for the first year and a half of my stay in Prague. It was infuriating to find that the man I had come to Prague to hear conduct, was, like the works of Mozart, erased from all concert programmes.

Nejedlý, who was hunchbacked and wizened when I knew him, would have made a splendid Kopecký puppet too! Certainly his dry, squeaky voice and his academic gobbledygook would have made excellent material for an impersonator like the brilliant Russian Arkadii Raikin, if Russo-Czech relations had permitted it.

It was a tragedy that this gifted man had gone off the rails: a tragedy for him and a torment for the Czech people. How had it come about? Some people whispered that he had been Suk's rival for the hand of Dvořák's daughter, Otilie, and when she rejected him in favour of the composer, he had got his revenge by taking it out on her whole family. It was not irrelevant that he was utterly lacking in a sense of humour. In this Kopecký had the edge on him.

I only managed to talk to him once in the 1960s, when he was over eighty and practically gaga. We spoke about Mozart and he commented drily: 'You see, I always maintained he was not a Czech composer. . . .'

Many if not most of the leading Czech and Slovak writers of the period were Communists or had Communist leanings, and the Party was well represented in the arts in general. Two of the most eminent Czech poets, František Halas and Vítězslav Nezval, were Party members and were departmental heads in the Ministry of Information. Both came from Moravia, that blessed land which has nourished so many poets and musicians as well as the founding fathers Comenius and Masaryk. Halas, one of the greatest Czech lyric poets, had a gentle character and was quite devoid of political prejudice. Nezval, the outstanding surrealist poet of the 1930s, was much more ebullient. His poetry flowed as spontaneously as Dvořák's music and when in 1936 he felt the doctrine of surrealism was a straitjacket on his verse, he published fifty-two beautiful poems under the name of the 'unknown student Robert David'. Like many other leftish Czech poets, he was much influenced by French and western poetry.

From a ministry presided over by poets and artists one could hardly expect much efficiency. My first step was to call on these various dignitaries, and I started with Nezval, who was Head of the Film Section. To my surprise, I found myself in a kind of glass palace which appeared to be completely uninhabited. I walked along corridor after corridor: I could only hear the sound of my own footsteps and there appeared to be no staff whatsoever. At length I stopped in front of a glass door, behind which I seemed to hear heavy breathing. I listened and wondered whether the breather was listening to mine. Then I gently knocked. At this, there was a tremendous racket, like the clatter of encyclopaedias falling on to the floor, and when I pushed the door open, I saw, half-lying before me, the corpulent figure of the poet himself, his hand raised to welcome me. I shook it warmly. In his sudden rush to greet me—he was an impetuous man, full of goodwill—he had fallen down but he could still, at least, grasp my hand.

Communist journalists readily attended my press conferences and parties. I must here make a terrible confession which *Rudé Právo* will certainly wish to note. When we first were in Prague, the diplomats, none of whom knew Czech, were quite in the dark about what was going on. (The government had not yet started to send out bulletins in English.) And so I used to distribute copies of our own review of the Czech press which was a quality document, brilliantly executed by a valued member of my staff. The Scandinavian Ambassadors, with whom I was in close contact because my wife was Norwegian, used to give us presents of cases of schnaps. I served this at my press conferences and the journalists then wrote very nice things about us. Their reports were carried in our review and the Ambassadors were impressed and gave me more schnaps. The majority of the reporters who attended these conferences were Communists. But journalists are human after all!

Many of the Communists I knew in Czechoslovakia in the mid-forties were not what I expected Communists to be like. They did not cold-shoulder the west: on the contrary, they were interested to learn about anything we were doing that was progressive especially in the spheres of social reform or education. Indeed the Health Service which Czechoslovakia adopted was ultimately modelled on our own. Communists were often seen climbing the steep hill to my office, which lay at the foot of the Castle steps, to get our books and publications, read our newspapers and borrow films from our film library. I was justified in feeling that British information work was a valuable activity in the Czechoslovakia of those days.

The Czechoslovak Communists were a great contrast to their Soviet counterparts. They had behind them years of democratic parliamentary practice, which Russian Communists had never had, and, unlike the Russians, they took democracy for granted. They were civilized and cultured, having been educated at Czechoslovak schools and universities, which were traditionally of a high standard. While in Russia many of the writers and artists were non-Party or unimportant in the Party hierarchy, Czech Communist intellectuals were at that period in influential posts in government and Party, and enjoyed the support of many other leading artists, writers, painters, actors and musicians. It was one of the secrets of the success of Communist propaganda in Czechoslovakia. The men who conducted it knew how to do the job.

Unluckily these men were idealistic and naïve enough to believe in a specifically Czech road to socialism, and many paid the penalty, languishing in gaol in the 1950s. Present-day western Communists— Italian, French and British—might take warning from their example. Nonetheless, I was nauseated by the Communist claptrap which poured out daily in the numerous Communist newspapers and journals, and which these intellectuals had not the courage to disavow. Above all, I hated the arrogance of the Communists: 'We shall be King of the castle. Get down, you dirty rascal.'

One of the young journalists I met at this time was Miroslav Galuška, a member of the staff of the leading Communist paper, *Rudé Právo*, who was to become head of the Press Department of the Czechoslovak Ministry of Foreign Affairs, Ambassador in London and finally Minister of Culture until he was swept from that post by the Soviet invasion. At that point he had a passion for everything Soviet. He gave me a blatant Soviet propaganda book called *Warmongers* or *Butchers of History* or something like that and invited me to come and see his editorial office to convince me that it was not the inferno I took it to be. He took me to see his editor, who proved to be affability itself, and as I looked out of his window over the buildings of the New Town (built by Charles IV in the fourteenth century) I could hardly believe I was really in the offices of our 'arch enemy' and was not dreaming. Although the newspaper continued to print venomous attacks on British policy, those in charge of it appeared to be friendly, reasonable men.

I said goodbye to my host and climbed into one of the 'paternoster' lifts used throughout the *Rudé Právo* building. These are open wooden lifts, which operate in continuous rotation as though on an assembly line. Unfortunately just as I was descending, the bell rang and all work stopped. The electric current was switched off and I was left hanging between the second and third floors. I was not in danger but had to retreat from the Communist Party headquarters in a rather undignified manner, scrambling with some difficulty out of the lift.

As was to be expected my visit did not check the flow of *Rudé Právo*'s hostile propaganda. But one day there was a startling development. I can best recount it by quoting from an article published by the People's Party's cultural weekly *Vývoj*.

Parrott sincerely likes our country and the Czech and Slovak people, but he does not hesitate to protest strongly against certain excesses in a section of the Czech press in connection with the publication of information and tendentiously untrue commentaries on British policy. *Rudé Právo*, which criticized very unfavourably Parrott's 'interference in the internal political affairs of Czechoslovakia' thought to teach the press attaché a lesson and invited him to write an article himself on India and British Imperialistic policy. Parrott wrote the article immediately and wrote it well; and *Rudé Právo* willy-nilly published the first objective and reliable article on the problems of India. . . . All the best, Mr Parrott!

What exactly was my undiplomatic 'interference' in the domestic affairs of the country? An editor of a friendly newspaper, *Lidové Noviny*, the *Guardian* of Czechoslovakia, published an interview with me, in which I complained of the way *Rudé Právo* had attacked our Foreign Secretary, Ernest Bevin, and our policy in India. As a result, with some sour comments from the Communist press, I received an invitation from the editor of *Rudé Právo* to contribute an article justifying British policy. The editor was as good as his word and the article was indeed published, with equal space given on the same page to an article from an Indian nationalist attacking British policy. It was fair enough. In what other country at that time could one have read the official British viewpoint in the main Communist Party organ? Later, when I met the editor after his release from gaol, he told me that he had got into serious trouble for what he had done and this figured among the charges levelled against him at his trial.

This act was not the only mark of sympathy which I received from the Communist press. The Communist cultural weekly *Kulturní politika*, edited by the gifted writer, composer and stage director, E. F. Burian, published the following remarkable write-up by A. Liehm, later a literary rebel against Novotný and a 'reformer':

Every Saturday in the editorial office you will get a small neat parcel containing the most valuable press material. Accompanying it is a card on which you are pleasantly greeted by the Press Attaché of the British Embassy. . . . This is not merely English politeness. Mr Parrott is the type of modern diplomat who knows what propaganda is, and of what importance it is even for such a great empire as the British in a country as small as ours. . . . You can ask our press, our film people, our publishers and anyone else you like if they do not know him, and if they knew anyone he has not accommodated in some way as though it were a matter of course.

Curious words about a person who had had no experience of public relations and who hated propaganda!

2. Treasons, Stratagems and Spoils 1946–1948

But the happy days passed, and the political scene began to darken. The first parliamentary elections took place in July 1946. The Communists, while emerging as the strongest party, failed to obtain an overall majority, mainly because of their heavy defeat in Slovakia where the Slovak Democratic Party secured sixty-two per cent of the votes. What was decisive was that in Bohemia and Prague the Communists were now in the majority and Klement Gottwald, their leader, became Prime Minister. However, the results did not quite match up to Communist hopes. They could only command a majority in the National Assembly if all the Social Democrats voted with them.

The next elections would not be held for two years and the Communists redoubled their efforts to achieve an overall majority, stepping up their demagogic agitation to a level at which they began to alienate voters and jeopardise their chances. A defeat in 1948 would have been an unacceptable blow to their prestige and that of their protector, the Soviet Union.

In 1947, relations between east and west deteriorated. In March came the 'Truman doctrine', by which the USA promised aid to the 'free peoples whose liberty is threatened'. In April, the four-power negotiations on Germany broke down. In France and Italy the Communist parties ended their three years' participation in the governments and went into opposition. In Czechoslovakia that summer there was a very bad harvest and a great shortage of grain. The overall food situation grew worse and even we, as diplomats, were affected by shortages of milk, butter, fresh vegetables and coal. Czechs rushed off to Slovakia to replenish stocks of butter, but, by the time we got there, there was none to be had. Eggs were in such short supply that we decided to get two hens from Slovakia and keep them in our garden. To our chagrin both birds turned out to be cocks when they came and made such a noise that the neighbours complained! In June there was the American offer of Marshall Aid under a European Recovery Plan followed by Stalin's refusal to allow the east European governments to accept it.

This last event broke like a thunder-clap in the country. The effect on the morale of the majority, which had up to that point been confident and buoyant, was shattering. The decision to attend the Marshall Aid Conference in Paris had been taken by the whole government, including Gottwald. Stalin's blunt intimation that if Czechoslovakia took part the Soviet government would regard it as a hostile act, struck a chill into the hearts of the people and brought home to them once and for all that they were no longer sovereign.

When this news was announced, I was on holiday with my family at a lakeside hotel at Medlov in Moravia. Among the other visitors there was a People's (Catholic) Party deputy, Bohdan Chudoba, who had seen the writing on the wall and was already anticipating exile. One day when I was out in a rubber dinghy with a red sail in glorious weather, my wife asked him where I was and he replied: 'The British Press Attaché was last seen sailing downstream under the Red Flag.' It was characteristic of the mood of the Democrats at this time, who regarded the British as too indulgent towards Communism. By the autumn of 1947, Stalin's ultimatum had begun to affect the local political scene. The Democratic parties were starting to panic as the Communists grew more and more domineering.

The establishment of the Cominform, which was designed to coordinate and intensify the struggle against the 'Imperialists', helped to make the already highly charged atmosphere still more explosive. The Czechoslovak Communist leaders had evidently received secret orders from Moscow to give up the idea of establishing their own road to socialism and to accept the Soviet one. The political struggle sharpened. Jan Masaryk and two other non-Communist Ministers received letter bombs, for which each political camp held the other responsible. In the worsening situation the Communists had the upper hand: control of the police, the ability to neutralize the army and, if necessary, Soviet armed support. Above all, as a party, they were monolithically solid and professionally organized. Their hold over police and factories was absolute and here lay the key to their final victory. The Democratic parties were disunited, disorganized and very shortsighted. The main anti-Communist Czech party, the National Socialist Party, did not trust the main anti-Communist

Slovak party, the Slovak Democratic Party, and would not rally to its defence when the Communists launched an all-out attack on it. The Social Democratic Party, which held the key voting position in the government and the Assembly, was split into pro-Communist and anti-Communist factions and its support could not be relied on.

It was at least some comfort when on 17 November elections were held in Brno for the leadership of the Social Democrats and the pro-Soviet Fierlinger was ousted and replaced by the more moderate but, alas, equally untrustworthy Laušman. After his defeat, Fierlinger is said to have arrived unannounced at the President's country seat of Sezimovo Ústí. Here he openly accused the President of having influenced the election against him and threatened that he would be held personally responsible for the consequences. This apparently upset Beneš so much that he had a stroke. It was his second one and affected his speech and his capacity for resolute action. So the man who should have been the strong arm of the Democratic parties was at this stage not fit enough to play the role expected of him.

My Ambassador told me at about this time that Beneš had said that he was absolutely certain of the army's loyalty to him. In the event he never put it to the test. But as he had not taken the precaution of ensuring that he had people in the higher military echelons on whom he could rely, it seems doubtful whether he could have mobilized the army, even if he had wanted to. Twenty years later Dubček too was to fail to take the necessary measures to prevent a Soviet military attack.

The tragedy was that the President, as the Communists well knew, was a champion of the old League of Nations, a man of peace, and anxious to avoid civil disturbance. The Communist leadership, on the other hand, had nothing to lose by confrontation as they could count, if need be, on covert—or overt—Soviet military support. Moreover, they knew by this point that the west would not intervene to save their opponents. The only possibility for the Democrats was a solution within the rules of parliamentary government. Thanks to their strong position in government and parliament and their well-organized grass-root structure, the Communists could not only take up the battle within the framework of the constitution but also mobilize extra-parliamentary pressures, what Beneš called 'the street'.

Soon after his victory at Brno, Laušman met the National Socialist Minister for Justice, Drtina, and both parties agreed that in the coming electoral campaign they would not attack each other, but that the Social Democrats would go their own way on questions of nationalization so as not to risk the loss of the working-class vote. They were unanimous that the rapid communization of the police, which was being pushed through by the Ministry of the Interior, must be checked at all costs. On Friday 13 February 1948, Drtina, impatient with the stalling methods adopted by the Minister of the Interior in the investigations of the bomb affair, presented to the cabinet a detailed report on the case and accompanied it with alarming details about the extent of Communist control in the police. He revealed that eight non-Communist commanders in the Prague security forces had recently been dismissed and replaced by Communists, and succeeded in carrying a proposal that this order be revoked and the commanders reinstated. The Communist Minister of the Interior was not present at the time, on grounds of illness, and Gottwald, who was in a bibulous state, not uncharacteristic of him, commented: 'If you think we are going to carry this out, you're very much mistaken.'

On Tuesday 17 February, Gottwald went to see President Beneš and accused the Democratic parties of sabotaging the work of the government and plotting to exclude the Communists. The President did not apparently raise the matter of the Prime Minister's failure to carry out the decision of the majority in the Cabinet. He simply promised Gottwald never to sanction a government which was not headed by Communists as the largest party.

Shortly afterwards, the Politburo met and decided to 'call the Party to a state of alertness and mobilize the nation against the reactionaries'. Couriers were sent to all the regional and to the more important district party headquarters to ensure that these decisions were carried out all along the line. They were the first open moves in the preparation of a *coup d'état*.

On their side, too, the Democrats 'mobilized' for action, but of a different kind. The ministers of all parties except the Social Democrats held a joint meeting at which Ripka, one of the National Socialist leaders, urged that if the Minister of the Interior stalled further, they should hand in their resignations *en bloc*. Government would become unworkable, Gottwald would have to resign, and new elections, involving a Communist defeat, would be unavoidable.

Ripka's plan was to have fatal consequences for the survival of democratic government in Czechoslovakia. If the ministers' resignations were accepted, they would at once forfeit their voice in the government, the machinery of office being left exclusively in Communist hands. For their gamble to succeed three conditions would have to be fulfilled. First, the Social Democrat ministers would have to resign too, thus putting the resigning ministers in the majority. Next, and more important, they would have to rely on the President's not accepting their resignations. Finally, they would need to be quite sure that Gottwald would abide by the constitutional rules and accept defeat.

The first mistake they made was to act before securing the support of the Social Democratic leaders. Had the Democratic parties shown greater solidarity, the President might have withstood Communist pressure.

There are conflicting views on whether the President was, in fact, informed of Ripka's proposal beforehand. According to his Chancellor, Jaroslav Smutný, the resignation of the ministers was presented to him as a *fait accompli*. The National Socialist ministers maintained that they informed Beneš beforehand and he either fully endorsed their plan or made no objection to it. All sources are agreed, however, that, when finally informed, Beneš expressed his determination not to accept their resignations. The National Socialists claim that Beneš specifically encouraged them to remain firm and not give way.

On Friday 20 February, therefore, twelve of the ministers sent in their resignations to the President. It was now of crucial importance to the Democrats that the President should not yield to Gottwald's pressure to accept them. The Communists redoubled their attacks on the ministers who had resigned, accusing them of plotting a *coup*. At the same time, they suborned one or two unknown Judases in the Democratic parties to accept posts in a new all-Communist government and brought to bear all the pressure they could upon the President to comply with their demands.

The following day the President was bombarded with thousands of Party inspired telegrams allegedly emanating from Communist factory councils and works committees demanding that he should accept the resignations, while workers' delegations similarly organized surged into the courtyard of the Castle to reinforce their demands. Other Communist organizations crowded into the Old

Town Square, where Gottwald, in a vehement speech, called for the formation of 'Action Committees of the National Front' throughout the country. A delegation from the rally went up to the Castle and insisted on seeing the President. In reply to their threats, Beneš gave them to understand that it was for him and not for 'the street' to decide which course of action he, as President, should take.

In the final event, however, it was the street which decided, because by this time the Communists had the street under their complete control. In Prague itself the main factories were being taken over by Communist workers, who had received weapons from their fellow workers in the armament works at Brno. Although the Communists were the minority party in Slovakia, the Communist leader Husák, who held the post of Chairman of the Slovak National Council, ruled that since the Democratic ministers had resigned in Prague, their counterparts in Slovakia had no right to continue functioning. And so they were summarily dismissed and Communists or crypto-Communists appointed in their places. To add to all this, the Soviet Deputy Foreign Minister, Zorin, formerly Soviet Ambassador in Prague, arrived in the capital, ostensibly 'to help the grain shortage'. The Soviet government evidently wished to support the Communists, if they needed it, and to leave no one in any doubt of it.

I well remember those fateful days. It was a severe winter, Moscow seemed already to have closed in on Prague, and when Gottwald spoke in the Old Town Square, he wore a Russian fur cap and his breath steamed in the frosty atmosphere. It was not a night when anyone would care to be outside. But thousands of trusted Communist Old Guard were moving stealthily but purposefully everywhere in Prague.

All of us had an icy premonition that Parliamentary government might soon be over, that the Communists were taking to the streets and that mob law would prevail. Only one man, perhaps, possessed the authority and influence to halt the process: the President. But, to our consternation, he did nothing.

Like others I too expected Beneš to take some political step on Saturday, and was astonished to hear that he had left Prague to spend the weekend at Lány, his country residence, without taking any action or making any pronouncement. Sunday came and there was still no word from him. He was reported to have spent most of the day listening to the radio, and what he heard in the speeches at a Communist-dominated Trades Union Rally did not strengthen his resolve.

He returned to Prague and received the National Socialist ministers supposedly to tell them, once more, that he would never yield to Communist pressure. They must have known, though, that by that time he was incapable of doing anything else. Action committees directed by the Communists were taking over every sector of national life and those who resisted Communist encroachment were dragged away and arrested. The Minister of National Defence, General Svoboda, took a leading part in the arrests. At a meeting he said: 'The Army goes with the people. Whoever disturbs the unity of the people is a menace and must be removed.'

Things were in fact moving very quickly. First, the leadership of the Social Democrat Party was forcibly taken over by the pro-Communist faction within it. Next, the National Socialist and People's Party strongholds—the Party headquarters, editorial offices and printing works—were seized by armed workers and police. Then it was the turn of the ministries. On Wednesday afternoon President Beneš, exhausted and isolated, finally gave in, accepted the resignations of the outgoing ministers and signed the list of Gottwald's new 'government'. It was called an 'all-party government', but it consisted exclusively of Communists and a few 'non-Communist' supporters, discredited stooges, who fawned on the Party leaders and were only too glad to accept seats in their government. The era of even qualified parliamentary democracy was over.

Beneš had yielded completely to Communist pressure. In so doing he sealed the fate of the Democratic leaders, of his own friends and former colleagues, of himself and of the country as a whole. What induced him to do this?

As we know, Beneš was a sick man, after his two strokes, and he was in no condition to stand up to exceedingly strong Communist pressure. Since he first stepped back onto Czechoslovak soil, he had stressed that he wanted to act strictly in accordance with the constitution and not seek personally to influence the domestic political scene. This *idée fixe* made him lean over backwards to avoid the charge that he was favouring the Democrats at the expense of the Communists. As things were, he probably saw that if he refused to accept the resignations, Communist pressure would be increased, creating dangerous tension, and civil disturbances would ensue in which the Democrats stood little chance of victory. Beneš at least realized that Gottwald would not play the game according to democratic rules. The Democratic leaders seem not to have taken this into account.

In justifying the legality of the Prague *coup d'état*, the Communists have always argued that the changes were not achieved by force and were wholly compatible with the constitution. The agreements reached between the parties in 1945 at Košice in Slovakia established a grand coalition—a National Front of all parties—and it was patently contrary to the spirit of those agreements that the Communist leader should form a government made up exclusively of Communists and persons who were only self-styled representatives of the other parties. Was it constitutional for a Prime Minister to refuse to implement the decision of the majority of his government and then, on the resignation in protest of three of the coalition parties, accuse their leaders of what amounted to treason, and outlaw them? And was it in accordance with the principles of democracy to resort to mob law in order to force a physically weak and almost incapacitated President to give his approval to what he knew was unlawful? If Czechoslovak Communists are reluctant to concede this, one Communist party at least has been prepared to do so—the Chinese. Since 1964 they have argued that a decisive factor in the February events in Prague was 'armed mass actions' or the Communist Party's use of para-military formations, and that the Communist takeover in Prague was by no means the 'peaceful transition to Socialism' Czechoslovak Communists claim it to have been.

These para-military formations consisted of the armed security forces of the police, the mobile security squads, the factory guards and the Workers' Militia. The collaboration of them all under the direction of the Central Committee of the Communist Party and the Ministry of the Interior not only ensured that maximum pressure could be exerted on all the Democratic forces from the President downwards, but also guaranteed that the Communists could not be defeated without civil war. And in the background was the Soviet government—represented by Zorin—which on future showing would not have hesitated to transform a civil war into a foreign invasion if the situation had demanded it.

The Communists claimed that the Workers' Militia was formed in the last stages of the crisis and in defence against an alleged 'plot' by the National Socialists. In reality, it had existed in embryo since 1945 and had never been disbanded, and plans for reactivating it were probably made in 1947. How else might one account for the 10,000 picked Communists who suddenly appeared fully armed on the Prague streets at the height of the crisis?

Ironically enough, some of the men who played a prominent part in the organization of this force, were the very people who were to stand up so valiantly to Soviet threats twenty years later. Dr Kriegel, one of the members of the Prague Party Committee elected to the general staff of this force, though treated shamelessly by the Russians in 1968, was courageous enough openly to condemn the Soviet invasion and to repeat his stand seven years later. The Militia's Chief of Staff was Josef Pavel,* from the 'Spanish Brigade', who, as Head of the Ministry of the Interior in 1968, tried to end all the abuses which had existed within it since the Communists had laid hands on it in 1945. Smrkovský is said to have played an active part in this as well.

In 1948 these three Communists were on the side of *force majeure* as against accepted parliamentary rules. They were among those idealists who genuinely believed that Communism would bring a new democratic order to their country, never reckoning that it would later recoil on their own heads, as it did in the fifties. Kriegel fell under a cloud and was arrested. Pavel was also arrested in 1951, imprisoned and tortured. And in the same year Smrkovský was deprived of all his posts and also imprisoned.

The Communists made great play in 1948, as did the Russians in 1968, of the existence of a 'western plot'. The utter unpreparedness of the Democratic parties—an unpreparedness I saw quite plainly at the time—is sufficient evidence to absolve them of this charge. The western powers themselves took no action and made it plain to the Czechoslovak Democrats that they could not help them. The American Ambassador was away during the important period before the crisis and only returned the day after Zorin arrived. If the British government had had any intention of trying to bolster Czech resistance, the crisis could not have come at a worse time. Nichols, who served as Ambassador to the Czechoslovak government in

* Miroslav Bouček, *Praha v Únoru*, 1948. The political organization of the Militia appears to have been entrusted to Novotný, the Chairman of the Prague Regional Committee of the Party, which no doubt partly explains his rapid rise to power.

London, and spent a further two and a half years in Prague, had just left and the new Ambassador, Sir Pierson Dixon, was totally unfamiliar with the situation. As a result, there was next to no contact between the Czechoslovak politicians and the British Ambassador before and during the *coup*.

There is little doubt that had Nichols been in Prague, he would never have remained passive while Beneš capitulated. If he had thought that the situation demanded it he would have gone straight up to the Hradčany to talk to the President. Dixon, who was in his first ambassadorial post and had no special relationship with the Czechs, could do nothing but await events. Thus the President and Democratic ministers remained incommunicado to us throughout the crisis.

Was 1948 merely a repetition of the Munich crisis of 1938, or did it anticipate the Soviet invasion of Czechoslovakia in 1968?

On each of these three occasions the Czechoslovak leadership was exposed to almost irresistible pressure and yielded. But for all their similarities, the crises were in fact very dissimilar. In 1938, pressure came from Czechoslovakia's traditional friends, who forced President Beneš to give way to Nazi demands but, at least, had no designs on its sovereignty themselves. In 1968, the pressure was from Czechoslovakia's new ally, the Soviet Union, who violated its sovereignty and still occupies it today. The crisis of 1948, however, had to be settled by the Czechs and Slovaks themselves without outside intervention. And on this occasion there was no unity. The country was split right down the middle.

On the evening of the capitulation I drove my car through vast crowds who made the Václavské Náměstí almost impassable. No one shook his fist at me or tried to bump my car. People laughed happily. I remember thinking to myself:

> Alas, unconscious of their fate
> The little victims play.

A few months after these events I was transferred to London. I left Czechoslovakia with a heavy heart, convinced that I would never return. In the weeks before I left the country was in a terrible state. Where, previously, people had not felt the need to disconnect their telephones, talk in whispers or avoid our house, a cold terror seemed now to have descended on them like a shroud. They crossed to the other side of the street when they saw me coming—I was comforted by the thought that Palacký, the Czech political leader, had experienced the same after 1848—and only those who wanted to flee the country came to my office or house. (The wife of a leading journalist even called on me to try to persuade me, a married man, to help her escape!)

Just at this time I received from my Norwegian father-in-law a present of the works of Bjórnsterne Bjórnson. I was glad that the writer who had in his day shown such sympathy for the oppressed Slovaks, had not lived to see what had become of their country.

When we left Prague in May 1948, of all our many Czech friends only one couple came to the station, the cellist František Smetana and his wife. He was arrested on Christmas Eve of the same year—not for seeing me off but because of the courageous stand he took elsewhere. After a considerable period of incarceration he was let out one day, and made to play before the President that very evening. He was later sent on a tour of China, Korea and Mongolia. On his way through Moscow he twice braved the Soviet militia men outside the British Embassy, where I was working, to call on me—a very hazardous step for someone from a Communist-dominated state. On the first occasion, I was out. The second time he came, although I was overjoyed to see him I could hardly speak Czech. I, too, had become Russianized.

INTERLUDE

3. The United Nations

After a preliminary run of a year in one of the Information Departments of the Foreign Office I was relieved when I was told that I should be transferred to the United Nations Political Department as Assistant.

The department was a small one consisting of the Head, the Assistant and three other First or Second Secretaries, and I was lucky enough to be sent to New York, at the outset, in place of my chief who had injured himself while skiing.

The world of the United Nations was entirely new to me. It was generally acknowledged that it took six months longer to learn the ropes in our Department than in any other. I despaired as I tried to drum into my head the clauses of the Charter, the rules of procedure in the different bodies and the enormous number of important resolutions taken in the past, to which one was continually referring back. Not only was I meant to be familiar with all these points at home when I had to advise ministers about the delegation in New York but also in New York I had the responsibility of sitting behind our principal delegate, who could turn round and ask me for an off-the-cuff briefing at any time. An inspector who had earlier discouraged me by saying I would not be equal to the job, had not been right after all.

However, human nature is such that, with time, one is often able to master things which at first sight seem impossible. It was not long before I had reached the conclusion—privately—that I was the last word in the Foreign Office on United Nations procedure! It happened that at the first meeting of the General Assembly of the United Nations in September 1949 I found myself in New York as adviser to Hector McNeil, who was then Minister of State in the Foreign Office in the Labour government and leader of the United Kingdom delegation.

Travelling out with the Foreign Secretary, Ernest Bevin, and his staff on the *Queen Mary* was an interesting experience. It was during

this period that Tito had started his quarrel with the Soviet government, and the Yugoslav delegation, under the leadership of Kardelj,
were on the boat with us. They were anxious to make contact with
the Foreign Secretary and I was called in to act as interpreter. It
had two pleasant consequences. First, Bevin invited me to have
lunch with him after the interview. He recalled his days of courtship
with his wife Flo—how they used to meet at the Strand Palace on
Saturdays after a Turkish bath, and go dancing afterwards at the
Trocadero or a Holborn restaurant. He still enjoyed dancing, he told
us, but now he was too fat and had no privacy from his detectives,
although he sometimes managed to escape from them. And, in
addition, the Yugoslav delegation, who were in a vulnerable
position, came to look upon me as a friend and often consulted me
in the United Nations building.

Our crossing was very rough. I remember how oranges fell off the
Foreign Secretary's table at dinner and rolled across the length of
the vast dining-room like billiard balls. Later, we were warned that
the ship might be struck by a hurricane and all the furniture was
corded up. Bevin resisted all the attempts of his staff to spare him.
As the ship rocked more and more, he said to Bob (Sir Pierson)
Dixon, 'I suppose you're going off and we'll have to do without you.
What are the crew going to do?' A meeting was arranged in Bob's
cabin. 'I'll sit and you all lie on your beds.' When at a small cocktail
party his Private Secretary, Roddie (Sir Roderic) Barclay, said to
him, 'Now it's time for us to go, so that you can have a nap,' Bevin
replied: 'You mean *you* want one.' Then he put his arms round Bob
Dixon and another Foreign Office mandarin and waddled out, saying, 'Don't let it get abroad that the Foreign Secretary left the party
propping up two of his senior advisers.'

When I first met Ernie I could hardly believe that this was the
Foreign Secretary. With his short, squat frame and his formidable
gig-lamps he reminded me of a landlady from my bachelor days.
But his kindness and humour earned him great affection in the
Office. When we had all gathered at his bidding to discuss the
Yugoslav situation, he began, good naturedly: 'Well, what are we
going to do about Tito? I'm sure I don't want to add to his
difficulties, poor chap.' Another of his endearing traits was his
pathetically uneducated handwriting, combined with his mistakes
in spelling and his childlike habit of trying out new words in
the margins of reports he read. If he saw, for example, the word

'unsophisticated', he would adopt it at once and use it himself.

I got on splendidly with Hector McNeil. We were fellow-sufferers in one particular respect. Next door to us sat the Soviet delegate, Vyshinsky, who was then at his peak in the United Nations and wasted the Assembly's time with his insufferably long speeches, which were often insulting to the western powers. For Hector, who was a somewhat impatient man, it was a boring and frustrating experience. For me there were advantages. Vyshinsky spoke beautiful Russian and, from the literary point of view, his speeches were far superior to those of the other Soviet delegates. He had been a bourgeois and a Menshevik and he spoke old-fashioned educated Russian, so that it was a delight to listen to his eloquence, however obnoxious the message. The other delegates used the simultaneous interpretations available on their headphones, but Vyshinsky, translated into English by an American interpreter of Galician origin, was definitely not the same thing as Vyshinsky speaking his own language. Anyone who knows the way educated Russians used to speak knows that Russian rhetoric is coaxing, flattering and beguiling rather than boisterous and fierce. Vyshinsky in Russian possessed considerable charm, but the interpreter made him sound sinister and intimidating. As I sat there and listened I thought it perhaps a blessing that he was unable to convey in English the full seductiveness of Vyshinsky's eloquence.

Khrushchev, we will remember, made frequent use of Russian proverbs in his speeches. Vyshinsky used them before him. No speech of his seemed to contain less than half a dozen of them. Not only did Hector McNeil find them tedious but he also smarted under them, especially when they were offensive to him and his American colleagues. One night when I was working with him over a bottle of whisky in his hotel room, he asked me if I could find a Russian proverb for him to throw back at Vyshinsky. I promised to go next day to the New York State Library, which has a remarkable Russian section. I had only time to do this in the evening and worked quite late at it, but in vain. I found many books of Russian proverbs, but nothing which Vyshinsky would not be able to cap at once with something better. Then it dawned upon me that we might do better if we quoted him one of Krylov's fables. Krylov was a kind of Russian La Fontaine, whose fables were political and sharply satirical. I soon laid my hands on one which I thought might do.

At this time Vyshinsky was trying to 'con' the United Nations into accepting some very dubious 'peace proposals'. Every year the Russians introduced some kind of 'resolution for peace', which was disingenuous and meaningless and patently designed as a move in the cold war. Mindful of this, I fished out of the book a fable called 'The Serpent'. The story went like this: the serpent once complained to Jupiter that he was being badly treated. He had not been given a beautiful voice. 'Look at the nightingale,' he said, 'when she perches on a tree and sings, all the beasts of the earth and the fowls of the air come from far and wide to hear her, so golden is her voice. Grant me a voice like that, Jupiter,' he begged.

Jupiter replied that he could have the voice of a nightingale, if he really wanted it, but he doubted very much whether it would have much influence on the other animals. Having acquired this wonderful gift, the serpent crawled up on to the branches of a tree and began singing. All the beasts of the earth and the birds of the air came and sat on the ground close by the tree to listen to his music. After drawing nearer at first, they soon ran or flew away one by one, until only a single old starling remained.

Astonished, the serpent asked him what the matter was. Did he not sing as beautifully as any nightingale, and if so, why did all the beasts and birds disappear so quickly? The starling shook his head and answered: 'Of course you sing as beautifully as any nightingale and we loved your charming voice, but when we came a little closer to you we saw your fangs and we thought it more prudent to move further away.' In other words the Soviet peace resolution sounded honeyed enough, but a closer look at it revealed its hidden teeth.

I read Hector the fable. He was delighted with it and planned to let the squib off in the General Assembly as soon as Vyshinsky started on one of his Russian proverbs. He was anxious, however, that Vyshinsky should not think he had got the fable from me, and he asked me to find him an English translation to show Vyshinsky that he had read the fable himself. Back I went to the New York Public Library and, after some difficulty, discovered an old-fashioned Victorian edition of the fables with illustrations reminiscent of those in *Reading without Tears*.

The next day Vyshinsky dazzled us again with his proverbs. My head was dizzy with them. When the time came for Hector to speak I waited to see the effect on Vyshinsky and his delegation. I also turned on the Russian translation to see how the speech would sound to them in their own language.

The Russians were at first taken completely by surprise. But they pricked up their ears when they heard the name Krylov. (A lady translator was on duty that day and she was completely flummoxed by Hector's Greenock accent. She thought that when he said *sarpent* he meant *sarvant* (servant), and used the Russian word *sluga* instead of *zmiya*. Later she righted herself and got back into the correct groove.) I observed Vyshinsky carefully. He swung round abruptly and whispered something to his closest adviser, who turned to the man behind him. So it went, all the way down the line, like the ball in a rugby football throw-in, until the last member of the delegation, having finally caught it, rushed out of the room. 'He's gone to the New York Public Library,' I thought. I felt like Alice and the jurymen in *Alice in Wonderland*.

My ploy had captured the imagination of the Russians, who were thoroughly enjoying themselves. I could well understand why! I calculated that, notwithstanding our initial advantage, their counter-attack would be crushing, as they had a much wider repertoire of Russian quotations to draw on. I was proved right.

The last member subsequently rejoined the Russian team, and a book was passed from hand to hand up to Vyshinsky. When Vyshinsky got up to speak again, he turned amiably towards Hector —but with the amiability of a serpent—and said how delighted he was that the British delegate had been reading the *great* Russian fabulist, Krylov. Here Vyshinsky went into raptures over Krylov, presenting him as one of the truly great masters of literature in the world. (Hector had in fact tossed his English edition of the fables towards Vyshinsky, who had picked it up and read it.) 'But,' continued Vyshinsky, 'I could wish that Mr McNeil had pursued his studies of our great Russian master further. If he had looked at Book 5 he would have found another fable called 'The Slanderer and the Serpent'. The slanderer and the serpent had an argument as to which was the more venomous. In the end they appealed to Beelzebub, who declared: 'The slanderer deserves the prize, because he can cast his spittle further.' Although this crude formulation is not, in fact, to be found in Krylov's writings and was Vyshinsky's own, all the members of the Russian delegation sat back, beaming with self-satisfaction and triumphantly eyeing the whole assembly.

At this point, the Chairman of the Political Committee of the General Assembly, who was Selim Sarper, the Turkish Foreign Minister, intervened and mildly rebuked both Hector and Vyshinsky.

'These zoological allusions are in doubtful taste,' he said. The whole affair received wide publicity and inspired the *New Yorker* to write about it in its 'Notes and Comments'.

Noting that McNeil and Vyshinsky had exchanged fables, the *New Yorker* commended to the delegates a fable of its own where the animals met to establish a community 'devoid of tooth and fang'. 'Each jungle session saw the Bears, Lions and Eagles at odds. . . . Once in a while a very small animal would make a speech—a Chipmunk or a Water Beetle—but nobody paid much attention!'

In the intervals between debates I used often to talk to Vyshinsky in Russian—not for long, because he did not linger in the bars or public rooms like the other delegates. Like the White Rabbit, he was always hurrying somewhere. It was typical of members of Russian delegations at all conferences. However, he once did me the honour of congratulating me on my Russian and, when I spoke of my love for the language, said: 'But English is a great language too. English is a strong language.' I went off wondering what he really meant.

When it became known through the grapevine that he was going to speak, the public galleries filled up an hour or more before the speech was scheduled. On these occasions, all countries were represented by their chief delegates, which was by no means the case with other speakers. It was less a tribute to Vyshinsky's oratory, though, which the listeners received secondhand through translation, than to the power of Russia. It appears that the same had applied at the League of Nations when Litvinov was scheduled to speak on an important issue. The growling of the bear seemed to mesmerize and attract people, unlike the serpent in the fable.

I well remember how on another occasion Vyshinsky wanted to quote something from Lenin in the middle of a speech. One of the other speakers had accused Lenin of saying that it was necessary 'to intrigue'. Vyshinsky had obviously instructed one of his delegation to find the appropriate reference and pass it to him. For some reason they had trouble finding it, and Vyshinsky was coming nearer and nearer to the point at which he would have to bring in the quotation. It was interesting to observe how he circled round the point for a long time, like an aeroplane wheeling round and round in the sky before at last deciding to alight. One never knew when he would land, but it was always at the right moment—bang on top of the quotation. Now he continued to heap praise on Lenin until he could finally clinch the argument by claiming that the Russian word 'intrigovat', used in this context meant 'excite the interest of' or 'charm'. Then he was off again with his eulogy of Lenin. His voice broke as he asked the assembly how 'dear Lenin' could possibly have stooped to intrigue.

I was fascinated by the way Vyshinsky conducted himself during the speeches of the other delegates. Although he had his headphones on all the time he did not appear to be listening. He was always immersed either in preparing his own speeches or in reading Soviet press reports of them. When, on certain occasions, I took the Minister's seat (if, for example, he were delayed at a lunch or another engagement) I was close enough to Vyshinsky to see exactly what he was doing. From this vantage-point I could even read the names of the papers he was going through. The impression I had was that he was desperately anxious to see how his speeches were getting across in the Soviet Union. Knowing how the fortunes of the Soviet leaders fluctuate, I could well understand his anxiety.

On my return to London I was promoted Counsellor and made Head of the Department, and then a problem began to rear its ugly head which was to plague the Foreign Office for many a long day. The question was: which China was to be represented on the various bodies in the United Nations? Those powers who recognized Chiang Kai Shek and the Formosan government naturally regarded them as the rightful occupants of the Chinese seat. Those, in turn, who recognized the Central People's (Communist) government of Peking, regarded Communist China as the true Chinese representative. Acting independently of the Americans, who continued to recognize Formosa, we had taken the premature step of recognizing the Central People's Republic. From this there flowed a duty to recognize the Communist representative as the rightful occupant of the seat. This meant that whenever questions concerning the Chinese came up, we and the Americans might find ourselves on opposite sides and this was difficult for our masters to stomach.

I held firmly to the belief that, having once recognized Communist China, we ought to nail our colours to the mast and vote its delegates into all United Nations seats. In order to prevent this reprehensible show of independence from America, however, a crude rigmarole called the 'moratorium' was thought up, under which it was prearranged that with every substantive vote, a friendly delegate would jump up and propose that the matter be post-poned. Then a procedural vote was taken on this (because by UN rules procedural questions had precedence in voting over sub-stantive questions). Since only a simple majority was required to pass a procedural resolution, that was easily secured and the issue was postponed and taken off the agenda until the next session. The masquerade continued year after year.

When we decided to recognize the Central People's government our Department was never consulted. Had our opinion been sought, we should undoubtedly have warned the Office that if we recog-nized Communist China, the question of which China was to be represented would come up again and again on every little body.

At that time Ernie Bevin was seriously ill. We had to go to his nursing home to consult with him, because the issue of Chinese representation would shortly arise for the first time at a politically unimportant body called the United Nations Children's Emergency Fund. The 'moratorium' policy had not been yet thought up and the question was whether or not we should stick to our guns. Bevin was most reluctant to take a decision on this. I was present at a meeting at the nursing home with (Sir) Kenneth Younger and Sir William (Lord) Strang, the then Permanent Under-Secretary. At one time Bevin bewailed his decision to recognize Communist China and moaned: 'I didn't ought never to have done it. It was you, Willie (William Strang), what put me up to it.' Here Kenneth Younger put in: 'On the contrary, Secretary of State, it was one of the finest things you ever did.' But Bevin was inconsolable. We could not go against the Americans, he said. He later became so ill that he could not continue and responsibility for Foreign Affairs was taken over by the Prime Minister, Clement Attlee.

I was very cut up by Bevin's death though it was not unexpected. I had watched him grow yellower and yellower, until one morning his temperature was found to be 104°. Even more alarming was his arrival, some weeks later, at his room in the House of Commons, occupied in his absence by Kenneth Younger. He staggered in un-announced, and, as we both sprang to our feet, collapsed gasping into a chair. He had been driven by car all the way from the West Country, over bumpy roads, to be present at a crucial division. Better care should have been taken of him. Whips can easily kill their Leaders.

Hector McNeil, as Minister of State, and Ernie Bevin had always influenced each other, whereas Kenneth Younger, who did not have the same standing with Bevin, got on much better with Attlee. Consequently, he was more favourably placed to get his way when Attlee took charge, and like me he wanted the government to stick to its guns.

However, when it appeared that we might soon commit the 'awful' crime of voting against the Americans all the power of the 'establishment' was mobilized to prevent him from taking the step he thought right. He began to receive various letters from influential people deploring the fact that we might be separated from the United States on such an issue. Finally, Bevin's Private Secretary wrote him a solemn letter saying that he felt sure that, had he been well enough, the Secretary of State himself would never have agreed to such a decision being taken—which was of course true—but Prime Minister is Prime Minister! As a result of all this backstage manoeuvring, in which some senior members of the Office took an active part, the 'moratorium' came about, barring the Chinese from the United Nations for some twenty years until the resolution of the problem in 1971. Hence Britain, after having been one of the first to recognize the Central People's government, had to be content with a Chargé d'Affaires at Peking throughout this long period, while Norwegians, Swedes, Danes and others had full ambassadors. It was surely absurd too that the Chinese representative in the World Postal Union should come from the tiny island of Formosa and the vast Chinese mainland be left without a voice!

The main objection to having China in the United Nations at all, of course, was that Russia appeared to be her greatest supporter. Even at that time, however, we had a shrewd suspicion that Russia did not really want her there because, once in, she could not be depended on to follow Russia's lead. We were not to know then that China would soon have an open breach with the Soviet Union, although there were indications that things were not well between the two powers. If we had stuck to our guns and voted for Communist China, China would probably have entered the United Nations much sooner which might well have precipitated the breach. Moreover, we should then have enjoyed full diplomatic relations with Peking which would have done us no harm.

I had now been four years at home and was utterly broke, and so I put out feelers for a Counsellor's post abroad. I suggested Brussels because my wife and children had not been well and it was close enough to England for us to return if they had health problems, or if we wanted to see the children at school. I was fortunate to be given the post and we spent a happy two years there. It was in fact the only post from which I thought I was moved too soon.

Once when I was in London on leave the Head of Personnel Department asked me if I would come and have lunch with him. I had a kind of inkling, I do not know why, that he was going to ask me to go to Moscow and my premonition proved correct. He broached the question very gingerly and hedged it with various reservations. It was a possibility they were talking about: I must not regard it in any way as definite but they would like to know my reactions.

I replied cautiously. I had always wanted to go to Moscow. It was my greatest dream. But I had never taken any active steps to get myself there because of my family. I felt I must not take the initiative in subjecting them to the possible insalubrities which Moscow might impose on them. I cannot remember much of what we spoke about. I seem to recall stressing that what was really important in the job was to know the Russians and their history. Knowledge of Marxism was not so important, because the Russians would always be guided by their own traditional and national interests. They bent Marxism to make it fit into the Russian national and imperialistic mould. 'What an interesting idea,' he commented. I casually mentioned that I knew Russian. He said drily: 'That will be a help too,' and changed the subject. This was a blow. I had always imagined I was known in the Foreign Office as a Russian speaker, and that it was precisely because of this that I had been nominated for the post. I came to learn afterwards that it was in fact because nobody else wanted to go! The post had been offered to three members of the Foreign Service of my rank and they had all refused. I learnt all this from the Austrian Ambassador in London whom I met in Brussels while he was visiting his colleague there. If you want to get the low-down on what your own Foreign Office is up to, ask one of the *chers collègues*!

However, when one day the Ambassador showed me the telegram asking him if he would spare me for the post of Minister at Moscow, I was much excited all the same. It was not just that it was promotion, and to a more important embassy, but for twenty years I had longed to be able to speak Russian in Russia itself, and sad as I was to leave Brussels, now, at the age of forty-five, the chance I had been waiting for had come at last.

BOOK II

Russia 1954-1957

FIG. 1. Map of western Russia

4. Fever and Thaw

I travelled out to Russia in July 1954 by the good ship *Molotov*. Like so many Russian towns and streets she changed her name frequently. Originally flying the Finnish flag, she had been surrendered to the Russians after the war as reparations, and had been rechristened *Molotov*. When that name was discredited in 1957 she took the more neutral name of *Balticum*. This name seemed reasonably safe anchorage for her.

It was a delight to see for the first time the Russian sailors in their sparkling white blouses and trousers and fluttering ribbons. They brought back to me images from the Tsar's visits to Reval and the *Battleship Potemkin*. I even enjoyed their waking me up at 6 a.m. with their singing, as they merrily scrubbed the decks.

After arriving at Leningrad I took the train to Moscow. Here was my first surprise. Everybody knows that Moscow is terribly cold, but no one had told me that it could also be very hot. I arrived in weather that was sultry and each day grew more and more torrid, ending with spectacular thunderstorms in the evening. Like everything in Russia, these seemed larger than life. The lightning flashed luridly around the spires of Moscow University on the Lenin Hills and torrents of rain brought my car to a sudden halt. Once inside my flat, I nearly had a heat stroke, trying to unpack my things and carry them down three flights of stairs by myself into the cellar, where everything had to be stored. There was no lift and no help to be had, because it was Sunday and even if the maids I had inherited had been there, it would not have been much use as they were elderly, if very helpful and efficient. The *dvornik* or concierge did not appear, and I was afraid to rout him out in case it was not in his contract to move heavy goods. To top it all, I had brought no light clothes with me. I suffered terribly during that first summer. Had I looked in the right place in my 1914 *Baedeker* of Russia (bought in Stockholm) I should have read that the July temperature in the environs of Moscow 'often rises to 100° Fahr'.

My Ambassador, Sir William Hayter, was champing to get away
on leave, and I had only a month to learn the ropes before taking
charge. In an unfamiliar post, such as Moscow, where at any
moment important issues might blow up which would go straight to
No. 10, I needed more time to be initiated. My chief was experienced
and competent, but though I was reassured by the calm and the
ease with which he dispatched business, I felt rudderless and adrift
when the storm broke after his departure.

One day the news was brought to me that two of our junior staff
had been arrested by the police and were in danger of standing trial.
They had gone to 'America House', one of the few places of entertainment in the capital where the staff of western missions could play
bingo, see film shows and have drinks. The Soviet police alleged that
the offending pair had emerged from the building late at night in a
highly intoxicated state, entered a garage underneath a bridge and
attacked four women workers. Two policemen were also said to be
victims of the rough house. The accused had then allegedly run on
to the bridge and demonstrated, in a most unseemly and ungentle-
manly way, their low opinion of the Soviet authorities. We immediately received a stern note from the Soviet Ministry summoning
the offenders to appear before the examining magistrate.

We had no idea whether the accused would be safe in their flats
or whether the Soviet police would come and fetch them away in the
middle of the night. I arranged for them to be transferred as soon
as possible to rooms in our compound where the police had no
authority to break in. I was advised that, under Soviet law, they
could, if convicted, be sentenced to five years in a labour camp. The
Home Office said that even in Britain, they might have received a
year's imprisonment—or more.

I arranged for them to be accompanied to the preliminary hearing
of their case by a senior member of staff, who spoke Russian. We
did not know whether they would be allowed to return. They could
not leave the country without Soviet permission, which would
certainly be withheld. There had been a case many years earlier of
an employee of the Embassy who had been accused of an offence
against a Soviet citizeness. He had also been moved into the compound, where he remained for five years at least, creating unending
problems for both the Embassy and himself.

As it happened, I caught tonsilitis while handling the case and
was confined to my bedroom. I received many visits from experienced

senior staff, as well as the American Ambassador, Charles (Chip) Bohlen, the most experienced of them all.

As far as I can remember, the affair dragged on for almost a year, the accused and their families having to live in uncertainty all that time. It was in the end solved by Eden's having a whispered word with Molotov at a conference. By this time the case had passed out of my hands and reverted to the Ambassador.

I had expected to be negotiating with the Soviet high-ups and here I was spending hours arguing with bureaucrats about the seamy side of life. My search for old Russia, to which I had been looking forward so much, had to be laid aside, and in the first few months, the beauties of Moscow almost passed me by.

But nonetheless I was glad to be living in the old capital of Muscovy rather than in Peter the Great's new-fangled capital, 'Sankt-Peterburg'. For all its grandeur and wide vistas, Leningrad was to me a completely western city, built by a Tsar who aped foreign ways and designed by Netherlanders, Germans, Frenchman, Italians *and* a Scot. I preferred the narrow winding streets, squat buildings and bulbed churches of Old Moscow. For me (and for many a Russian too) this was the true Russia. 'It smells of Old Rus', a writer once said—and it was literally true! Shalyapin claimed that the Muscovites had more of the Russian soil, the Russian 'black-earthness' about them, than the inhabitants of 'Piter', the half-derogatory, half-affectionate name for St Petersburg. Moscow had its western architecture too but it was mainly confined to the Kremlin. If one wanted to see what Italians could do with traditional Russian architectural forms one had only to look there and see Fioravanti's Cathedral of the Assumption and Alevisio Novi's Cathedral of the Archangel Michael.

It was also fortunate that my place of work for the next three years was to be the British Embassy building on what was then called the Sofiiskaya Naberezhnaya. On summer evenings it was wonderful to sit with the Ambassador on his balcony and feast one's eyes on the gleaming Kremlin domes, while immediately below, fast-moving diesel boats carried tourists up and down the river. The British, who have a remarkable eye for ambassadorial residences, had succeeded in snapping up the best site in Moscow. Understandably, they lived in a permanent state of fear lest the Soviet government should take it away from them. It was supposed to have been sentenced to destruction by Stalin, but it was saved from that fate by his death.

But by the time I came to Moscow, plans to raze most of the buildings in that quarter and build a special park had been abandoned, and British ambassadors could continue to dine on their balcony in peace, dreaming, perhaps, of the times of Ivan the Terrible and Boris Godunov, accounts of whom we owe to the reports of their sixteenth-century predecessors.

Although it could blow hot and cold in Moscow, we were luckily just on the threshold of a more favourable climate in our diplomatic relations when I arrived there. Stalin had died on 5 March 1953, and it was now July 1954. The new ruler of the Soviet Union was Malenkov and the first foreign diplomat he received was Sir William Hayter—an unusual mark of favour for a western representative. Things moved slowly in Russia, however, and one had to wait some time before one could be sure which way the wind was set.

A sure touchstone was the Soviet reception of the Labour Party high-level delegation which passed through Moscow on its way to China. The Party, then in opposition, had picked a powerful team led by Attlee, and including Nye Bevan and Morgan Phillips, then General Secretary. Hayter naturally wished to hold a dinner in their honour and figuring out, rather oddly, that perhaps Khrushchev was the nearest person to the leader of the Opposition, because he held no government appointment, asked Vyshinsky, the then Foreign Minister, to invite him on his behalf. To his surprise Vyshinsky replied next day that almost *all* the members of the Presidium would come. On the day of days, we were astonished to see the whole Presidium led by Malenkov assembling in the entrance hall of the residence. Vyshinsky, who was soon to be removed from his position and replaced by Gromyko, brought up the rear. I could see by his servile attitude to the others that he knew he counted for nothing in their eyes. By the end of that year he had died. He was not overmuch missed by anyone, I suspect, except myself, whose Russian had derived considerable benefit from his speeches. He had, after all, played up quite well to my practical joke against him in the United Nations.

The presence in our Embassy of all this Soviet 'brass' was an unprecedented event in Moscow's diplomatic life, let alone in the field of Anglo-Soviet relations. As the great men trooped up the stairs into the reception rooms above, they were confronted by a painting of George V. One of them, either Malenkov or Khrushchev, observed that we had the portrait of the last Tsar hanging on the wall. We hastily explained that the two monarchs were cousins and rather alike, but that this portrait was in fact that of our Queen's grandfather.

As both the Labour Party and Soviet delegations were numerous, there was not room for many members of the Embassy staff. I was included; but otherwise, as far as I can remember, only two of the staff who could speak Russian and act as interpreters were detailed to come. Consequently I had to act as interpreter too and was placed at the table between the two most important guests, Attlee and Malenkov.

I have never worked harder in my life. It was not that it was difficult to interpret. My varied experience with Russians in Yugoslavia, Sweden and Czechoslovakia and at the United Nations had kept my Russian up to the mark. It was the fact that Attlee was such a bad conversationalist and Malenkov little better. In the end, in order to dispel the stony silence, I had to turn myself into a kind of question master in a BBC guessing-game feature. It was like *What's My Line?*, because both men when seeking to explain what they were trying to say supplemented their efforts by making dumb crambo actions with their hands.

Attlee appeared so tired after his journey that my immediate objective was to try and prevent him falling asleep, and so I invented questions for him to ask Malenkov. I said to Malenkov: 'Mr Attlee would like to know, etc.', and then whispered to Attlee: 'I have asked him this. . . .' I was amazed that the leader of Her Majesty's Opposition, when offered this unique opportunity of having a long talk with the newly emerged leader of the Soviet regime, should have almost nothing to say to him and exhibit such indifference.

Malenkov, who was a fat, flabby little man with oriental eyes, which could be benign but also, no doubt, very cruel, could not have been particularly at ease at the Embassy table, though if he was at all uncomfortable, he gave few signs of it. He was genial enough, but his conversation just ran out. I asked him what he had done during his holidays. He said he had gone fishing because that was his favourite sport. After a long pause he added, 'Is Mr Attlee a fisherman?' I passed the ball quickly to Attlee, who replied promptly: 'No, I don't fish.' The conversation then dropped dead.

After another interminable pause Malenkov came to life again and asked: 'What did Mr Attlee do in the holidays?' I bowled this one along to Attlee who replied: 'Went on a motoring tour.' The ball went back to Malenkov, who caught it and said, 'Ah, then Mr Attlee likes driving?' 'No,' replied Attlee, 'My wife does.' There was another dead silence. Attlee looked like the dormouse at the Mad-Hatter's tea-party, and I felt it might be better to let him doze off for a while, in the hope that after forty winks he would return to the fray with renewed vigour. Meanwhile, I started up a conversation with Malenkov myself. He told me some interesting things: how they had changed the nocturnal office hours which Stalin kept and now worked till five o'clock in the afternoon; how he had thrown or was about to throw the Kremlin open to the public; how it was a bad thing that the Russian leaders had not seen more people up to now and how this would be changed; and, finally, how he believed in more contact between the peoples of Russia and was going to arrange for the inhabitants of the various Soviet republics to visit each other. There would be many festivals which would bring people from the provinces to the capital. All of this, in fact, took place.

Observing that Attlee was coming back to life and wanted to say something, I leaned over to him, all agog. Very slowly he drawled: 'I once met Kropotkin. Ask him if he knew him.'

Prince Kropotkin was a leading anarchist who opposed Marxist dialectics, the doctrine of class warfare and the dictatorship of the proletariat, and had been unacceptable to Lenin. Malenkov not unexpectedly failed to register, confining himself to the remark that he was too young to have known him. He was indeed only nineteen when Kropotkin died. So all conversation between them ended there.

After dinner the Ambassador divided us up into small groups, with interpreters where necessary. I had to act as interpreter between Malenkov and Nye Bevan. After exchanging a few opening politenesses Bevan came quickly to the point. Unlike Attlee, he wanted to make full use of the occasion. My services were for the moment irreplaceable. 'This kind of arrangement is no good,' he started. 'What we want to have is a proper get-together.' Malenkov raised his eyebrows and said, 'No good? Is it our people's fault or yours?' Bevan indicated that it was not Malenkov's. Then he lowered his voice and said deliberately: 'I want to come here again in the spring, you know, and this time alone.' Malenkov suggested that this could be easily arranged and he would welcome it. 'Let's arrange things,' he began, and then the Soviet interpreter turned up. Bevan paused and looked fixedly at me. Finally, he said, 'Mr Parrott, would you mind?' It was not very polite of him, but I, naturally, got up and went. I wondered whether he had intended to tell his colleagues about his conversation, or had sent me away because he was afraid I might do so.

From then on diplomatic life began to change in Moscow. At every National Day party Malenkov (as long as he was still a member of the Presidium), Khrushchev and one or two of the other top men appeared regularly. There were endless opportunities for speaking with them. I was to find Malenkov a congenial table companion again. When he acted as host to a delegation from the Electrical Trades Union led by Lord Citrine we sat next to each other and amused ourselves by exchanging Latin tags we could remember from school. Malenkov was not afraid to tell us how journalists in England had quizzed him about the death of Beria, nor to recommend, privately, that I read the novels of Andreyev, then condemned in the Soviet Union as decadent. One evening he played a trick on me. At a dinner given in honour of the New Zealand Vice-Premier he asked me—in front of the whole company —whether I preferred Soviet or French champagne. I hesitated. 'Soviet champagne is very . . .' I began. 'Now, don't hedge,' he said banteringly. 'Don't be a diplomat. Tell the truth.'

I cannot remember what I said, but when Malenkov was host once more, I was listening to a conversation he was having with Iris Hayter, and heard the trick repeated: 'Tell me, Lady Hayter, which do you prefer—Soviet or French champagne?' She looked straight at Malenkov with her wide, innocent blue eyes and replied, unequivocally: 'Oh, French.' I admired her.

When the Ambassador was away and I was left in charge something unusual generally happened. When he had gone home for Christmas in December 1955, the Soviet government decided, at short notice, to invite all heads of missions to see the New Year in with them. It was something they had done regularly with the Communist diplomats, but never with us.

When I received the invitation I was advised by the Foreign Office to attend the function, but to keep well in the background. Our government was not pleased with the anti-British speeches Khrushchev had recently made in India and Burma.

It was not so easy to keep in the background. At any moment you
c

might suddenly find Khrushchev bearing down upon you, and once
he started to wag his finger in your direction, even if his face was
wreathed in smiles, you knew you might have to face the worst. To
increase your embarrassment, swarms of journalists would immediately come up and huddle round you like a rugby scrum, busily
taking down every one of his sallies and all your feeble repartees.

At this party the Soviet top brass were sitting at a kind of high
table and we were all placed in the well of the hall, rather like
students in a college. There must have been some five or six hundred
people sitting there, among them the élite of the Party, and it was a
chastening thought that when the men seated at the high table
disappeared from the Soviet scene there would be no one better to
replace them than the hard-faced robots surrounding us. As we
came in, we were simply given a table number. Once you had found
your table, at each of which there were some forty places, it was
'first come first served'. Thus the French Chargé d'Affaires found
himself squeezed between on the one side two of the bodyguards of
one of the Soviet high-ups and on the other a very bibulous and
obscure Party official. The bodyguards refused to make conversation
with him at all and nearly elbowed him out as they reached for their
food. The Party official's only interest was to drink as many
Armenian cognacs as possible. When Bulganin proposed a toast to
the Communist Party, Khrushchev said in an audible aside: 'This
won't suit some people,' and then added publicly, 'It is the only
toast that is not obligatory.' Just before midnight President
Voroshilov left the table to go into another room in the Kremlin to
broadcast his traditional New Year's speech. He returned at midnight and then, as the Kremlin bells pealed forth, the curtains on
the stage behind the high table were drawn back to reveal a
dazzling projection of a Russian lake. The lights went out, and by
the kind of transformation effect that Russians love—and are
supremely good at—this picture dissolved into the new hydroelectric power station at Kuibyshev.

At the same time, a Christmas tree, which was some forty feet
high, burst into colour, and it revolved whenever Bulganin proposed a new toast. When the lights went up again, the scene in the
St George's Hall was exceptionally festive, and in the 'minstrels'
gallery' a band in the uniform of the Kremlin guards played
'establishment' music.

One notable feature of the evening was that Zhukov, who was

usually not given a very high place, was made to sit on Khrushchev's right. It was not the *placement* intended for him. He should have been sitting at one of the lower tables, but was invited by Khrushchev to come and sit between himself and Malenkov. Absolutely everybody who counted in the Communist world was there.

When the members of the Presidium had finished their dinner, again, as in a college, they left through a door on the dais. This meant, I hoped, that they would not come into direct contact with us and that I could remain inconspicuous and leave the party early and unseen.

Alas, I was deceived. As I walked past the tables in the general scramble, with Bohlen, the American Ambassador, beside me, I saw to my consternation that Khrushchev was standing opposite me. He put his hand out across the table and I slightly withdrew as I imagined it was Bohlen he wanted to greet. Khrushchev's advance had been towards me, as it happened, and he interpreted my withdrawal as some kind of diplomatic coyness, which it certainly was not. A huge schoolboy grin came over his face and he shook his finger at me. 'Don't pout now, Mr Parrott, don't sulk,' he said.

Now I don't know whether Khrushchev had been able to read my telegrams to the Foreign Office and their instructions to me, but he had certainly divined the situation and was reacting in his usual undiplomatic but human way.

That same Christmas the diplomats' children were not forgotten. For the first time they were invited to a Christmas (New Year) Party held regularly in the Kremlin for Russian boys and girls selected for their good examination results. The parties went on for a week and were held two or three times a day. We were invited to bring our children to any one of them we liked.

When we arrived at the Kremlin door an extraordinary sight met our eyes. On every one of the fifty-eight steps of the granite Ceremonial Staircase, was a young pioneer dressed as a fairy, elf, animal or fairy-story character. At the top, we were ushered into the St George's Hall, which this time sparkled in white and gold. There were some dozen or half-dozen—I do not know how many—Christmas trees, and in the centre of the hall children, dressed as Red Riding Hood and the Wolf, Puss-in-Boots, Cinderella and so on, had formed rings and were dancing and singing. They stretched out friendly hands to our two boys, who were soon caught up—

somewhat shyly and unwillingly—in the round. It was a fantastic
occasion, quite like a dream. It was not one, however, as every child
who received a present to take home as a memory of the event, will
confirm.

There was no doubt that, at that time, the Soviet government
could charm and show their human face—something they were later
to grudge Dubček in Czechoslovakia. A British ambassador once
said to me: 'The Soviet leaders are very pleasant people. They are
much nicer than HMG.' And in one sense, they were: they went out
of their way to take notice of you and never appeared to be looking
over their shoulder to see if there was anyone more interesting
around. In short, they were excellent diplomats.

Perhaps the best example of the way the Russians could rival the
west in entertainment was the famous garden party, held the
following summer. Again, the Ambassador was away, and I am sure
that, this time, he was sorry to have missed it. One afternoon the
Ministry of Foreign Affairs rang to inform me that Bulganin had
invited all the Heads of Missions and their families, my wife and
three sons included, to spend Sunday with him at his dacha outside
Moscow. There would be opportunities for the guests to bathe, boat,
relax in the grounds and listen to a concert.

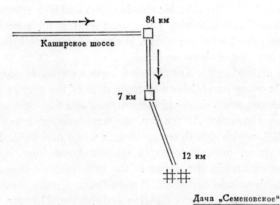

Fig. 2. Directions for finding the garden party dacha

We were given a diagram showing us how to get to the dacha. This was in itself an innovation, because such locations were generally kept strictly secret. The dacha was situated in a place called Semyonovskoye and the route to it was clearly and simply marked. On the diagram it lay some sixty miles south-east of Moscow and we had no difficulty getting there at the appropriate hour of 2 p.m. There was a long procession of diplomatic cars on the private road leading to it, which ran through some seven miles of beautiful undulating meadows and woodland.

It was difficult to form any idea of the dacha itself, as we were led straight through it on arrival, to a verandah, on the steps of which the Deputy Foreign Ministers, Kuznetsov and Zorin, stood waiting to welcome us.

We followed a small path down into the garden and found the whole Presidium grouped before a small spring at the bottom. Bulganin and Khrushchev were dressed in light tropical suits, the latter wearing a Ukrainian shirt. The rest were in their Sunday best. As I greeted the host and introduced my sons, Mikoyan stepped forward and insisted on our putting our hands into the spring to feel its icy freshness.

We walked on and saw ponds on either side, where dinghies were moored, and on the banks fishing rods were propped against the trees, complete with tins full of worms. A military band was playing. All the diplomats were taken care of by the heads of the appropriate territorial departments of the Ministry of Foreign Affairs, who seemed eager to provide any form of amusement they might desire. The whole of Soviet high society could be observed strolling under the trees and on the lawns, among them ministerial overlords, Ministers, Deputy Ministers, Marshals and Admirals. The surrounding woods were full of uniformed militia, and plain-clothed detectives wearing red armbands and acting as guides were scattered through the crowds.

The arrival of the American Ambassador seemed to be the signal for the host to leave his receiving point and escort his guests on a tour of the estate. Here, for once, it was Khrushchev who took charge, and he did so with something of the proprietorial pride of a country squire. He drew our attention to the hammocks hung between the trees and the sunshades erected on the banks of the water, indicating that there were facilities for an afternoon nap. Otherwise Bulganin dominated the proceedings. Soon the whole company, proceeding in a very straggling file, reached the shores of a lake where several landing stages had been constructed. Here, Mikoyan invited Mrs Bohlen and her young daughter to step into a dinghy and rowed them energetically across the water to an island, amid good-humoured cheers from the rest of the Presidium. Molotov, somewhat diffidently, followed suit, taking the Argentine Ambassador and the Indonesian Ambassadress in another boat. The stern of his dinghy was hardly more than half an inch above the water, and when he put in again, he gave his distinguished passengers a royal wetting.

Meanwhile, Malenkov and Suslov seized hold of me and ushered us towards a motor boat. Malenkov invited Admiral Gorshkov, at that time Deputy Commander-in-Chief of the Soviet Navy, to take us on a trip and advised us against running down Mikoyan *en route*! It was as if Lord Mountbatten had been conducting pleasure boat trips on the Serpentine.

I should not have been a bit surprised if I had suddenly seen Suslov turn into a white rabbit, take out several watches from his pocket and disappear down a hole, muttering that he would be late for the meeting of the Central Committee. Nor would it have struck me as strange if one of the worms which had been prepared for the fishing called out in a thin small voice 'Try me!' and then helpfully jumped on to the hook. Khrushchev and Bulganin might have turned into Tweedledum and Tweedledee—after all, they were much the same size and dressed alike—though I should have been severely alarmed if they had started quarrelling about a rattle. Indeed, there was a moment when I really believed that Malenkov had become the Red Queen, as he took me very seriously by the arm and led me at a great pace towards the table, overtaking all the ambassadors and Soviet dignitaries on the way. 'To the luncheon table,' he kept repeating. I had to look at him closely to make sure he was not saying 'faster and faster'!

After washing in splendidly equipped mobile lavatories, which Mikoyan showed us with great pride, we were all escorted to the lunch tables, which were shielded from the inclement Moscow skies by an ample awning. The high table at which the Presidium sat had a magnificent beech wood as a natural backcloth, and during the courses Russian serving maids with kerchiefs on their heads and holding trays on high could be seen passing through the shadows of the trees. It was a beautiful sight, reminiscent of the work of a nineteenth-century Russian landscape painter, and it added to the atmosphere of unreality I had sensed so strongly when I had first stepped into the garden.

At the table members of the Ministry were seated at strategic points to look after us. I sat near Kuznetsov, colleague of the Deputy Foreign Minister, Zarubin, and he frequently toasted me and chaffed me about the fishery negotiations I was having with him at the time. During the lunch we were regaled with an excellent concert by the best singers of the Bolshoi. Perhaps the climax of the meal was the exquisite hushed singing to the guitar by the Russian

М Е Н Ю

Икра зернистая и паюсная, растегаи
Балык, лососина, шемая копченая
Индейка с фруктами, ветчина
Салат из дичи
Огурцы, помидоры, редис

Раки в пиве
Бульон куриный
Судак в белом вине
Седло оленя с гарниром
Жаркое — индейка, рябчики, цыплята

Парфе сливочное, мороженое фруктовое
Кофе, чай, печенье, фрукты, арбуз, дыня

7 августа 1955 года

Fig. 3. Menu for the garden party, 7 August 1955. For translation see p. 77

tenor Kozlovsky. The silence was so intense that nothing seemed to stir for miles, except occasionally the rushes at the water's edge.

During the meal Bulganin, who was conviviality itself, made a speech in which he recalled the success of the Geneva meetings and expressed the wish that festivities such as the present ones should take place more frequently. I am told that Khrushchev interjected something to the effect that they should not be allowed to interfere too much with people's work, and this prompted some of the press correspondents present to conclude that he did not really approve of so un-Soviet a form of hospitality. Indeed, the American Ambassador maintained that neither Khrushchev nor Molotov were really in favour of the 'new look' in Soviet foreign policy. In Khrushchev's case, however, this was wrong. It was simply that he was a great deal more at ease wandering around a collective farm, laying down agricultural law in the company of his party cronies than in making himself agreeable to diplomats.

The Russians had thoughtfully mounted a television set on a table to enable the guests to watch the football match between our Wolves and Spartak, which was being played in Moscow that day. There was always a crowd round it and the game was much discussed during lunch. When lunch was over I was on my way to the television set when I observed Khrushchev walking towards me. I invited him to come and watch. Presently we were joined by Mikoyan and Malenkov; then I felt an arm round my shoulder, and Bulganin himself came to complete the group. We were photographed by the correspondent of *Time* and our picture appeared on the front page with the caption: 'Mr Khrushchev and a friend—Mr Parrott, British Chargé d'Affaires in Moscow.' We had a pleasant time watching the last minutes of the match, disappointing though the result was.

We next wandered into the garden again, where guests were picking strawberries and raspberries. Near them the Marshals Zhukov and Konev asked us, winking, whether we had noticed that the 'peaceful marshals' of the Soviet Union were picking berries— unlike certain other military leaders in the west. They posed amiably for my son Michael to photograph them. He was an excellent amateur cameraman and found it hard to resist the offer of £100 made to him for one of the photos by Sefton Delmer of the *Daily Express*. I exchanged some good-natured banter with them, but it was interrupted by an urgent summons from Bulganin to bring our children to see the deer. Five large black Zis's—Soviet cars reserved for VIPs—were waiting in the beech glade, but unfortunately my family were so scattered by that time that I could not collect them, and Bulganin set off without us. The American Ambassador and his daughter went with them, however, and told me that when Bulganin was asked whom the dacha had originally belonged to, he showed some embarrassment in having to say before the young Avis Bohlen that it had belonged to Count Orlov, the lover of Catherine the Great.

As lunch had not started till about 3 p.m. and had lasted several hours, the evening was now advanced and most of the guests began to abandon their fishing and boating. I noticed that the Presidium had formed a little ring and were enjoying a quiet private sing-song. Mikoyan did a short Armenian dance. Reizen, a Chalyapin-like bass, and Ivanov, with his warm baritone, sang 'Stenka Razin', and all the Presidium, including Molotov, joined lustily in the chorus. Many of the guests joined the ring and Bulganin brought my youngest son, Jasper, into the middle and held him in a paternal handclasp. There was much laughter when Shepilov, then editor of *Pravda* and a Secretary of the Communist Party, was pushed forward on the alleged grounds that he had a really fine baritone voice.

Perhaps the most striking feature of the day was the easy atmosphere. It was no mean achievement on the part of the Soviet leaders, if one takes into consideration the fact that they had had next to no experience of this sort of entertaining, and they neither overdid it nor underplayed it. They did it as to the manner born. Indeed they did more. They created an atmosphere of enchantment. At its most prosaic it reminded me of a Chelsea fête or flower show, but, at its most sublime, of a Shakespearean fairyland, through which Bulganin seemed to move, now like Prospero and now like the Duke in the Forest of Arden. And it was Bulganin's genial personality which irradiated the festivities throughout. When we said goodbye and shook hands with him, he took my youngest son by the hand and put his spectacles on his nose. Jasper can boast that, for a moment, he saw the world through the eyes of the Prime Minister of the Soviet Union.

The events of the day were prominently reported in the Soviet press, but the Russian correspondents were incapable of conveying its atmosphere in their reports. The phrases 'lively conversations quickly began', 'N. S. Khrushchev invites all persons to look at the park', 'Foreign and Soviet guests walk along shaded alleys, admire the mirror-like surface of the ponds' had the stilted tone of a recorded language course.

The Soviet government had clearly given thought to the selection of pictures to be published, and the Yugoslav Ambassador and the head of the Yugoslav Parliamentary Delegation were not left out.

The American Ambassador was shown—always in conversation with Molotov. When I had occasion to call on Bulganin three days later he asked me eagerly how we had all enjoyed ourselves. He had even prepared a collection of newspaper articles and photographs and took evident pleasure in showing them to me. It may be that he was anxious to have his efforts appreciated, particularly if Khrushchev and others of his colleagues were sceptical about its value. But I think that on this occasion he was inspired by a genuine wish to be friendly to the representative of one of the three powers he had met at Geneva, and particularly of Great Britain. It was in fact a follow-up of the Geneva spirit.

A typical feature of diplomatic life in Moscow was the National Day receptions. These, of course, were held in all diplomatic posts, but nowhere made such a fetish of as behind the Iron Curtain. Under Stalin western National Days in Communist countries were generally attended by only one or two ministers of the government who, as is well known, were never top-ranking Communists. But in Khruschev's time an exception was made for the Queen's birthday party and other similar functions. Here the host could count on the presence of a nucleus of the top leaders. This made these parties valuable diplomatic events, since the Soviet leaders mixed freely with diplomats and journalists and were fair game for anyone who wanted to accost them. They were, as I said, courteous and friendly, the best 'Party men' in the true sense of the word. They would not, it goes without saying, do anything to mar the occasion for the host, but if the reception were to be held at the embassy of another Communist country or an uncommitted country, they would not scruple to make speeches or toasts at times which were embarrassing for some of the guests.

Here I must say something about the notorious issue of the 'walk out' which created something of a furore during my time in Moscow. It is impossible for an ambassador to remain unconcerned if his government is attacked in his presence on a public social occasion. Even if he affects to ignore the slight, he cannot do so because people will be watching his every reaction, and his colleagues will report back on this to their governments. At the same time, he has a duty not to be discourteous to his host and the government his host represents.

In Moscow there is, for political (and human) reasons, a great feeling of *esprit de corps* among western diplomats and if, for instance, the United States or the Italian governments were to be attacked, and the American or Italian Ambassadors felt they should walk out, their western colleagues would feel that they should act in sympathy with them and do the same.

The 'walk out' craze started when the Burmese Ambassador, who was a socialist idealist, thought he might contribute to international understanding if he organized a big dinner in a Moscow hotel for all the Heads of Missions in Moscow sitting around one table. The exalted guests, who had not been warned of this, were aghast when they arrived and saw the table plan. The American Ambassador found he would be sitting at the same table as the Chinese and the British Ambassador the same as the East German. The guests hurriedly huddled together to discuss the course they should follow. They decided they must express their apologies to their host and insist on withdrawing—which they did. Going down the stairway, however, they were unlucky enough to run straight into Mr Molotov, who was just coming up. Nothing is more discourteous than to leave a dinner where the Minister of Foreign Affairs of the government to which you are accredited is the guest of honour and, especially, to do so just as he enters! This episode resulted in a lot of head-shaking and heart-searching among the *chers collègues*.

It inspired the famous Osbert Lancaster cartoon in which a whole phalanx of ambassadors is shown in full regalia (never the case in Moscow, of course, where at Soviet receptions not even a black tie is worn), blazing with medals and sashes, descending a staircase, to be confronted by another ambassador, similarly accoutred, coming up. 'Now really, *mon cher collègue*,' says the doyen, 'we must insist that you arrive in time to walk out with us.'

Arising out of this, the Netherlands Ambassador, who had taken part in the historic 'walk out', played an amusing practical joke on some of his closest colleagues. He invited them to a private dinner and put a false table plan up outside the hall. He did not include the Chinese or the East Germans in the plan because he knew that his guests would see that he was joking. Instead, he wrote down the names of the worst bores in the corps and pretended to seat each beside one of his colleagues at the dinner table.

The guests were furious. The party was supposed to be an informal one where everybody could relax. They formed an indignant group outside muttering, 'Monstrous of "Tex" to do this to us.' They soon joined in their resourceful host's laughter, however, when they discovered that they were in fact completely alone with him.

There were other less amusing forms of diplomacy in Russia. I was there when the Suez campaign took place. This sparked off the first of those massive demonstrations at the buildings of the western embassies, which were to become a regular part of diplomatic life during the next ten years. On the whole, those staged against our embassies behind the Iron Curtain were less savage than those directed against some of the others: against the Americans and Belgians at the time of the Congo troubles or, later, the Russians by the Chinese in Peking, or against us by the Indonesians in Djakarta or the Irish in Dublin. Needless to say, however, we were not very happy when, at the time of the Suez crisis, we found our whole courtyard filled with surging Russians who cut our main building off from its subsidiary building, climbed on to the roof and posted offensive placards on the windows of our offices and our ambassadress's drawing room. Moreover, we were kept prisoner in the building for most of the day.

Yet when I looked at the crowds I could not be frightened. They were all young and attractive people, and seemed to be full of good humour, which contrasted curiously with the venomous words on their posters. Most of them behaved as if they were on holiday and were obviously getting an enormous kick out of walking over our Embassy gardens and grounds. What was reassuring about the demonstrations was that, contrary to reports in the Soviet press, they were not spontaneous but most punctiliously organized. Had they reflected a spontaneous upsurge of feeling, it might have been rather nasty. Thus, when the Ambassador sent me to protest to Zorin and I had to pass through the crowds to find my Russian chauffeur who had bolted in panic, I was not frightened at all. I knew that the demonstrators had respect, if not liking, for us; they were just doing a job and cared little about the purpose of their demonstration. I had to ask the crowds to give me a passage and they did this immediately—in spite of isolated jeers. For a moment I was strongly tempted to climb on to a tub and tell them the facts about Hungary and urge them to go home. They might well have given me a hearing, if I had done so. Given a little forensic skill I might have engineered their orderly dispersal.

As it happened, I could not locate my chauffeur and had to return to the Embassy to find some other means of transport. This was somewhat humiliating and I feared I had suffered a loss of face, but all went well. On the way, I noticed a general of militia in the garden. Now, this is a very rare bird indeed and not often observable in Moscow. I could not recall having seen one before, and when I got into the sanctuary of the Embassy, I suggested to my Ambassador that he might like to call him in and ask him how long our siege was going to last. This he did. The scene which followed was unforgetable. 'When are these disgraceful proceedings going to end?' the indignant Ambassador asked. The general stiffened like a ramrod, clicked his heels, saluted and replied: 'At a quarter to two, your Excellency.'

Poor general. He was honest and no doubt he paid for it. I felt obliged to quote his words to Zorin as proof that the demonstrations had been officially sponsored, and I felt a cad doing so. Indeed, I hate to think of that nice old man, more like a Zoshchenko character than a commissar, being possibly torn from the bosom of his family and shunted off to Siberia.

Caviare soft and pressed. Rastegais (pies).
Balyk (cured fillet of sturgeon). Salmon. Smoked Russian carp.
Turkey with compote. Ham.
Game salad.
Cucumbers. Tomatoes. Radishes.

Crawfish in beer.
Chicken Bouillon.
Russian pike-perch in white wine.
Saddle of venison with garnishings.
Roast-turkey, hazel grouse, chickens.

Parfait. Fruit ice.
Coffee. Tea. Pastries. Fruit. Water melon. Melon.

The garden party menu (translation) (see p. 71)

5. Musical Chairs

My wife arrived about two months after I did and soon afterwards I happened to notice that a concert was being given in Moscow of organ works and arias by Bach. Organ music was a rarity in a country where there were no organs in the churches, and a Bach concert was quite an event. The bearded organist, Alexander Gedike, who was performing, was almost eighty and looked as if he had come straight out of a play by Chekhov.

If the instrument was not impressive, the playing was. But I was more struck by the singer who sang the arias. We were so charmed by the music and the intimacy of the occasion (because the audience was not very numerous and rather special) that we ventured to do what we had done in Prague and went behind the scenes at the end of the concert to congratulate the performers. It was a bold move for us so soon after our arrival: we were not known to any of the musical people and diplomats did not usually do such things in Moscow. When we had groped our way behind the platform, we were received formally by the artists. The giant bear-like organist bowed respectfully but reticently, and the lady singer, Nina Dorliak, preserved her distance. Later, when I started talking Russian with them, congratulated them on their performance, asked the singer if she knew Purcell's music, and drew from her that she did but had not sung any of it, the atmosphere became much less frigid. Imagine my surprise when I discovered that she was none other than the wife of the pianist, Sviatoslav Richter.

She was allegedly descended from an old aristocratic French family who came to Russia like many other French emigrés at the time of the French Revolution. According to reports (although I cannot vouch for their truth), her mother, Ksenia Dorliak, had been a lady-in-waiting to the last Empress of Russia. After the Revolution she taught singing at one of the Leningrad music schools, eventually being appointed Professor of Singing at the Moscow Conservatoire.

Richter, whom I often met at concerts, was very knowledgeable about music and it was an intellectual treat to talk to him. At that time he was not known in the international arena but discriminating critics at home had recognized his exceptional talent.

Through meeting musicians at concerts and sometimes going backstage and talking to the artists I gradually got to know quite a lot of them. I sometimes had a chance to meet them again at receptions in the Kremlin—if they were important enough—and carry the acquaintance further. Eventually I was emboldened to try and organize a dinner party for all the most eminent composers in the Soviet Union. I realized that this was an exceedingly ambitious plan and did not stand much chance of success. Normally, artists did not come to the British Embassy for private dinners and were, indeed, hard to secure even at important diplomatic functions. However, if there was a visit from an English musician and the Ambassador gave a party for him, Russian artists were more likely to turn up, because they would probably get blanket approval, or even orders, to attend an Anglo-Russian function. To ask them to one's house rather than to the official residence was a most hazardous operation. I therefore determined to seek aid in this from the Russians themselves.

I had met at a reception the representative of VOKS, a one-time equivalent of the British Council. His name was, I think, Yakovlev, and he seemed pleasant and forthcoming, so I confided to him what I wanted to do. He thought it a good idea and promised to help. I planned the dinner several months in advance so as to give the operation plenty of time to develop.

The people I particularly wanted to get together were Shostakovich, Khachaturyan, Kabalevsky and Khrennikov, the influential Secretary of the Union of Soviet Composers. Yakovlev was as good as his word and, to my amazement, when the day arrived, they were all assembled in my house for dinner—all, that is, except for one and a very important exception at that: Shostakovich. Although it was him I wanted most to have, I felt I had been handsomely treated by the presence of so many other eminent composers.

I afterwards learnt, or at any rate guessed, why Shostakovich had not come. Shostakovich and Khrennikov were enemies. Khrennikov never failed to remind the Soviet public that Shostakovich was a deviationist, that his work was full of contradictions and that it was only by virtue of a few of his compositions (and these were his least good works) that he deserved a place in the Soviet musical hierarchy. It was said that Shostakovich would not attend a social function where Khrennikov was present. This may have been true, because I later saw these musicians again and never remember seeing Shostakovich in Khrennikov's company.

The dinner went very well. The composers came without their wives and mine was the only woman present. Our Russian cook produced a marvellous cake with several orchestral instruments executed faultlessly on it in icing and marzipan. There was plenty to drink and in the course of the evening both Kabalevsky and Khrennikov played their own compositions, Khrennikov singing songs from his incidental music to *Much Ado About Nothing* and accompanying himself on the piano. They all teased each other in a friendly way, and one would not have suspected any divisions among them. Kabalevsky pretended that he was no pianist, but the others laughingly insisted that he was a pupil of Goldenweiser, who was one of Moscow's great piano teachers many years ago. The atmosphere was happy and I learnt a lot about Soviet music which was very valuable to me. It was difficult to get any information in England about such things at the time.

The next day I went to a concert where I knew I should meet them in the interval. To my disappointment I found that not one of them came up to thank me for dinner. In fact, the few I saw walked away when they caught sight of me. I was soon to accustom myself to this. It was the Russian way of life.

Still, on one or two occasions when I had difficulty getting seats for concerts, some of the musicians took me into a special box they had in the Large Hall of the Conservatoire, which was reserved for members of the Union of Soviet Composers. I felt proud to be sitting among these distinguished musicians, and other diplomats who were not granted this facility stared at me in some perplexity from their normal seats. I finally succeeded in persuading Shostakovich to come to lunch, when he was kind enough to advise me which modern Soviet composers to look out for. At the opera I seldom ventured backstage. This would have been rash, because there were too many 'extras' about, but I got to know the singers through meeting them at receptions.

Oddly enough, when I did this sort of thing in Prague I was accused of being a spy but no such charge was brought against me by the Russians—as far as concerned my actions in Russia.

One day Peter Brook came on a visit, bringing with him his production of *Hamlet*, with Paul Scofield playing the leading role. The Russians put on marvellous entertainment for them, including a concert where the best ballerina, Maya Plisetskaya, appeared in *The Dying Swan*. The tenor Kozlovsky was due to sing there too and sent a message to me saying that he would like me to accompany him on the piano on this occasion. On the day of the concert he made an appointment for me to come to the Artists' Club, where the concert was to be held so that we could rehearse.

The building was full of small concert halls and club rooms and after welcoming me he marched me off to a room where he thought we could start working. It was already occupied by the Soviet Army Choir who were heartily rehearsing 'It's a Long Long Way to Tipperary' in English. We moved to several other rooms which were also taken up by people practising, until at last we found one where we could be alone. I sat down at the piano and we began. Kozlovsky was known to be a prima donna (once *Pravda* called him —ironically—Lohengrin Lohengrinovich). The piece we had picked together was a famous song by Pushkin set to music by Glinka. It was a simple ballad with an easy accompaniment of the um-pum-um-pum kind—flowing quavers in four beats to the bar. Any amateur could play this, but Kozlovsky's *rubato* was so incalculable that I was never quite sure when we would come together. At last, feeling a bit put off by his temperamental sallies, I made a diversion. 'I can't play on this piano,' I said. 'It's out of tune.' 'Out of tune! Out of tune!' he exclaimed crossly. 'It can't be out of tune.' He then tried playing on it. 'Yes,' he said suddenly. 'Mr Minister is right, it *is* out of tune.' He raced me off into yet another room where there was another piano, and here we concluded our practice. I was a little shy at the prospect of the performance. No one had told me when we were to appear, or how, and I sat in the front of the audience with our British actors. After *The Dying Swan*, exquisitely performed by Plisetskaya, the curtain went up again to reveal Kozlovsky standing alone with a piano in the background. He strode to the footlights and beckoned me to come up.

I scrambled with some difficulty on to the elevated platform and walked to the piano seat in the full blaze of the footlights. Again I felt like Alice—this time passing through the looking-glass. Kozlovsky sang the ballad beautifully, and by this time I had learnt to follow him and all went well. The next day there was a Kremlin reception and I was talking to some of the Soviet leaders, when Kozlovsky came up, took me by the arm and said, 'This is the British Minister, you know. He loves our *Poosh*kin and *Gleen*-ka and he was playing for me yesterday.' In most countries I suppose such a statement would not make a great impression on the members of the government. It was different in Russia. The eyes of the Soviet leaders lit up and they congratulated me in a most amicable way. As everyone knows, both Pushkin and Glinka mean a great deal to the Russians; a combination of both is irresistible, even for a member of the Presidium!

Singers and musicians appeared to occupy a higher place in the Communist hierarchy than actors. This did not mean that the Soviet high-ups were normally seen at concerts, even if Khrushchev and Bulganin sometimes attended the song and dance ensembles which came from the provinces to perform in Moscow. There was one exception, however, when they attended a concert of classical music. At a period when our relations were getting warmer, a group of distinguished musicians headed by Sir Arthur Bliss visited Moscow. They represented the flower of English musical life and included Leon Goossens, Jennifer Vyvyan, Gerald Moore, Cyril Smith and Phyllis Sellick, Alfred Campoli and Clarence Raybold. Such a team would certainly have commanded top-level artistic attention in Russia at any time, but we did not expect the government to be represented by anyone more important than the Minister of Culture. The Ambassador and I attended with our respective wives and had seats in the stalls. We looked across at the equivalent of the royal box and we saw three people bob up inside it just before the concert began. They were Khrushchev, Bulganin and Mikoyan. The orchestra was tuning up, when a man came and said something in the ear of the Ambassador. He and his wife then disappeared and, after what seemed an eternity, they surfaced in the royal box. We had hardly recovered from this shock when the same enigmatic figure, rather like the mysterious visitor who visited Mozart before his death, came and whispered something in my ear. It was: 'Mr Khrushchev and Mr Bulganin invite you and your wife to hear the concert in their box.' We had to thread our way through a be-wildering labyrinth before we found ourselves on steps mounting to B. and K.'s box. I then realized why it was that the Ambassador and Ambassadress had been such a long time on the way. The box had been built for Stalin and our devious route was all a part of the intricate security system arranged for him. Defensive catacombs as a sub-structure to celestial harmony above! A somewhat wasted effort, I thought, if the *generalissimo* never came there at all.

During the music I carefully observed the behaviour of the leaders. Although they must have been bored they did not show it. The one thing I noticed was that when Leon Goossens played an oboe solo Khrushchev seemed to be full of an inner tension and looked as if he was trying to suppress his laughter. At any rate, he was bursting to say something and could hardly check himself. When the applause came, he beckoned to me to sit near him and said, 'This reminds me of when we were in Belgrade. You know, we went to a concert like this and someone brought out a national instrument of some kind and blew on it, and blew on it, and blew on it all the time. And when I looked round what did I see but Mikoyan, fast asleep.' Mikoyan was the favourite butt of Khrushchev and he was always making jokes about him. When we sat down to supper afterwards in the box and Khrushchev was arranging the *placement*, he said to my wife, 'Mrs Parrott, sit next to Mikoyan. He's our cavalier. At least he's the best one we've got.' I can remember that the evening passed with more digs at Mikoyan, which the latter took quite phlegmatically.

During the meal we were served with quails on toast, and when we tried to cut them with a knife they jumped off the plate. Khrushchev watched me with a condescending smile. Then he said: 'That reminds me of when we were in India and Burma.' Since on that occasion he had made a very anti-British speech, which the British government particularly resented, it was not exactly the most tactful thing for him to say. We all held our breaths and he went on as follows: 'Once at a dinner there Bulganin and I were given quails, and I saw a Burmese official trying hard to cut them just as you were. Finally I said to him: "Use your fingers, man!" And the official replied, "I'd very much like to, Mr Khrushchev, but unfortunately those British colonists taught me to use a knife and fork".'

It was an immense compliment to us that these Soviet leaders who never turned up at their own concerts, should come to hear a concert of our musicians. It may seem bizarre to some readers that we should think of measuring our success by the presence at a concert of leading members of the Soviet Presidium. But in Russia this had enormous significance. For many years one gauged the position of the leaders in the struggle for power by the kinds of occasion on which they appeared in public. The appearance of Khrushchev in a royal box, which was otherwise rarely used, during this visit showed the whole of Moscow the *political* importance which the Soviet government attributed to it.

I cannot conclude without saying a word about dear Yuri Davidov, Tchaikovsky's nephew. I met this wonderful man at his uncle's museum at Klin, where he was the curator. He showed us the trees which he had helped his uncle to plant when he was composing his Sixth Symphony. It was the custom on a visit to Klin to ask for a record of the composer's music to be played. I asked for the *1812 Overture*. I could see that Davidov was unwilling to play it. He kept on suggesting something else. Afterwards he came and whispered in my ear, 'You know they have changed it. They took out the old Russian national anthem and put in the *Slava** instead.'

Conscious of the importance of the occasion for my children, I asked Davidov to tell them something about his uncle which they would remember all their lives. He thought for a moment and said to my second son, Michael, who was a bright and keen fourteen-year-old: 'You know, Tchaikovsky was a very industrious man. He always worked hard and was most conscientious in everything he did.' Then, turning to my youngest, Jasper, to whom music and musicians were in time to mean so much, he said: 'Tchaikovsky was a very clean man and he used to wash every day. Yes, all over, even his feet.' I looked at Jasper. He was standing goggle-eyed at this prodigious revelation.

---

* A famous chorus from Borodin's opera *Prince Igor*.

6. Southward Bound

One of the things we enjoyed most in Russia was making trips to the provinces. After having been confined to the capital for ten months I felt we deserved an outing. We decided not to go too far afield. I was particularly anxious to see something of the Ukraine and the Crimea, which was now part of it.

The train to Kiev, which we boarded on 24 May 1955, went so slowly that we could easily have jumped off, picked flowers and caught up with it again. In fact, the journey from Moscow took us twenty-one hours, which was exactly the time scheduled for it in the 1914 *Baedeker*!

There was no restaurant car, but at the end of the carriage sat a wizened little old man, who seemed himself to be a relic of pre-revolutionary days and who served us with innumerable glasses of hot watery tea from a samovar installed in the corridor. For solid food, passengers relied on buying boiled eggs, chicken, radishes, pickled apples and wild berries from vendors on the platforms. As soon as Russian travellers got into the train and prepared themselves for a long journey they took off their coats and dresses and put on pyjamas and peignoirs. At every stop thereafter they could be seen strolling up and down the platform in these garments, a somewhat exotic sight for western eyes!

Kiev seemed much more relaxed than Moscow. The people looked happier and better off; the houses were in good repair; the streets were lined with avenues of lime trees; and the parks and gardens were well kept and full of flowers. I remember that the Austrian poet Rainer Maria Rilke, who was so enthusiastic about Russia, was not attracted to Kiev. I understand why. Kiev looked like a town in the Austro-Hungarian rather than the Russian Empire. And that no doubt explained why it disappointed him and attracted me.

No one seeing Kiev today could escape some feeling of disappoint-

ment. It had once been the proud capital of Russia and the seat of
her Metropolitan. Foreign merchants, catching their first glimpse of
the golden city, would marvel at its beauty. Prince Vladimir, its
ruler, introduced Christianity and brought the first culture to
Russia. It was here that Russians began to learn from Greek masters
the art of icon and fresco painting. The city state had formerly been
so powerful that it dominated all of Russia which was not overrun
by Asiatic nomads. It even threatened Constantinople. The oldest
stone church in Russia had once stood here.

But when the royal dynasty began to quarrel among themselves,
Kiev, lying in the midst of the steppe, and an easy prey to the nomad
hordes, was lost. The city was sacked many times by the princes of
the blood, and when it was left unprotected it was destroyed by
Pechenegs and Tartars. When Catherine the Great saw the city for
the first time in 1787 she wrote: 'I keep on looking to find the city:
up to now I have only found two fortresses and suburbs. All the
ruined parts are called Kiev and remind one of the past grandeur
of the ancient capital.' If on top of this one bears in mind the severe
destruction wrought on the city by German and Romanian forces
in the last war, one can understand how disappointing old historic
Kiev looks today. I visited the wonderful eleventh-century Cathedral
of St Sophia. Its exterior has been reconstructed many times and
only its interior is still to a great extent original. It has some remarkable secular frescoes depicting eleventh-century Byzantine court
life, including circus scenes.

The Lavra—formerly one of the four most important monasteries
in Russia—is now heavily restored and forms part of what is called
a 'State Reservation Museum'. One could not help being struck by
the contrast between the emphasis placed on the historical value of
the buildings on the various signs and notices and the crude anti-
religious note sounded in the party texts which were posted up at
key points inside. It was like inviting people to look over
Tchaikovsky's house, praising him as a great Russian and plaster-
ing the walls with posters saying what a pernicious thing music
was.

I examined all the guide books on sale in Kiev and found that in
none was there any mention of the famous Lavra Caves. It seemed
indeed that everything was done to make it difficult for visitors to
get to them. The road from the Lavra to the caves appeared to be
barred, but a friendly Russian workman said we should take no

notice and led us through to where they began. The scene outside them was unexpected and seemed like an old religious pilgrimage with crowds of visitors, mostly of the poorest class, bunching up to get their candles and go down below. In the past, of course, this crowd would have been a hundred times bigger.

It was uncanny being given a taper and being escorted by a monk down narrow steps into the bowels of the earth. The pressure of his warm and clammy hand seemed sinister in the darkness. We passed by the diminutive subterranean cells where the old monks lay embalmed and in full regalia, including the famous first chronicler of Russian history, Nestor.

We left Kiev by boat on the evening of the following day for a three-day trip down the Dnieper to Kherson—a port on the Black Sea. It was an enchanting experience to have a parting glimpse of the Ukrainian capital in the evening light, and hear the nightingales singing from the shrubs on the banks as we cruised along. Unhappily, their music was soon to be drowned by the ubiquitous Soviet loud-speaker which kept up its interminable blaring for most of the trip.

The captain of the boat greeted us hospitably when we came on board and kept a fatherly eye on us. His behaviour was always most correct and he was impeccably dressed. However, we were rather perplexed one afternoon to see him emerge from his cabin in blue pyjamas, empty his shaving water over the side, and give a casual eye to the navigation.

One particular thing puzzled us. The restaurant always seemed closed when we wanted a meal. It was open at the oddest hours—mostly when we did not want to eat, like from 10 to 12 a.m. or from 2 to 4 p.m. After we had suffered this for a day, we then found that they would unlock it specially for us whenever we felt hungry. But this made little difference because there was hardly anything to eat except eggs. We had the kindest attention from the restaurant stewardess, Olga, who asked us before the boat stopped at the main ports what food we would like her to buy at the local 'bazaar', so that we should have the meals we liked. Yet at every stop, on visit-ing the bazaars, we saw there was absolutely nothing to be had except eggs, potatoes and poppy seeds which the Russians ate then as we would sweets. However, at Buzhin we saw *one* ancient hen held on a lead by a muzhik wearing a long-tailed coat in the old Russian style. I said: 'Olga will certainly snap that up,' and, sure enough, we got it for dinner that evening. But as was to be expected in a Communist society, the skinny fowl was divided up among all the passengers, so we did not get a very full meal!

There was plenty of space in our cabin and we were very comfortable. The only thing which disturbed us was that our paddle-steamer insisted on greeting every other craft on the river with blood-curdling shrieks from its hooter, and this continued all night. After a whole night of it, though, I began to sleep very well and I can heartily recommend a Russian steamer trip for anyone suffering from insomnia. You will not have an overloaded stomach and the paddle motion and the variety of sounds, like the cries in a jungle, will finally deaden your nerves so that you no longer respond to any external stimulus.

Throughout the voyage the scenery along the Dnieper was beautiful, if somewhat monotonous, as the objects of interest to be seen from the boat were few and far between. It was fascinating, none the less, to be able to stop at so many small Ukrainian towns and villages, which one could probably never reach by rail or road. Moreover, the districts through which the Dnieper flowed were full of historical memories. Not far away lay the battlefield of Poltava where the Swedish King Charles XII was defeated by Peter the Great. Everywhere there were links with famous Ukrainians of the past from Mazeppa to Shevchenko. Memories of the Zaporozhe Cossacks seemed ever present too. At Perevolochno we reached the point in the river where Charles XII, fleeing from Poltava, attempted to lead his defeated army across to the other bank, but was prevented by the Russian armies and the Ukrainian Cossacks. Only the Swedish king, Mazeppa, and their immediate suite succeeded in reaching the other bank. We were also made only too conscious of more recent history by the plight of so many towns and villages that had been destroyed in the war.

We generally had from half an hour to two hours at the most important stops, most of which were indescribably primitive, although Ukrainian houses were mostly cleaner and better kept than those in the Moscow area. Wherever we landed, we realized that, unless it was a very small place, there were miles to tramp before we got to the centre of the settlement, and then there might be nothing to see. At Cherkassi, for instance, the centre of the town seemed to be some two miles from the landing stage, and it was a matter for conjecture whether we were going along the main road or not, since it was nothing more than a broad grass field interspersed with impassable mud or deep ponds. Cherkassi was described in a 1951 Soviet guide book as a town of marvellous fruit orchards, but we could see nothing of them. The sole life visible was a steady trickle of old women going to and fro on their way to a market we could never find. The so-called main road bore the pretentious if anachronistic title of 'the Boulevard of the Comintern'.

Seventeen miles below Dniepropetrovsk the boat crossed what used to be the Zaporozhe rapids, now covered over by the Dnieper Dam. Until the last year before the war, when the dam was completed, these rapids—there were nine of them, of which the most formidable was called 'the Insatiable One'—formed a barrier some sixty miles long between the upper and lower reaches of the Dnieper, through which small craft and rafts alone could penetrate and then only at high water. Otherwise the navigation of the rapids was nothing short of daredevilry. To guide the boats through this difficult passage, Catherine the Great founded a special school of pilots.

Although the Dnieper is now so well regulated that one can hardly believe the rapids ever existed, the river is by no means easy to navigate. In spite of its width, it is shallow, and the channel along which our boat went was a narrow one. It happened frequently during our voyage that we had to cast anchor and wait just off the channel while a slow convoy of barges passed by. This made the journey tedious. The boat never kept to schedule and arrived at the terminus of Kherson about six hours late. That must have been a feature of the river services in the Soviet Union, because there was a cartoon about delays on the Volga journeys published in *Crocodile*, the main comic weekly of the country. Passengers were shown waiting at the quayside and one of them was saying: 'We have scarcely got used to the boat coming twenty-four hours late, when it starts coming forty-eight hours late.'

It was an intriguing experience passing through the sluice gates of the great Dnieper Dam. The ships went through three locks, each of which lowered the water by nearly forty feet. The passengers (none of whom were foreigners) took great interest in the lock. I asked the officers of the boat who were lunching in the dining room how great the drop was, but fear of giving away any kind of information is so ingrained in the Russians that their replies were all evasive.

Below the Dnieper Dam the river divided into two channels—the new and old Dnieper. In between lay Khortitsa, an island where at the time of the Byzantine emperors, trade caravans used to rest and make offerings in gratitude for their safe passage over the rapids. Here it was that the princes of Kiev made their base for their campaign against the Polovtsians and Tartars in the twelfth and thirteenth centuries.

The passengers came and went. None of them, as far as we were aware, travelled all the way from Kiev to Kherson, and indeed the captain expressed surprise and pleasure when he heard we were staying so long. Things were quiet on the first-class deck, but there was tremendous activity in the hold below, where peasant women travelled from stop to stop, buying and selling goods at various bazaars. There was a kind of shop on the second-class deck where goods were sold to passengers.

It was the time of the elections in Britain. Newspapers were difficult to obtain and wireless programmes either ignored them or reported on them in Ukrainian, which was not always easy to understand on account of the distortion by the loudspeakers. I found it a good opening gambit in conversations with the various passengers to ask them whether they had, by any chance, heard the results. In this way I got into a long conversation with a university lecturer, who told me he had never left the Soviet Union and had never before exchanged a word with an Englishman. He spoke with unexpected frankness and lamented the lot of historians in the country. He said that he had been forced to study economic history, since the study of political history was impossible on the basis of the one-sided documentation available. He had tried to write about the rise of the working class, but failing to make any headway there, he had had to limit himself to a study of the history of the railway system in Russia, where he hoped to get better documentation. He asked me whether it was possible to get hold of any books on railways from England, since England was a pioneer in railway development. Later, I went with him to his cabin and he questioned me at great length about books on Russian history published in England. His particular interest was nineteenth-century history. I mentioned the names of various books which had been published and his eyes grew more and more hungry. He said that if he could only get these books, he had someone who could translate them for him. He was forced to go, at his own expense, to Moscow for two months every year to continue his researches. He referred to Khrushchev's speech in Belgrade and cited the Soviet dispute with Tito as a case where it was absolutely essential to see the documents before one could form any opinions. Soviet intellectuals were skilful at reading between the lines in their newspapers and there was a tremendous rage among the young for more information about everything. I lent him Mannerheim's biography which my wife brought with her. After reading it, he said that the Finnish war was another subject on which one should suspend judgement until one had seen the complete documentation.

He told me some curious things about the behaviour of the students at the university, emphasizing the tremendous solidarity between them. Cribbing was quite common in examinations but students never betrayed each other when the authorities attempted to break this down. Any student who informed was given the cold shoulder.

He listened to the BBC broadcasts in Russian, which were clearly audible in his area. He complained that there was too much politics in them and what the BBC should do was give the Russians the latest news of progress made in Britain and of new books published in all fields, particularly scientific and literary. When we talked about the elections he seemed quite well informed about the British political scene. I gave him my address in Moscow and offered to show him some of our books, if he felt like coming to see me. With great hesitation he gave me his own name and address. Before he left he came especially into our cabin to implore me under no circumstances to write to him.

Much later when I had returned to Moscow and was working in my office in the Embassy, I was surprised when a Russian was put through to me on the telephone. This was most unusual. The caller was obviously using an assumed name and said he had now come up to Moscow and would like to see me. I suspected that it was my lecturer, but his boldness struck me as being quite out of character. It would have been highly dangerous to attempt to carry on a conversation with someone under an assumed name, when one knew that everything that was said was being taken down and reported to the KGB. In cases like this the wisest thing was to play it straight. I asked him if he would not rather come and have a cup of tea with me in my flat. He told me that he could not do this and suggested that we should meet in a particular restaurant. I said that I was not free to do that, unfortunately, and the only place I could see him was at home. He then turned nasty and made unpleasant remarks about Britain, which satisfied me that he was speaking with 'his master's voice' and not his own.

We never met again. This was one of the sad things about life in Moscow. I simply could not risk continuing an acquaintanceship in this way. He may have been an unusually bold and fearless intellectual (he was a Jew), but he could also have been in the hands of the KGB already, after consorting with me on the boat, and was now perhaps being used as their stool-pigeon. Perhaps he had been one from the very beginning. How was I to know?

The captain escorted us off the boat at Kherson and found a taxi to take us to our hotel. From the balcony of our room we could see a vast expanse of water and many sailing boats. The town was full of sailors and there were models of Soviet warships on sale in one of the shops. We went into the market and bought our first strawberries, but otherwise there was not much to be found, although the market here was the best supplied of all we visited. The population was noisy and excited and we became aware of the great difference between southern and northern Russians. We went to the garrison church, which was founded by Catherine the Great and saw Potemkin's tomb and the chair in which Catherine had sat.

We left in the late afternoon to take the train to Dzhankoi. Ours was a typical Russian departure. The station was crowded with a seething mass of peasants, none of whom seemed to have tickets. There was no porter to be seen and, as we could not possibly leave any of our cases, we had some difficulty piloting ourselves and all our baggage through deep puddles of mud to our carriage, which turned out to be at the very end of the platform. It was only when we got to the carriage that we met the smartly dressed station master, who was waiting to receive us. The fact that we were weighed down by baggage seemed to make no impression on him. However, he was concerned about our comfort in the train—at least! There were only 'hard' compartments on the train, but he had done his best to try and make one of them appear 'soft'.

Though we should have had a compartment to ourselves, a Russian had booked a seat in it. The station master said that he could easily be asked to sit elsewhere. When he finally turned up, he gave every indication of wanting to leave immediately, but we pressed him to stay, and he proved at first to be a lively companion. He was frank about his own personal life, which is characteristic of Russians, and he told us within about twenty minutes that he had lost his wife, because Russian doctors had not understood how to use penicillin at the time of her illness, and had given her too little of it.

He appeared to know that we were English and subsequently asked what part of the country we came from. When I said that I was in the Embassy in Moscow a horrifying change came over his face. It was alarming to see how he blenched. 'I thought you were a member of a *delegation*,' he said. 'Well, I suppose we are,' I said. 'To be a member of an Embassy *is* to be a member of a delegation, only you stay two years instead of two weeks in a country.' He had obviously taken us for 'fellow travellers' (he had probably been misinformed by the station master) and never seemed to recover from the shock.

On our arrival at Dzhankoi, where we had intended to stay the night, we were welcomed by the official responsible for accommodation, who told us that there was going to be a conference there (I could scarcely believe this as the place was so tiny), and that he could not offer us the rooms which had been promised us. Instead he had arranged accommodation for us at Simferopol, which was an hour and a half's drive away. We found ourselves thrust into what appeared to be a taxi but in fact was not. The driver introduced himself as the director of the local cinema, and he had agreed to drive us to our destination in his own car. We were grateful to him for this, but it soon became apparent that he had come straight from a wedding and was completely tipsy. He talked and gesticulated wildly and his hands were seldom on the wheel. This kept us in a constant state of tension, as it was late at night and the road was full of drunks reeling in all directions, mostly young people coming from dances, or perhaps from the same wedding. (We were fairly horrified by the amount of drunkenness we encountered during our trip, particularly among young people.) I eventually succeeded in making him stop so that I could sit beside him in the front seat and prevent him from constantly turning round and talking to us in the back. I did my best to keep him in as calm a frame of mind as possible.

He was overcome with delight, if bewildered, to find that he was talking to an Englishman, and when he detected any sign of agreement in our views, declared that he would go to the office of his local *Obkom* (Provincial Party Committee) the next day and tell them about it. Twice he pressed me to go to the offices of the Yalta newspaper so that we could give them the substance of our conversation.

He had a few things on his mind. There was some kind of mystery with regard to Churchill's retirement. Would I tell him the truth about it? It could not be explained merely on grounds of age. (Here he had obviously swallowed Soviet newspapers' innuendoes that Churchill had been hastily 'put away'.)

He was outraged by Beria's treason. He said over and over again: 'How could we know that this might happen? There were we, believing that they were all sitting there in our government looking after our interests, and all the time that scoundrel was working against us.'

He was a great supporter of Khrushchev, repeating most of his favourite notions, like 'heavy industry', 'the cultivation of maize', etc. When I said that Khrushchev must be an able man, he nearly kissed me. In general, his ravings were interesting in that they revealed that, like many other Russians, he had a lot of questions preying on his mind to which the Party line did not provide a totally satisfactory answer. He also had difficulty in reconciling what he read in the papers with the facts, even in the garbled state in which he received them.

While lunching in a restaurant in Simferopol we had an experience which was to recur several times during our trip. A group of Russians came to sit at our table, but a waitress appeared and told them to sit elsewhere. Though the husband obeyed, the wife became sulky and remained where she was. She then began to make unpleasant remarks about 'not being good enough for foreigners'. Finally, she 'swept out'. When people in restaurants wanted to sit at our table and asked us, 'Are these places free?', we always gave a friendly reply. But they soon received some directive from someone that they should sit elsewhere, and resented it. Incidentally, contrary to the English custom, Russians always seemed to prefer to 'fill up' a table rather than sit at an empty one. Presumably communal life made them uneasy about solitude.

When we reached the Crimea we took the opportunity of paying a visit to Bakhchisarai, the palace of the Tartar Khans. Our driver was himself a Tartar, which was appropriate. We saw the palace and received a good grounding in the history of the Crimea from a lady graduate in archaeology.

Next we took a car to Yalta. It was typical of conditions in the

Soviet Union that it was impossible to approach the door of the main hotel at this famous resort, as the road was up all the way. The balcony of our room looked out on to the street, and the noise of pneumatic drills throughout the day was most nerve-racking.

In the evening after dinner, an amusing incident occurred. In accordance with continental practice, Russians come up to ladies they do not know, including foreigners, present themselves and ask for a dance. I told my wife that, tired as she was, she *must* accept, if asked. Not to do so would be undiplomatic.

As she was whirled away in an unknown Russian's arms, a lady who was sitting with a man at a nearby table, leaned across to me and said in excellent English: 'He wants to dance with me. Please ask me for a dance and save me from him.' I pretended to look stupid. 'Now, come on,' she said, 'you Englishman, be a gentleman, and help a lady in distress.' I remained stolidly silent, because I liked neither her looks nor her approach. I felt awkward, however, when my wife came back.

On the esplanade at Yalta a young wounded sailor asked to borrow my field glasses. It turned out that he was in the severest category of war disablement and unfit for any work at all. He wore dark glasses, walked with a stick and his hand shook all the time. He was a heartrending sight. He said that he had been sent down to Yalta for a brief stay, but it was not enough, and he was getting worse all the time. His limbs trembled so much at times, that he could hardly stand. He told me he had a sister living in America and said he supposed things were pretty bad in England, but did not argue when I said that they were not. He asked me about unemployment in the United States and continued with the familiar argument that peace was necessary and there must never be a war again. He told me that his wife had run away from him and he was left with a little boy, whom he had to try and look after. He was helped by his family, and the state had given him a house with three rooms in which five other people lived. When I assured him that no country wanted war and asked who he thought was planning it, he growled out almost automatically, with a macabre grin, 'Churchill'. All the people I talked with came out sooner or later with this sort of remark.

Later we went to visit Chekhov's house in Yalta which was remarkably well kept. Chekhov's sister had refused to allow any alterations to be made to it since the day of her brother's death. She managed to defend it against both Russian Bolsheviks and German invaders. Even the visiting cards of people who called on Chekhov during the last year of his life were still to be seen on a tray under a glass. There had been no attempt to tamper with them, and good aristocratic and bourgeois names were left on top as they had been in his lifetime. In Chekhov's dining room and bedroom were icons. The notices hanging on the walls of each room went out of their way to explain that this was not because Chekhov was religious. They quoted passages to prove that he was not a believer but had to submit to the conventions of the times. It would have been easier for them to remove the icons, but this would have meant tampering with Chekhov's possessions. Suvorin, the publisher of the very reactionary newspaper *Novoe vremya*, to which Chekhov contributed, and who was at one time a great friend of his, had given him a small statuette of himself. There was also a photograph on the wall of the two men together in a group. The authorities would probably have liked to remove it and instead plaster the walls with photographs of Chekhov arm in arm with Gorky.

In Levadia we talked to some Russians who had taken us for Germans. Others assumed we were either Balts, Czechs or Poles. It was not the only occasion on which this happened.

We returned to Simferopol by taxi. Interestingly enough, the driver was again a Tartar, but this time he came from Moscow and had never lived in the Crimea. His original home was in Kazan. He said he had forgotten most of his native language and anyhow Kazan Tartar differed from Crimean Tartar. Since the forced removal of the Tartars, the Crimea had lost most of its real character. It was now populated by an extraordinary mixture of Great Russians and Ukrainians, drawn from all parts of the Soviet Union. Most of the notices were put up in the Ukrainian language, as the Crimea was now part of the Ukrainian Soviet Republic. The presence of blond Great Russians in Tartar villages with big notices stuck up in Ukrainian produced an odd effect.

Driving along the main road from Simferopol to Moscow we found a number of newly built roadhouses which offered primitive board and lodging to motorists as well as service for their cars. We stayed at one of these—Zelyony Gai—and were rather attracted by it. The facilities it offered were not of a high order, but it was clean and contrasted favourably with the sordid conditions one had to expect in hotels in the towns. Probably not all the roadhouses were

1. The invincible Bohemian nobility—still invincible after 1948. Countess Waldstein in the Waldstein (Wallenstein) Palace at the age of nearly 100.

2. The Waldstein Palace in Prague: the Cult of Personality—Wallenstein as Mars, the God of War.

3. Concert given by Beneš at the Hradčany after the war. Note the three harps (in tune) and the three Ambassadors, American, Soviet and British (out of tune).

4. The British Film Festival: I talk (down)to Beneš.

5. 1948: police and 'armed militia' holding the Red flag. They are there 'to keep law and order'. Whose? The Chinese maintain that there was no 'peaceful transition to socialism'.

6. February 1948: 'exhausted and isolated', Benš esuccumbs to Gottwald's pressure.

7. The 'yawning' gap between east and west: Vyshinsky and myself at the UN.

8. The amiability of the Serpent. Vyshinsky has already reported unfavourably on Clementis, the Czechoslovak Foreign Minister. As a result, he will be summoned back to Prague and executed.

9. 'Have you come from Moscow to destroy our dear church?' He suspects us of wanting to pull down the church we have been admiring.

10. Up the Wolves! Bulganin, and I watching the match on TV, with Krushchev Malenkov, Mikoyan, Kaganovich, Zhukov and other high-ups.

11. B. and K.'s famous garden party—a cross between an English fête and *Alice in Wonderland*.

12. 'Uncle' Bulganin chats with my three boys.

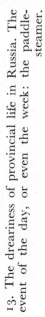

13. The dreariness of provincial life in Russia. The event of the day, or even the week: the paddle-steamer.

14. One of the countless
churches in Vologda.

15. The Thun Palace, the British Embassy in Prague.

16. The Thun Palace
from the air.

17. A cosy chat with Novotný.

18. The great days of Bohemian silver: Fischer von Erlach's tomb of St John of Nepomuk.

19. The pride of Prague Cathedral, the Wenceslas Chapel.

20. The pride of Prague, the Charles Bridge.

21. Draining the historic Bohemian fish-ponds.

22. *Yakee dar!* Peter Thomas arrives in Prague.

23. 1968: Russian tanks in Wenceslas Square, Prague, under the statue of the saint.

24. 1968: Goodbye to culture! Russian tanks in the Old Town Square by the side of the monument to Hus, and in front of the building where Kafka went to school.

as good; still, one welcomed them as a sign of growing civilization. There were roadhouses on the main Moscow–Simferopol road every ninety-five miles. Around one of the petrol pumps was a cluster of hoopoes—an unexpected sight!

Our last day on the journey back was Whit Sunday. It was the Russian custom on this day for girls to go into the woods to make garlands of flowers and wear them. Houses were decorated with birch trees, and churchgoers brought flowers and birch branches into the churches. We became conscious of this as soon as we left the Ukraine, where there appeared to be few churches (the influence of Polish and Catholic rule) and crossed into the Great Russian district, where there seemed almost too many. Whenever we stopped and looked at a church the peasant women seemed delighted. When I took a photograph of one in Novomoskovsk a woman asked me if she could have a print of it.

The speed with which we returned did not give us much opportunity for observation, but what struck us most were the appalling living conditions in the country, which were worse than those we were accustomed to see in the towns. Even in the Crimea I saw people living in places which were little better than holes in the ground. Returning to Moscow I read an article in *The Times* on Soviet housing, which contained these words: 'Housing has been an outstanding example of the failure of Communist reality to live up to the predictions of the prophets.' The writer mentioned that at the time of the Revolution peasant dwellings were often not much more than hovels and went on to say: 'And even today the individual peasant farmer tends more often than not to live in conditions identical with those of his father and grandfather.' The impressions which I formed after a fairly wide sweep of the Soviet countryside in what was a fertile part only confirmed the truth of this. In the villages and small towns hardly any houses were being built at all. In the larger towns attention was mostly concentrated on 'Houses of Culture', stations and other public buildings. Otherwise there was little that was new and what was being put up was jerry-built. Between Kursk and Orel the houses seemed quite medieval. Indeed, by and large the vast bulk of the houses in central and southern Russia seemed exactly as they were depicted in an old Russian book I had, which was published in about 1910—except that now every village boasted its cheap plaster statues of Lenin, Stalin and Komsomol heroines.

D

7. Security

One problem in carrying out official or even private business in Moscow was that we could never talk without being overheard because all rooms were presumed to be 'bugged'. As in other embassies at this time we had our own 'safe room' downstairs, where we were supposed to be able to speak freely and had our most important conferences with the Ambassador. I used to hate going in there since I was afraid there might be a short circuit, the ventilation would stop working and we would find ourselves cooped up like men in a submarine when the oxygen is exhausted. I asked Hayter once whether it would still be secure if the current failed. He answered grimly, 'It would be secure in this sense that we should all be dead.' Dead men tell no tales!

The same applied at our homes and everywhere else. We were supposed to be on our guard against talking about official business or discussing the habits and peculiarities of our colleagues, particularly members of our own staff, as this would enable the Soviet authorities to fill up the dossiers they held on them. The staff were continually warned to be vigilant. The weakness here was that we had not yet been able to point to a case where the Soviet had actually obtained vital information through somebody talking out of turn in a 'bugged' room. I myself doubted whether the Soviet authorities had the manpower to overhear and record everything that was said by every member of the numerous missions quartered in Moscow, but one could never be sure. In any case, it soon became simple to keep our conversation within safe channels and only speak about anything confidential or other people's foibles when we were in the open air. Bars were dangerous and even parks and gardens were vulnerable, as we were later told.

In my opinion the effectiveness of this bugging lay mainly in its potential for undermining morale. If you feel that Big Brother is watching and listening to you, and you are far away from home,

you begin to imagine things. Occasionally in this sinister and artificial atmosphere members of our staff broke down. Bohlen told me
that when he was in Moscow he found himself speaking to his wife
in a different tone from the one he used anywhere else. It was like a
state of chronic hypertension and great humanity and understanding were required when dealing with people.

From time to time, I used to help the Ambassador on security
matters. It was not strictly my job; it was the responsibility of the
Head of Chancery, who would normally report direct to the Ambassador on such questions. But I used to give a helping hand by talking seriously to the staff about the dangers of getting involved with
the Russians or breaking the Soviet laws. When the Ambassador
went away I had to take full responsibility for security in his place.
There were not as many 'breaches' as there were subsequently to be
in Prague, but each case was more serious because it took place in
the Soviet Union.

Normally on the few occasions when the staff acted foolishly,
they came and told us in time for us to be able to save their bacon.
One lady in a rather key position was rash enough to start an affair
with a Russian provocateur rejoicing in the seductive name of
Terpsichorov. The sad end of the story was that she was blackmailed
and pressurized to betray classified information. As far as I can
recollect she confessed to us before she did anything treasonable,
and we got her out of the country, making sure that nothing happened to her in East Berlin where she had to change planes for the west.

The only case I know of where a member of the staff compromised
himself with the Russians without telling us was that of the Naval
Attaché's clerk, John Vassall, though there might have been more
cases we never knew about.

Vassall had been sent out to Moscow four or five months before I
arrived; so I had not seen him when he came, or been involved in
any of the routine warning briefings given to him as a new member
of staff on arrival. By the time I was conscious of his existence and
was able to put a name to him, the Russians had already compromised him.

From the first I had been quite strict about the staff's relations
with Russians and felt that the Service Attachés were resentful when
I refused to let them and their families accept private invitations
from their own local teachers of Russian. They understandably
took the view that they were capable of looking after themselves.

This was true, but I had to take into account that for most Service Attachés or their assistants, this was their first experience of diplomatic life anywhere, let alone in Russia. They entertained generously in the good service tradition and did much to keep up the morale of the staff, but we could not exclude the possibility that under the effects of hospitality their wives, at least, might say or do something indiscreet. It was a delicate task discussing this with them and I often wondered whether out of excess of zeal I was not perhaps making myself into an unpopular Mrs Grundy.

Vassall tried afterwards to defend his actions by claiming that little was done for the junior staff by the senior members of the Embassy, and that he could not have made a clean breast of it to Hayter, as he was not the sort of man one could approach in a matter of that kind. He also said that after hearing me give a warning talk to the staff about the dire consequences of getting involved with the Russians (illustrated by the case of the lady and Terpsichorov) it was clear to him that 'no one would dare admit a thing to anyone in authority in future'.

Of course if a member of the junior staff got into trouble he did not need to go to his Ambassador or Minister (as I was at the time). There were plenty of senior officials nearer his age to whom he could turn. And in Vassall's case his first duty was to tell his chief, the Naval Attaché, or one of the latter's two assistants. However, he not only said nothing to any member of the staff but deliberately denied that he had had contact with Russians when the Naval Attaché put a direct question to him after my same talk to the staff. I remember urging the staff that if they were in trouble, they should tell us at once, before it was too late. But by that time Vassall was 'so far steeped in gore, that returning was as tedious as go o'er'.

In the spring of 1956, Vassall did actually come to see me in my office in the Embassy and spoke to me frankly about his fears for his future. He said that he was coming to the end of his two-year tour of duty in Moscow and was not at all sure whether the Admiralty would go on employing him or, if they did, what kind of a posting he would get. He said he had several Swedish friends whom he liked, and asked me if, through my Swedish connections, I could help him get a job in Scandinavian Air Lines. Although I hardly knew him, he did not strike me as someone who could not speak openly about his personal affairs to any senior member of the Embassy who showed himself a sympathetic listener. And I certainly was one. I rang up a friend at the Swedish Embassy and asked him if he could help. I cannot remember what the outcome was, but I imagine that my colleague suggested that Vassall should come to the Embassy and talk about it. In any case, if we can believe what Vassall wrote, he had so many friends among the higher personnel of the Swedish Embassy that he hardly needed my assistance.

The Radcliffe Tribunal which was set up to enquire into the Vassall case, completely disposed of the false reports published in some of the newspapers to the effect that Vassall was well known in the Embassy as a homosexual who had contacts with the Russians. The journalists responsible for them, when cross-examined by the Attorney-General, could not produce any facts to document their story. It was impossible, however good our relations with the staff, to know in detail how they spent their private lives when so many of them lived in scattered parts of Moscow. Occasionally it came out that someone had been drunk or behaved indiscreetly at parties. But I do not remember hearing of anything which involved serious contact with Russians.

The Mephistopheles in the Vassall case was the Soviet agent, Mikhailsky, who worked in the administration of the Embassy. He would help the staff in various ways, seeing that necessary repairs were done in their flats, assisting them with their shopping orders, getting theatre tickets for them or making their travel arrangements.

It was a key position for any Soviet agent, since such a person was indispensable in the Embassy whose staff would otherwise not be able to get what they needed. Whoever was appointed to the post had to be a Soviet citizen and would inevitably be used by the KGB.

I observed Mikhailsky carefully, because he was a Pole, and I had long been interested in non-Russian Slavic peoples. I remember that he struck me as a most undesirable character and was apprehensive about his position in relation to the staff. Indeed I made a point of engaging him in long conversation when I met him at a staff party. How did he come to be taken on? A temporary member of our staff, an academic who should have known better, had met him in Gorki Park and suggested we should employ him! I thought Mikhailsky might be a homosexual, although I did not assume Vassall was one, or connect the two. In the end, when I was acting as Chargé d'Affaires, I took the drastic step of sacking Mikhailsky as a flagrant 'contriver of undesirable contacts'. But that was closing the stable door after the horse had fled, since Vassall was already in Britain by then.

It was in November 1962, when I had been Ambassador in Prague for two years, that the Radcliffe Tribunal was set up by the Home Secretary to enquire into allegations with regard to the Vassall case and to determine any negligence which might have taken place. Early in 1963 I was asked to come over to give evidence, and I was fairly confident that I would be able to show that the Embassy had paid great attention to security matters and done all in their power to keep the staff from being dragged into perilous relationships with Soviet citizens. I was to receive a shock when I arrived in London.

I had a telephone call from the Treasury Solicitor asking me to come and see him. He showed me a minute written on 13 January 1956 to the Acting Head of Chancery by the Military Attaché in Moscow, reporting that his typist had volunteered the information that Mikhailsky's recent 'targets' had been not only herself (which she had allegedly reported before) but the Military Attaché's clerk, two junior members of the Embassy who had left Moscow and— Vassall. The Military Attaché added: 'I have no evidence, however, that his friendly approaches have been other than innocent.' On this minute Patrick O'Regan, the Acting Head of Chancery, had written: 'I have at any rate several times observed him going to Narodnaya and Sadovaya (where some of the junior staff lived) on Sundays and after hours. HMM has informed HE.'

The last sentence conveyed the impression that HM Minister (myself) had told the Ambassador about these suspicions. On the other hand, there was no evidence on the paper that I had ever read it, since normally, the Head of Chancery would have marked it to me and I would have minuted it myself and signed it. Neither the Ambassador not I could remember having seen it.

Unfortunately O'Regan had died some years before. He was a delightful, lovable Irishman, but he seldom acted as Head of Chancery and lacked experience in the post. The Commission might very well have concluded that we had been presented with an important clue on the Vassall-Mikhailsky relationship, and had taken no action on it, since there was no record of this having been done.

The only explanation I could offer, if I did indeed see this minute, was that we were all aware by this time of Mikhailsky's attempts to ingratiate himself with certain key members of the junior staff. Evidence of this is that at about that time the question had come up as to whether Mikhailsky should be sacked, and after some discussion, the Ambassador had decided that he should be retained, on the ground that the KGB would only replace him by another agent and 'better the devil you know'. In any case it would have been the responsibility of the Acting Head of Chancery, or the Head of Chancery, when he came back, to take action on the minute even if neither of them had received any specific guidance from the Ambassador or from me.

However, it was not only difficult to explain this to the Commission, but it put paid to my hopes that I would be able to show that we had been very much on the ball over security matters in the Embassy. A great handicap was that all these events had taken place seven years earlier and our memories of them were very shaky. When I asked if I could read the Embassy papers which led up to and followed the minute, and would have contained accounts of the positive security measures we had taken, I was told that they had all been burnt. Only this minute had been salvaged.

By the time the minute was written, Vassall had been working for the Russians for over six months, and a cross-examination of him on his relations with Mikhailsky at that late stage would probably not have yielded much result. Nonetheless, even if Vassall had not confessed then, his reactions might have strengthened our suspicions and induced us to transmit a much-needed warning to London.

The Commission accepted my assurance that I had no recollection of ever having seen the minute and that if I had done so, I should have minuted it or initialled it. What probably happened is that O'Regan never showed me the minute but merely mentioned the information to me. How he could have written that I had informed the Ambassador, I do not know, because this would have meant (a) my reading it, (b) my speaking to the Ambassador about it, and (c) my telling the Acting Head of Chancery that I had done so and one of us minuting it or signing it off. Surely the Ambassador would have commented and I would have conveyed that comment back to the Acting Head of Chancery?

There is little doubt that Vassall came to Moscow seeking adventure, and once it presented itself he was not the sort of character to resist it. He had a yearning for high life and Soviet money was welcome to him. Any suggestion that his treatment by the Embassy was the cause of his secret defection was contradicted by his diary and his own accounts of all the parties he attended at our and other embassies. A Naval Attaché's clerk was hardly likely to find his way into the society of senior members of foreign missions unless they had met him at our own Embassy parties. Moreover, he admitted that he was once asked to accompany the wife of our Ambassador in Vienna to the ballet in Moscow, and on another occasion helped entertain the Commander-in-Chief of the British Home Fleet and his wife in Leningrad. I can say that in all my diplomatic career as a Foreign Service officer such social responsibilities never came my way until I was quite senior. I think Vassall was shown quite unusual attention for an attaché's clerk.

The truth was that he preferred the hospitality of foreigners—particularly that of the Russians—to that of his own compatriots. He was a bad choice for such a post, and it is clear that those who selected him were gravely at fault. If you have someone in a sensitive position on your staff, who is disloyal, there is absolutely nothing you can do about it. You cannot act against him unless you have proof, and he may be able to cause untold mischief before that proof comes your way. In the case of Vassall, to the best of my belief, it never came our way until we read about his arrest in England.

I remember our Naval Attaché telling me that he had noticed that Vassall had been going on picnics with counsellors' wives in other embassies, and he had had to warn him to 'stick to his own grade'. Sensible advice, I suppose, since such company might have gone to his head, but it would have provided safer anchorage than where he eventually got moored and shanghaied.

8. Northward Bound

Another successful trip we went on was to the former Kirillo-Beloozersky and Ferapontov monasteries, both at or near Kirillov. Our inspiration came from an article I had seen in a Soviet periodical in which the complaint was made that these great monuments of Russia were not being properly looked after, as any tourist who went there would confirm. A Moscow art expert who had visited them privately promised to write on our behalf to the director of the local museum.

Belo-Ozero is a large lake at about the same latitude as Leningrad, but a good deal to the east. St Cyril of Belo-Ozero founded a monastery at the nearby settlement of Kirillov in the fourteenth century. The Ferapontov Monastery, which was some ten to fifteen miles away from Kirillov, was founded at about the same time by St Therapontus, a friend and supporter of St Cyril.

The normal procedure on these tours was for us to inform the Ministry of Foreign Affairs forty-eight hours beforehand and if we heard nothing more from them it meant we could proceed. We applied simultaneously to the Russian authorities for bookings by boat as far as Vologda, which we obtained without difficulty. I did not tell the Ministry where I was going after Vologda, but left it vague because I was not sure how I would ever get to such a remote town as Kirillov where no western diplomat seemed to have gone in recent times. I was surprised that the authorities did not press me for more precise information about the rest of our trip.

The first part of the journey was by boat over the Moscow Canal and the Volga to Cherepovets. It must have been dull at the best of times, but on this occasion the water was so rough that most of the passengers had to remain in their cabins. Visibility was nil and it was so cold that it was seldom possible to be on deck. From time to time I caught an unhappy glimpse of one of the heaviest forms of female labour in the Soviet Union—the carrying of huge sacks of peat across marshy territory and the dumping of it into lighters. Unluckily, all the interesting places were passed at night. A historic spot on the route which I specially wanted to see was the town of Uglich, the scene of the murder of the young Tsarevich Dimitri, the son of Ivan the Terrible, which had provided the plot for Pushkin's play and Mussorgsky's opera, *Boris Godunov*. At 3.30 a.m. the light and the weather just allowed us to catch a glimpse of the town, which like so many other historic Russian towns was in a state of almost barbaric neglect. I was particularly sorry not to be able to stop and see the Prince's palace with its beautiful ornamental brick-work frieze. From the Volga the ship passed into the Rybinskoye reservoir, where it made a zigzag passage, and we found ourselves several times midway across in heavy seas. It was a depressing sight, when we steered nearer the shore, to see the inhabitants at the various stops braving the drenching rain so as not to miss the weekly call of the big steamer, which meant so much in their lives.

From Cherepovets we took the train to Vologda where we stayed the night and were very well accommodated in the Northern Hotel —the Golden Anchor of pre-revolutionary times. The food which was served in our room was excellent. We had a special waitress of our own, all dressed up like a maid in *Upstairs, Downstairs* and complete with cap. She turned out to be the English teacher at the local school. There were various reasons why she was allotted to us. First she could understand what we said (which was unnecessary from our point of view because we both spoke Russian). Secondly she made a good impression. Thirdly we were kept out of the dining room and confined to our room for meals. Fourthly we could be sure of unbelievable delicacies like strawberries and cream! That afternoon I queued in the drenching rain to secure a passage by ship to Kirillov, but was told by the booking clerk at the quay that there were no berths free that day. We therefore decided to stay another night in Vologda.

Vologda was a great centre of agriculture and dairy production. It was therefore peculiar that the queues at the shops were a great deal longer than those in Moscow. Our guide told us loudly, so that several other visitors could hear, 'At last we're getting some of our own butter in Vologda now. For years we've had to send it all to Leningrad and Moscow.'

Although enjoying a superb situation on the river and possessing many fine churches and buildings, it was, alas, a dreary provincial town now, very much of the type, no doubt, which the three sisters in Chekhov's play found so monotonous. The people looked terribly poor. The only redeeming feature of the place was that it had been comparatively untouched by the Revolution and the war. There were consequently a large number of decent houses which made living conditions appear better than in Moscow.

Before the Revolution Vologda had fifty-five churches and of these twenty-five were still in evidence, though only two were being used for services. In almost all cases the churches bore shields to say that they were monuments of culture and should not be damaged, but very little attempt had been made to respect this. Some of them were being used for 'peaceful' military purposes, i.e. for the stores of army archives and were guarded after dusk by bayonetted sentries.

At the time of the intervention in 1918 the British Embassy had been evacuated to Vologda and I went to have a look at the building they occupied then. It was an attractive wooden building, built in a sort of 'neo-Palladian' style some hundred years previously by one of the wealthier Vologda merchants. The town was rich in wooden houses with fine carvings, some of them peasant dwellings, but some clearly the former residences of prosperous patricians.

When I told the lady-manager of our hotel that there was no room on the boat to Kirillov, she immediately offered to make special bookings for us. We gratefully accepted and left Vologda the following night at eight o'clock in a tiny steamer which was to take us up the river Sukhona. There were no first-class cabins and we occupied the only second-class one they had for passengers. It was primitive and provided no washing facilities. There were three other cabins and all of these, including the captain's, opened out into a small dining room, where the wireless played at full strength all day. This was the most presentable part of the boat and was completely self-contained. When we left it, we had to thread our way over recumbent forms in the holds, clutching various goods and market produce which were intended eventually for sale. There was no protective deck and the weather was too cold to be out in for long.

The boat was an ancient paddle steamer which forged ahead extremely slowly. The river was so meandering and shallow in places that from time to time it had to cut off its engines and progress by funny manoeuvres like a dog wagging its tail. It seemed we would run aground but somehow we never did. The scenery was very splendid with trees in blossom and rich meadows full of flowers.

Most of the people on the steamer were peasants and there were not many opportunities for conversation. All the ship's personnel worked hard to look after us. They said they had never seen foreigners before and were surprised to find them so like themselves.

We eventually passed out of the winding Sukhona into the Kubenskoye Lake, where the boat hugged the shore and went up various estuaries—in one case going quite far inland. The country became more and more isolated. Such settlements as we passed were remote from any railway route and were linked to Vologda only by water, or by road which was pretty well impassable owing to the swamps and mud. At the various landing stages there was a busy coming and going. One of our fellow passengers was a priest who had come to take the weekend service at a church by the shore, and while other passengers rowed themselves across from the steamer to the village, he was taken off in the village's one motor boat. With my glasses I watched the black monastic figures descending the church steps to receive the priest and his attendants as they landed. After the meeting and greeting they went into a newly built low wooden house near the church, no doubt to celebrate with vodka. Leaving the lake we passed into the Porozovitsa river, which we saw only by night.

We arrived at Kirillov at about 4 a.m. and found the director of the local museum on the quay to meet us. We shall always remember with gratitude that although he had an artificial leg the good man walked all the way to meet us at that God-forsaken hour and piloted us across the long series of perilous planks, which bridged the morasses, where a road had once been. He took us to a simple collective-farm lodging house, where we slept the rest of the night.

We had a room to ourselves, but the other guests were lying on the landings and even on the stairs. The sanitation was, as usual, primitive. The 'communal' washing facilities consisted of a little cupboard on the landing with a small water container not much bigger than a soap container on a train. Underneath was a button which released a tiny trickle of water over our hands and into a basin. (The Russians have always preferred to wash their hands under running water, if you could call the trickle 'running'.) I gave one look at it and resolved to go down to the kitchen to beg for some hot water in a samovar and use our own portable basin which we had brought with us.

No food was provided, even for breakfast, although we were in an agricultural district. We had to go to an eating house down the road, which was distinctly unattractive.

Next day we were rewarded with the sight of the impressive Kirillo-Beloozersky Monastery with its immense surrounding walls more than a mile in circumference, thirty-five feet high and eighteen feet thick. In the sixteenth century, Ivan the Terrible had fortified and extended the walls. It was his policy to use monasteries as a chain of defences against invaders from the east or west.

Within the walls were two monasteries, the Large Monastery (itself enclosed by an older inner wall) and the Small Monastery. All in all, there were within the wider ramparts a cathedral and three other churches, as well as one or two secular buildings.

A river ran through the heart of the citadel, flowing from one part of the small Siverskoye Lake to another. Each of the four towers, which formed the bastions of the outer defence ring, was capped with a conical roof rising to a small cupola surmounted by a spire. The Cathedral of the Dormition in the Great Monastery was built in 1497 in one year by twenty stonemasons from Novgorod and Pskov. The view of the citadel across the lake was grandiose with the church buildings towering above the massive walls.

It was in this monastery that Ivan the Terrible's father built a chapel of thanksgiving for the birth of his son. Here also the patriarch Nikon spent five years in exile, following his earlier exile at the Ferapontov Monastery in 1666. (He was the patriarch of Moscow who brought about the Great Schism in the Russian Church by drastically revising its ritual and liturgy. Those who disapproved of the innovation left the Church and maintained their own liturgy. They were called Old Believers, and still exist as a separate sect today. They have their own churches and some of the rarest icons.)

Contrary to what had been written, the monastery was not badly maintained at all, if one compared it with monuments elsewhere in Russia, especially those at Yaroslavl.

In the afternoon we set out for the Ferapontov Monastery which also stood on a lake, but a smaller one. The museum director had managed to get hold of the only car in the neighbourhood—it belonged to the collective farm. After half an hour's journey over the most ghastly roads imaginable, we reached the monastery. Between the fifteenth and seventeenth centuries it had gradually grown into a large complex, although it was not to be compared in size with the Kirillo-Beloozersky monasteries. An original feature of its silhouette was its gateway with twin 'tent' or pyramid-shaped spires—a rare phenomenon in Russian church architecture.

But what made a visit to the cathedral of this monastery unique was its frescoes painted by Dionisii and his sons. There were three great fresco- and icon-painters in Russia—Theophanes the Greek in the fourteenth century, and Andrei Rublov and Dionisii in the fifteenth.

The outstanding quality of Dionisii's work was its buoyancy, grace and joyfulness. His figures were so light and airy that they seemed scarcely to touch the ground. They had moved far from the severe Byzantine models where the Saviour and saints were stern and inexorable figures which inspired only fear. Instead of depressing and frightening the spectator, they elevated him. Dionisii made a cult of the Virgin, whom he even painted in the place of the usual Pankrator or God the Father. He omitted the Dormition from the conventional sequence about her, because he did not want to disturb the harmony and spiritual warmth by introducing the jarring note of the Virgin's death.

We found a young artist working on the restoration of the frescoes and he was an invaluable guide to have since he knew the techniques. We were allowed to climb up on the scaffolding and feast our eyes on them. To our delight we saw that it was only the lower registers which had been painted over and were now being cleaned. The top registers had never been touched and were just as perfect as when they were painted. It is the lower paintings in Russian churches that the heat of candles and human bodies always causes to deteriorate.

On our return to Kirillov we made plans for getting back to Vologda. I had already tried to order a taxi but the taxi station had refused to send a car to make the seven-hour journey over the abominable roads. We were warned against the daily carrier lorry, which would have broken our bones, and our only alternative was to go to the airport and attempt to negotiate plane passages. The airport consisted of a farmhouse on a grassy hill, looking out over the magnificent lake with the Kirillov monastery at the end of it. The wife of the director asked us to come in and drink tea around the samovar, where her family were gathered. She was a schoolmistress and was intrigued to hear about education in England. The director himself promised to call up a plane for us the next day, as there was no regular service on Sunday. Afterwards he and a friend took us back over the lake to the monastery in a motor boat. They were going out fishing on the lake and other small lakes, which were linked by channels.

The next day, soon after lunch, we set off for the airport, as we could get no information about the time of the plane's departure. Since there was no transport of any kind in Kirillov the director of the airport was kind enough to come out on his bicycle and walk with us, suspending our four bags on his handlebars. It was a lovely day and the two and a half hours we had to pass lying on the grass waiting for the plane to come were not wasted. As soon as the sound of the plane was heard the director and his wife came rushing out of the house and spread white sheets in the form of a cross to show where the plane should land. When it came down (it was one of the most rudimentary bi-planes I have seen) all the passengers jumped out, their faces green, and threw themselves on the ground. It was not a very encouraging sight. However, the weather conditions were in fact excellent and we got back to Vologda in half an hour—having spent nearly thirty hours getting there by boat. On the way we had the most magnificent aerial views of the province of Vologda, which consisted mainly of forest that was broken occasionally by clearings where there were churches and monasteries, all of them apparently untouched by the Revolution or the war.

From Vologda we travelled by train to Yaroslavl. This turned out to be a typically beautiful historic town which had been neglected by the Soviet authorities. One was always being told that it had been destroyed by the White Guards (sometimes, it was added, 'at the instigation of the allied diplomats in military missions'), but, in actual fact, it was the Red Army who had resorted to the most ruthless vandalism in their attempt to destroy the White Guards who were in possession of it for a short time. Here is an extract from the warning issued by the Red forces: 'After the expiration of twenty-four hours there will be quarter for no one; the most pitiless hurricane of fire will be opened on the city from heavy guns and also with chemical shells. All who remain will perish under the ruins of the town along with the rebels, traitors and enemies of the Revolution, the workers and poorest peasants.' This threat was carried out and a considerable part of the city was smashed to pieces by land and air bombardments. We met an old woman on the street who said to us: 'Everything that was beautiful here they have destroyed' and there was no mistaking who she meant by 'they'. Nonetheless a certain amount of work was being done on the monasteries and churches and nothing could really spoil the superb appearance of the town as viewed from the river. We went to see almost all the churches, one of the finest being part of a factory. A single small church far outside the centre of the town was used for services. We spoke to the verger, whose son had worked for Vickers in the old days. He said that at Easter there were 4,000 worshippers at his church and as they could not be accommodated inside they filled the surrounding roads and fields.

We were delighted when we found an enormous bath in our bedroom at the hotel at Yaroslavl—complete with plug. (When baths or washbasins were available *en route* they were generally useless because the water ran out as soon as you let it in.) Eagerly we turned on the taps, only to retreat from the room at top speed. The water was musty yellow and a stifling odour of bad eggs choked our lungs.

Our most striking experience in Yaroslavl otherwise was trying to get away from it. No one in Russia ever knows whether he can get a seat in a train until shortly before it comes into the station. Only then is he allowed to go on to the platform. In our case, this involved spending five hours on the station making visits to the station master. He was barely courteous to begin with because he thought we were Poles, but when he discovered we were English, he immediately warmed to us and we got our places in the train. It was four hours late, apparently because the lines were packed with people travelling to the 'Virgin Lands'.*

The conclusion we drew from our journey was that it was possible to go across Russia without official help but that to do so, one needed loads of time and an inexhaustible reserve of patience.

---

* It was one of Krushchev's schemes to sow grain in reclaimed areas in Kazakhstan and Western Siberia.

9. Trespassers Won't Be Prosecuted

Moscow was once called the city of 'forty times forty churches', but only about fifty were actually functioning. The rest had fallen into neglect or been pulled down, turned into museums or cinemas or used as private dwellings. Those churches which were in use were often well kept up, because the parishioners paid for them to be repainted and repaired. Some of them shone out beside the secular buildings. But they were of course only a minority among the fifty.

In the year I arrived in the Soviet Union, the government had let up on their attacks on churchgoing, particularly on Communists who went to church. In the first decree which Khrushchev himself signed, he gave special orders that people should not 'hurt the feelings of believers'. 'Clergy or believers are being unjustifiably depicted as being unworthy of political trust,' he declared. The large modern Cathedral of St Saviour, which was built towards the end of the nineteenth century on the Kremlin bank of the Moscow river, just beyond the point where the river began to divide, was demolished long ago on Stalin's orders and the site had been left unoccupied ever since. It was as if a superstitious people had been afraid to commit the sacrilege of erecting a secular building on it. There was now no proper cathedral left for the many who wanted to attend Easter or Christmas services. An eighteenth-century church in the suburbs of Moscow, the Church of the Epiphany in Yelokhov, was therefore put at the disposal of the Moscow patriarch. It possessed the precious icon of Our Lady of Kazan and had had the relics of St Alexis transferred to it from the Cathedral of the Dormition in the Kremlin. It was to the Church at Yelokhov that most of us went for the Easter services. When we walked out of our flat to look for a trolley bus to take us to the cathedral on Easter night, I was amazed to see a conductress leaning out of one and shouting: 'This way for the midnight service'. I had never imagined that I should be *invited* to take a ride to the cathedral for the Easter service in the Soviet Union.

It was the only church where the choir was up to the standard of the old days. Indeed several of the leading opera singers of the time had started their careers there. But it was not nearly big enough to house everyone. It was practically impossible to push one's way through the seething mass of people which lack of room had forced to stay outside. Sometimes I had to pretend that I was ushering a VIP along, shouting out, 'Make way for the—Delegation!' The crowd was docile enough and made a pathway. As diplomats we were allowed to go in through a side door quite close to the altar, where we could watch the service from a privileged position.

Russian services are often an extraordinary mixture of the sublime and the ridiculous. There are moments of quite agonizing beauty and solemnity. If you are in the nave a member of the congregation standing beside you may suddenly throw himself prostrate on the ground—rather disconcerting when you are packed like sardines. The atmosphere in a Moscow church service was more intense than at others I have attended elsewhere—much more so than at services in the Orthodox cathedral in Paris. On the other hand, watching from a privileged position in the wings, we were only too conscious of the lighter side of the ceremony. In the Orthodox church service, attention is concentrated all the time on the priest and his rites—his robing and unrobing, his movements in and out of the Tsar's doors or inner sanctuary, where only he may go— all of which have a symbolic meaning. Once, at one of the most solemn parts of the ritual, a candle started dripping on to the carpet in front of the sanctuary. An old nun rushed out with newspaper and an iron, and began to iron the carpet to remove the stains. The contrast between the spiritual exaltation of the service and the everyday act of ironing was a shock. At the end of the service, the same nun started feverishly tidying up. She wanted to roll up the carpet and a berobed server, who was standing in front of the Tsar's doors, nearly somersaulted when she pulled it away from under him. This was Russia, the country of paradox.

I never missed an opportunity of dropping into a church on a Sunday if I happened to pass one on my various promenades around Moscow, and it was intriguing to find that services were still being held all the time and that there were always parishioners in them, even if they were mostly women and elderly men. An interesting feature of my 'church-crawling' was the frequent christenings I found taking place in them. The parents of the infants were mostly not churchgoers themselves and had to be instructed and prompted by the priest throughout the ceremony. However, a *babushka*, either the husband's or wife's mother, who was a believer and was used to church ritual, was generally there. She had obviously worked on her non-believing children and persuaded them to bring their babies to be christened, which they seemed anxious to do just to insure them against the future in case God proved right after all.

I remember once going into a church and finding that a child was being christened on one side while, on the other, there was an open coffin with a dead man in it. I was haunted by this Dostoyevskian synthesis of life and death, youth and age, God and the Devil. On the way we passed five or six beggars in a line with mugs tied to them, who might have stepped out of *Boris Godunov*. The Soviet authorities encouraged beggars and cripples to congregate round church doors and on church steps so that the people should connect with the church the bad old days of poverty. Otherwise they were not favoured on the streets. Drunkards were treated with greater respect!

Russia was always the land of the unexpected, the paradoxical, the juxtaposition of the compatible and the incompatible. I can remember how well this was illustrated by an adventure which befell me when I was on a Sunday walk looking for churches.

I had become interested in a particular style of church in Moscow of which there were very few examples to be seen. It was 'Moscow baroque'. Up to the seventeenth century, when the age of the baroque began, the Russian churches continued to follow the strict canons of Byzantine architecture, according to which there must be no sculpture and very little decoration on the outside of a church. For a century and a half at least the external façades of the churches remained completely bare, and later, when at the end of the twelfth century small carvings began to make their appearance at Vladimir and Novgorod, they were not comparable with the wealth of stone carving which we find on western cathedrals.

In the seventeenth century, however, at the beginning of the reign of Peter the Great who opened a 'window in the west', some of the rich patrons of Russia went abroad and learnt foreign ways. The result was that a certain number of churches in Moscow and its surroundings began to be built by Russian architects in the style of western architecture. These churches are called 'Moscow baroque' and there are only four of them still surviving.

I was particularly anxious to see all these churches. One of them, the Church of the Apparition of the Virgin in Dubrovitsi, was not difficult to get to. It was about an hour to the south of Moscow. Another—the Church of the Intercession at Fili—was still nearer. It was on the outskirts of Moscow. The remaining two were the Church of the Redemption V Uborakh, in the country outside Moscow, and the Church of the Trinity in Troitsky-Lykov. The last two were possibly in forbidden areas and it was a long time before I ventured to go in search of them. One of the difficulties of our life at that period was that we never clearly knew where the dividing lines ran between where we were allowed to go and where we were not. It was so unpleasant to be caught in a forbidden area that one was most reluctant, however adventurous one's spirit, to risk such an experience.

The Church of Dubrovitsi was like a wedding cake. And when one looks at some of the large modern buildings built in Stalin's time, which are in their way a kind of perverted baroque, one understands where the Soviet architects got their ideas from. However, there were two things which were particularly fascinating about this church. First, it was very strange to see a church of this form and outward appearance in the Russian countryside at all, especially in central Russia. It might not have been out of place in St Petersburg, but in the surroundings of Moscow—the great village—it seemed to be flaunting its somewhat meretricious ornamentation. Next, it was built of dazzling white stone and stood out in summer against the greenness of the fields and in winter against the scruffy buildings in the neighbourhood. The ground plan of the church was concentric and consisted of a basic square with four semicircular apses (which were not in fact apses at all). Both outside and in, the church was decorated with sculpture and Latin inscriptions, which were foreign to Russian architectural traditions, and inside took the place of the normal frescoes on the walls. Instead of the traditional Russian round cupola it was surmounted by a gilded crown of beaten iron. On the steps leading up to the church were two statues on pedestals.

There were various stories about the origin of this church. It was built by a friend of Peter the Great, Prince Golitsyn, and therefore could safely be built in defiance of church conventions. Indeed, it is probable that Peter, who took part in the consecration of the church, enjoyed shocking the local priests with a building which must have appeared to them like the Whore of Babylon. Golitsyn had just returned from a visit to Europe and, no doubt, came back with these new ideas. Needless to say, a church of this type had few imitators.

The second example of Moscow baroque was the Church of the Intercession at Fili. Fili was famous in Russian history as the place where the Russian High Command under Kutuzov had their last meeting before the advance of Napoleon's armies in 1812. Today it is part of a rather boring Moscow suburb. Here was the same ground plan with the four semicircular apses, but this time, there was an open gallery with wide open stairways surrounding them. The wedding cake construction was perhaps even more apparent, because on top of the apses were two octagons, in tiers, each being smaller than the one below and all ending in an eight-faceted drum which supported the minute cupola. The striking silhouette of the church, marked by its square and octagon tiers, was enhanced by its colours—warm red-painted walls with windows, mouldings and sculptured decorations picked out in white. Above each of the apses was a small cupola—each carried by its own little octagon. There were statues outside—as at Dubrovitsi—but these were more impressive and less bizarre.

I stumbled on the third example—the Church of the Redemption in the village of Ubory—when I went bathing because it stood in isolated beauty in a field not far from Uspenskoe on the Moscow River. (All the same to get to it I had to go through the grounds of a hospital and be prepared to pose as a patient or visitor.) In my search for the fourth and last of these churches—the Church of the Trinity in the village of Troitsky-Lykov—I was in a quandary because it seemed to me that it was likely to be on forbidden ground.

I went to the limits of what I knew to be safe territory and then ventured, somewhat rashly, into the unknown. I found myself in a very beautiful part of the countryside on a road between two stretches of the Russian forest. But it was not the trees which held my attention. In the distance, advancing towards me, was a most curious procession. At first, it much resembled a funeral but I could hardly credit this, as there was no sign of a hearse. As it came nearer, I saw that it consisted of a certain formation of people mainly in civilian clothes. In the front walked two people in earnest conversation and outside, on the wings, as it were, were two others who appeared to be guards. Behind, at a certain distance, followed about ten others in rank and file. I was wondering who on earth these people could be when all of a sudden I recognized the leading two as Kaganovich, a member of the Presidium, who was shortly to be expelled as a member of the Anti-Party group, and Shepilov, the Soviet Foreign Minister, who was to share the same fate. Curiously enough, Kaganovich seemed to be dressed in a dressing gown and pyjamas, but when they came closer I realized that he was wearing a sort of hospital garb. I quickly jumped to the conclusion that he was recuperating in a sanatorium nearby and that I must be treading on very dangerous ground, having, in fact, stumbled on to the spot where the great ones received their medical attention.

It was too late to withdraw and I could hardly walk past the cavalcade without making some signs of recognition. I knew Kaganovich and Shepilov, of course, and they would almost certainly recognize me. As I came closer to them and greeted them, they both left the procession and walked to the side of the road to speak to me while the suite halted at a respectful distance.

It was awkward, to say the least, that I had a camera hanging round my neck and I felt extremely self-conscious about it. However, the two Soviet leaders were most amiable, as was usually the case. Nonetheless, after our opening formalities, I thought I ought to explain to them why I was there. I told them that I was looking for some churches and particularly the Church of the Trinity in Troitsky-Lykov and that I felt I must be near it. Was it in fact anywhere near here? 'Yes, indeed,' answered Kaganovich, 'it's a few hundred yards as you go down that road.' While he said this he stared pointedly at my camera. Luckily it was a Soviet one.

Feeling that I should make some further explanation, I said, 'I am a little hesitant about walking here, because I am not quite sure whether this is a protected area where diplomats are not supposed to come. Is it all right for me to be here, because, if it is not, I will naturally withdraw to permitted territory.'

Once more Kaganovich stared at my camera, and I added, 'Yes, I've brought this camera with me because I wanted to take a photograph of the church which is of a rare type. I suppose it will be in order for me to do this?'

High Soviet leaders are not usually placed in a position where they have to give snap answers to questions of this kind and Kaganovich's reply was amusing.

'Well,' he said, turning to Shepilov, 'that church is no longer a church and is now being used as the headquarters for all the army bands in Russia. All the same I don't think it is a military objective, is it, Shepilov?' He said it with a twinkle in his eye and the Foreign Minister's answer was reassuring. Kaganovich asked Shepilov how to say *Do svidaniya* in English and after he had made a rather comical attempt to say 'goodbye' the cavalcade moved off and I felt secure and was able to carry out my 'non-military objective' and photograph the church.

One of the disillusioning experiences in this kind of hunt for the memorials of old Russia was that the present-day reality never measured up to pictures in old Russian or even Soviet books. In Soviet publications the churches are seldom photographed as they actually were, rather as they used to be. In fact, illustrations from pre-Soviet books were often used. I remember once going to see a building which marked an important stage in Russian church architecture, because, although of stone, it was built entirely in the style of traditional wooden church architecture. The church in Tainina near Moscow figured in all the old Russian books on church architecture and Soviet ones too, but when I at last found it —and that involved tramping through mud and across fields—I discovered that it was being used as a massive dung-heap. The vapours arising from the manure completely concealed the outlines of the church and made it impossible for me to photograph it. Similarly, the Church of the Trinity in Troitsky-Lykov was in a shabby state and the surroundings terribly neglected. Even so, comparing it with pre-revolutionary pictures, I could see its great beauty. It was, in its delicacy, the loveliest of the four. It was built on the same plan as the others (except for Dubrovitsi) but, like Dubrovitsi, it was completely white. Had it been in proper condition it would have been a dazzling sight.

Most of these churches had been built on the property of the landed aristocracy and those at Fili and Troitsky-Lykov were on the estate belonging to the relatives of Peter the Great's mother, the Boyar family of the Naryshkins. For this reason, they are referred to in Russian architecture as the churches of 'Naryshkin' baroque. One could not get into any of these in the country. They were barricaded and desecrated. Grass was growing in the floors and walls of Dubrovitsi.

The historical development of Russian architecture is easy to follow because it moves from city to city. It begins with Kiev, then moves to Vladimir and Suzdal, next to Novgorod and, finally, to

Moscow, where it is interrupted by Peter the Great's decision to create his new capital of St Petersburg and stop all building in the old style.

It was by no means easy—even for diplomats—to get to some of the towns I visited. Kolomna, for instance, which is an old and interesting town with some remarkable buildings, was on the route in a tour I was making to Ryazan. Although it was on the river and my boat would be stopping there, it was out of bounds for foreigners and we should not be able to land. When we arrived, however, something went wrong with the propeller of the steamer and we halted there many hours. My wife and I dutifully remained on board until every member of the ship had gone off to gallivant round the town, leaving us completely alone. Then we decided to follow suit. In this way, I was able to see it without any hindrance and photograph it to my heart's content. The element of the accidental and unexpected is never to be excluded in Russia and it may bring surprising windfalls. I suppose the reason we were not supposed to stop was because there was an ugly railway bridge which spanned the river. I could not have cared less about it and would never have dreamt of wasting a film on it. Let me again direct your attention to a remark in the 1914 *Baedeker* of Russia, to bring the matter into perspective: 'The taking of photographs near fortresses is naturally forbidden; and even in *less important places* the guardians of the law are apt to be over-vigilant. In order *to escape molestation* the photographer should join the Russian Photographic Society. Its headquarters are in Moscow (Kuznetski Most) and the entrance fee is two roubles and the annual subscription six. Imperial chateaux and the like may not be photographed without the permission of the major domo.' *Plus ça change, plus c'est la même chose.*

On another occasion we went to Novgorod—that resplendent city whose prince, Alexander Nevsky, won three historic victories against the Swedes, the Germans and the Lithuanians. It was to become a city republic ruled by an oligarchy of merchant patricians. In spite of frightful destruction during the Second World War its cathedrals and churches, and some of the frescoes in them, survived. It was one of the most imposing cities in Russia, gleaming over the lush green meadows and the rich blue of Lake Ilmen, beside which the merchant minstrel Sadko lay down to sleep in Rimsky-Korsakov's opera of that name.

The Intourist hotel lay on the bank of the river Volkhov. Across the water could be seen the warm red walls of the Kremlin fortress and, above them, the gleaming gold of the central dome of the Cathedral of St Sofia, and the eleventh-century cathedral of Novgorod. The five other domes on the skyline looked like the helmets of an advancing Viking army. The colours were superb. Green banks sloped gently down to the blue waters of the river and in the evening, when I used to look across the waters from the hotel window, and the sun was setting behind the hills, the towers and walls of the Kremlin and the dome of the cathedral were covered in a roseate glow.

Novgorod owed its prosperity and its westernness in no small measure to the fact that it was the sole Russian city which the Tartars failed to occupy. After capturing Moscow and Vladimir they prepared to advance on Novgorod in 1238, calculating that their operations would be made easier in the winter by the freezing of the surrounding lakes and marshes. But it was already March and they feared that a sudden thaw might make the route impassable for their horses and transport. They reached a point sixty-five miles from the city, changed plan and marched south. Novgorod was saved.

Apart from the cathedral, the great treasures of the city were the frescoes of the Byzantine master-painter who worked in Russia called Theophanes the Greek—really the first 'El Greco'. In 1378 he painted the interior of the church of the Cathedral of the Saviour of the Transfiguration in Ilyina Street. The frescoes were only uncovered in 1912 and it is one of the great artistic experiences in Russia to climb up scaffolding and see Theophanes' sublime impressionist gallery of church fathers, saints, martyrs and ascetics.

One attraction in looking over historic Russian cities was that we were generally shown round by some historian or art expert from the local museum. We were dying to see Theophanes' famous frescoes and we kept on asking our guide to show them to us. But each time we did he took us into another church and showed us something else. After going through this about twelve times, we realized that he was deliberately keeping the Theophanes' frescoes till the end. When we at last reached the church we felt that we had no strength to climb the ladders, but as soon as we caught a glimpse of the famous picture of St Macarios, which like most of Theophanes' figures rose up out of the darkness as though illuminated by a lightning flash, we would gladly have suffered any martyrdom. There was something extraordinarily modern in the powerful expression of this saint. Hair, moustache, beard and clothes formed a mass of white and were differentiated only by the forceful thrusts of the artist's brush, like lines of force round a magnet. Everything in the portrait was white except the nimbus, the small uncovered part of the saint's face and the two hands upturned in a gesture of resignation.

Unfortunately, the murals in the Church of the Assumption at Volotovo were utterly destroyed by the Germans in the last war. Whether they were executed by Theophanes or not, their stark convulsive vitality made them one of the most striking examples of Novgorod art. In them the painter reduced expressionist art to a few eloquent strokes and lines.

10. The Anti-Party Plot

I was in charge of the Embassy during the momentous days when Khrushchev eliminated Malenkov, Molotov, Kaganovich and Shepilov. As is now known, this was carried out at a meeting of the Central Committee from 22 to 29 June 1957. None of us in Moscow were aware at the time that the Central Committee was meeting. We only began to suspect that something was up when it was all over.

The last any of us had seen of Malenkov and Molotov was at the reception given on 13 June at our Embassy to mark the Queen's birthday. It is true that Khrushchev, who was there, had complimented our Assistant Naval Attaché on his fine beard and contrasted it with Bulganin's 'scruffy one'. This might have boded ill for Bulganin or it might have been a normal piece of Khrushchev tomfoolery. Malenkov and Molotov appeared to be in perfectly good spirits on that occasion. They were not seen after that. But it was a holiday period, when the leaders often went away for several weeks to their dachas in the Crimea or the Caucasus, and there was nothing abnormal in their absence. As a result of the tremendous burden of social duties which the thaw in the Soviet Union had imposed on them they had started staggering their functions and their holidays.

Whenever an embassy gives a reception for its National Day there is always speculation about which of the Soviet leaders will attend. Much depends upon the importance of the country in Soviet eyes, the degree of friendship existing with that country (this takes second place) and, in addition, the attitude the government of the country has taken towards any receptions which the Soviet Ambassador has held there. On one occasion the Swedish Ambassador, who was the doyen of the Diplomatic Corps, had felt deeply humiliated when only one member of the Presidium turned up for his National Day. The reason for this was made abundantly clear to him. At least three Russians said to him or members of his staff: 'It is true, is it not, that at the reception given by the Soviet Ambassador in Stockholm, in honour of the anniversary of the October Revolution, only one member of the Swedish government was present?' An eye for an eye and a tooth for a tooth was the guiding principle.

The first of July was the Canadian National Day. The Canadians, as members of the Commonwealth and NATO, did not expect to be the object of any signal demonstration of friendship on the part of the Russians, but they could reckon on two or three of the leaders attending. Everyone was surprised to see that the sole member of the Presidium who came was Pervukhin, who was considered to be relatively unimportant. Another thing that struck observers as strange was that the only other important Soviet official present was one of the Party Secretaries, Aristov. Under normal circumstances, the Party Secretaries, who have no state positions, do not fulfil representational functions. If they attend diplomatic receptions, they come as normal 'Soviet guests'. In this case, Aristov acted as though he were a top Soviet representative and seemed to take precedence over Pervukhin.

Our suspicions were confirmed the next day when the Soviet press reported that the two Soviet representatives at the Canadian National Day had been Aristov and Pervukhin. Although Aristov was given no new title, he was placed before Pervukhin and since a member of the Presidium always had precedence over a Party Secretary, this suggested that Pervukhin might have been downgraded and Aristov promoted. (Members of equal rank were generally listed in alphabetical order.)

From the Canadian reception we all rushed off to a special performance at the Bolshoi given by dancers from one of the Caucasian republics. It so happened that I was put in a box which was next to that of the Presidium. It was interesting watching them. Khrushchev was in a prominent position, looking as if he had solved his most important problem and was on top of the world. With him was Voroshilov, who was senile by now, Bulganin, who looked completely broken, and close by his side, talking and laughing with Khrushchev, Suslov. But there was no Malenkov, Molotov, Kaganovich or Shepilov. This implied that something was up, but there was no hard evidence as yet, not at least until we read the report of the Canadian reception in *Pravda* the following day.

The news of the removal of the Malenkov group, subsequently

called the 'Anti-Party Group', broke in the British Embassy in a way which, though not unusual by Soviet standards, must seem peculiar to those who have not lived in Russia. On the morning of 3 July, *Pravda* carried an important article warning that party members who broke discipline, *however important they might be,* were likely to be expelled like Kamenev and Zinoviev.

It went on to state that 'individuals' within the Party, taking a 'dogmatic' view of Marxism-Leninism, had opposed the Party's policies on peaceful coexistence, strengthening the Socialist camp, improving the direction of industry, developing agriculture and broadening the rights of the Union republics. These individuals, it claimed, wanted to return to the incorrect method of leadership condemned by the 20th Congress.

I discussed the article with one of our Embassy experts. I was inclined to think that they were gunning for Molotov. My colleague was more cautious and thought that it meant a group of lesser men. Luckily, I did not take his advice and sent a telegram suggesting that the article was directed at 'people at the very top'. However, because of discussions and hesitations, I only warned the Foreign Office a few hours before the sensational news broke. At about 4 p.m. the correspondent of the *Daily Worker* confirmed to a member of our staff that Malenkov, Molotov, Kaganovich and Shepilov were to be the victims of an immediate purge.

It was almost impossible to believe it at first, especially as western correspondents, when attempting to telegraph the story at 6 p.m. had been refused permission. The story made its official public appearance in Russia at 9 p.m. as a Moscow radio broadcast in Arabic. The whole thing came out next day in the press, with long accusations against the 'Anti-Party Group'. Later, Pervukhin was made Ambassador to the German Democratic Republic—a degradation for a member of the Presidium—and Bulganin was cashiered.

We afterwards learnt that there had, in fact, been a two-week fight within the Presidium. It appeared that the members of the 'Anti-Party Group' had long been in disagreement with Khrushchev, each of them probably for different reasons. Collectively, they were agreed that his policies were a danger to the power structure of the leadership. They used the opportunity of Khrushchev's absence from the country in Finland in June to stage a palace revolution. On Khrushchev's return to Moscow on 19 June he was informed by the other ten members of the Presidium that he was being removed from office as First Secretary. Instead of accepting the decision in the spirit of 'collective government', he insisted that the Presidium could not fire him. Backed by three of the members, he called a special meeting of the Central Committee to argue his case. Marshal Zhukov helped by sending military planes to fetch its members. At a stormy eight-day meeting the Committee voted to reverse the decision of the Presidium and to keep Khrushchev in power. (Khrushchev had in recent years seen to it that he was supported by more and more members of the Central Committee.) But we knew nothing of this at the time. How could we?

Russians seldom gave one a straight answer. At times they refused to answer at all, but more often they provided one with misleading answers. This was by no means confined to the Soviet leaders or to Party members. Russians do not necessarily tell you what they think is true: they often tell you only what they believe is good for you to hear or what they think will please you.

I am reminded, here, of a little episode in *The Brothers Karamazov* by Dostoyevsky, who was, perhaps, the most Russian of all Russian writers, and from whose books one can glean a mass of information about Russian and Soviet psychology. Admission of failure and confession of guilt is something that is considered among them as more pardonable than it is in the west. So is the word *vrat*, which means 'to fib, boast or talk nonsense'. In Dostoyevsky's book there is an entertaining thirteen-year-old called Krasochkin who has progressive ideas and claims to be a socialist. Had he lived later, he would have become a leading figure in the Komsomol, but he might have become quickly disillusioned and defected or committed suicide. His mentality is characteristic of the way many Russians think, even today. He gives himself airs and likes to talk to the shop-keepers and the peasants in a patronizing and sophisticated way. He has a cheery conversation with a muzhik, who asks him, 'Oh, you're at school, are you? I suppose they beat you pretty badly?' Krasochkin replies, 'Yes, pretty badly.' Afterwards Krasochkin's young friend, who worships him like a god, asks him: 'Why did you tell that muzhik that they beat us at school? You know it isn't true.' Krasochkin replies: 'You don't understand. That muzhik thinks they beat us at school. He'll be disappointed if I say they don't. I had to keep him happy.'

It is astonishing how misinformed the Russians are, and how little they seem to care about it. If you go to a Russian railway station and ask about a train, you will be told one thing by a porter, another by the clerk at the booking office, another by the inspector and yet another by the station master—not to mention your fellow passengers. If you are not used to this, it may seem that there is a deliberate conspiracy of silence or deceit among the Russians.

The difficulty was that, at that time, information in the Soviet Union was passed on very much by word of mouth. Things were not always printed and written down, so Russians did not expect to know many routine details which western people feel that they should know. It exasperated westerners living in Moscow that they could not tell what play was being given on what day, what dancers were going to appear in the Bolshoi, and so on. Nothing was ever known until a day or two, sometimes an hour or so, before it happened. When I was in Russia there were no bus timetables, no train timetables, no telephone directories. Concerts were not announced in the newspapers. You had to go to the concert halls every few days to see what was going to be given, or you could buy a monthly calendar which was always published late, so you missed the performance on the first days of the month. It was the same when you bought a ticket for a train. This is the reason why Russian stations have, from time immemorial, worn the appearance of vast transit camps, with whole families including women and babies sleeping, eating and camping in the waiting rooms outside. Was this secrecy? Was it security? In most cases, it was just the Russian way of life, which the Communists had not altered, because it was not in their interest to do so. This is why the Revolution was, in some ways, so half-baked. It only swept away what the Bolsheviks wanted swept away. The rest remained. (Please note that I have put all this in the past tense, although people tell me that even if much has changed in Russia in the last twenty years, much remains the same.)

If this inability to give factual answers and to provide information on simple things causes difficulties for the Russians, how much more complicated is it when it concerns information that really matters? It is a cause of desperation to all westerners but it earns the Soviet regime infinite benefits. A tradition of keeping people in the dark is useful to an unscrupulous dictatorship, not least in furthering its policies abroad. Russian leaders can read about all our plans and projects in our papers, learn their advantages and disadvantages and gauge the opposition to them in this section of the country or that. We, on the other hand, have scarcely more knowledge of what is going on in the heads of the Soviet leaders, now when there is supposed to be 'collective leadership', than we did when it was all locked up in the inscrutable head of one man, Josef Stalin.

The Russians had undoubtedly let up a great deal since the death of Stalin and since the emergence of Khrushchev as the leading figure. In the days of Stalin, Soviet official announcements were rare and resembled Papal encyclicals. Members of the Soviet government kept their mouths shut and this saved them from making the ill-judged pronouncements which politicians in the rest of the world make sooner or later. At the same time it had the advantage of giving greater emphasis to their words on the few occasions that they did speak. Stalin was a man of few words. Khrushchev was a man of too many. Stalin was mysterious. Khrushchev often seemed to be thinking aloud.

Stalin carried on the traditions of the Russian Tsars and patriarchs to whose few words miraculous significance was attributed. Khrushchev belonged to a newer age; like Peter the Great he cut across many old Russian traditions, including that of monosyllabic caution, and displayed a remarkable understanding of the need for public relations. He was garrulous and liked to occupy the centre of the stage, while Stalin preferred to watch and direct invisibly from the wings.

The accession of Khrushchev to the 'throne' of Russia had considerable significance for east-west relations. For the first time perhaps for many centuries we had at the head of the powerful Russian state an unblushing extrovert. He had no hesitation in calling a spade a spade. This should have made it easier—in theory at any rate—for the western leaders to find common ground with him than with his Byzantine predecessors. He also understood the practical limitations of a problem and this brought him closer to our turn of mind. His habit of saying the first thing that came into his head (and that did not necessarily mean saying something silly, because he was extremely shrewd) gave us an opportunity of judging his real intentions. Sometimes, he voiced his ideas so freely at celebrations in Moscow that people thought he had drunk too much vodka. Contrary to what is generally believed, he did not drink excessively and, unlike Bulganin, rarely succumbed to the bottle in spite of the great temptation to which the lavishness of Soviet hospitality must have exposed him. There was no doubt that his remarks often caused his colleagues in the Presidium to do some head-shaking and it was quite common for the reports of his speeches to be delayed several days, while they were being vetted and corrected. I imagine that Khrushchev submitted to this operation and agreed that it was necessary, but, at the same time probably argued pretty tenaciously about what should be retained and what left out.

An important result of his frankness was that other leading Russians began to talk more overtly than they had done before. They were still extremely cautious, unless they were at the very top, and even then, they kept close to the Party line. But when Khrushchev delivered his famous talk on Stalin and the news of this got around, the floodgates opened among the Russian intellectuals, and it was surprising reading speeches made by artists, musicians, writers, etc., at congresses, in which many of the traditional concepts of Marxism-Leninism seemed to be called into question. The Hungarian rising in October 1956 put a stop to this salutary process. It was thought that Khrushchev had gone too far and that public opinion must be dragooned again, otherwise Communism in the Soviet Union would have found itself on the slippery slope.

In the summer of 1956 all sorts of changes hitherto undreamed of seemed possible. Western plays were coming back to the theatres. One could see *Dial M For Murder* advertised on the boards. Russian authors who had long been frowned on by the regime were being published again; a public dialogue went on as to whether contemporary Russian painters could learn something from French Impressionists, whereas 'Impressionism' had previously been a dirty word. Most westerners believed things had gone so far that the Soviet leadership could not put the clock back. Others, perhaps wiser, said that the Russian people would revert to the old attitudes, if the leaders cracked the whip again. Later, the intellectuals *were* driven back into their sheepfolds and became uncomfortable and uncertain about what their next step should be. Khrushchev found it necessary to have a garden party for them in the summer, followed by a big Kremlin reception in the winter, to try to restore their faith in the regime. Russian intellectuals were not men who spoke out. It was before the days of Solzhenitsyn and Sakharov. In the past, many Russian intellectuals had chosen the safe way and it was over-optimistic to expect any significant action from them.

However, the breath of fresh air which Khrushchev's disavowal of Stalin and the evils of his regime had brought into the Soviet

E

Union made it easier for the Russian people to know what was happening in the outside world and how the west thought, and the *détente* brought about enabled more Russians to go abroad. Did this lead to any change in the relationship between the foreigners and ordinary Russian man in the street? I cannot say it did.

Fear had always weighed heavily on Russians who lived in the capital, whether it was St Petersburg or Moscow. Writing over a hundred years ago, the Marquis de Custine described how, on the ship which took him to Russia, he conversed with a Russian prince who was afraid to criticize Russia in the hearing of any of his countrymen, in case they were police spies. This feeling existed long before Stalin and it will take many centuries before it is completely eradicated.

These are other reasons why Russians are uncommunicative. They have deeply patriotic feelings and any question put to them which seems to be critical of their government or their way of life evokes a sharp defensive reaction. They are never sure whether they are going to fall for provocation or not; whether they are going to be caught out by a hostile intelligence service. They have been told so often about the powerful operations of the secret services of the west that one must not be puzzled if their suspicions are swiftly aroused, when they are asked searching questions. Beria had scared them into vigilance and vigilant they remain.

I remember one day finding myself sitting next to a Russian girl in the Bolshoi theatre. She was unexpectedly communicative and told me that she worked in the Virgin Lands and had come to Moscow for a holiday tour. (I smiled as I recalled how at our Embassy Christmas show, performed before the diplomatic corps, some of the young male members of the staff had appeared dressed as 'land girls' and sung: 'We are the virgins of the Virgin Lands.') She introduced me to a friend of hers from the same collective farm who was sitting some seats away, and we had an amicable conversation in the interval. The two girls entreated me to come and see them in Barnaul, if I should happen to be in the neighbourhood. As I could not exclude the possibility of one day being in that area I took out my notebook and asked, more out of politeness than curiosity, if they would tell me their names and addresses. This produced an amazing change in one of the girls, who became quite hostile to me, asking me why I wanted to know. It was obvious that if I were to visit her I would have to know her address. But the fear of having one's name appear in a foreigner's notebook is deeply rooted in every Russian.

Another disagreeable incident was when I drove out in the car to visit Tolstoy's house, Yasnaya Polyana, now a museum. I had notified the Soviet authorities in accordance with the regulations and on the way back I stopped to picnic in the car. As there was a lot of traffic on the main road and it was pelting with rain, I turned about fifty yards up a side road and parked there. I realized that in doing this I was technically in breach of a Soviet regulation, since there was a security belt just outside Moscow which one could drive through provided one did not stop. But it was the spring of 1956 and I did not think, in that political atmosphere, it would be taken too seriously.

I was greatly deceived. An officer with his wife and family in a private car drove past and peered at us as he did so. Presently he returned, got out and gave a prolonged dirty look. A few minutes later, my picnic lunch was disturbed by a militia squad, motor cycle and lorry, which rushed on me as though I were a master spy. Now militia men were supposed to observe politeness and courtesy to foreign diplomats, even if they offended against Soviet laws. It said as much on the diplomatic legitimation cards we all had. Displaying the kind of Dutch courage which diplomatic inviolability gives one, I coolly went on munching my lunch and refused to allow the militia man, who wanted to take down my particulars, shelter from the pouring rain inside my car. Finally, as the rain, coming down in almost tropical intensity, began to make his notebook quite sodden, he rushed, in despair, to the lorry behind, jumped inside it and continued his reporting from there, much handicapped by the fact that I refused to get out of the car. In the end my trackers were forced to go away, discomfited to find that my papers were in perfect order. They rebuked me mildly for being fifty yards out of bounds and I heard nothing more about it. The unpleasant aspect of this episode was that, while peacefully picnicking, I had been informed on and reported to the militia. The regime has its spies and agents everywhere, but these spies and agents can count on the loyal co-operation of a very large number of Russians who are probably not convinced Communists but feel at one with the Communist regime when it comes to the question of protecting their country from the undesirable attentions of 'foreign agents'. The Russians have learnt this attitude to foreigners from Lenin. In my

Russian dictionary I remember finding the word *rylo* for 'snout'. The book gave only one example of how this word was used: it was a quotation from Lenin. 'Don't stick your swinish snout in our Soviet garden.'

On another occasion we found a delicious bathing spot in the river at Uspenskoye outside Moscow. In order to get to as remote a stretch of the stream as possible, I had to drive my car some half a mile over fields. Later, while swimming in mid-stream, I saw a building on the other bank with a high watch-tower where a guard appeared to be vigorously waving his hand. It augured ill and I did not know what to do. In no time a police squad arrived and ordered me to take my car away at once. It was not until later that I learned this had in fact been the country house of the Moscow merchant, Mamontov, and was now used as a dacha by one of the Soviet high-ups. I was Chargé d'Affaires and the Soviet government was playing host to an international conference on whaling. I was to give a dinner that night for some of the delegates, including Soviet official representatives. It seemed unnecessarily humiliating for me to be ordered by the police to come out in my bathing dress and dress before them, and so I remonstrated with the officer in charge. 'Look,' he said, 'I suppose at some time or other in your life you have been in a subordinate position and have had to carry out orders whether you liked them or not?' I had to agree that I had. 'Then please show some understanding for my position.' I gave him full marks for his diplomacy and made no trouble. The incident ended on a comradely note.

Was Khrushchev a convinced Communist and did he believe in his own propaganda? I think he was, though there is no doubt that his approach to Marxism-Leninism was a very pragmatic one and he was able to find loopholes in it if it suited his book. I am sure that he genuinely believed that the Communist system was superior to the capitalistic order and that the vast majority of mankind would be happier united in the camp of Socialism. He and his colleagues also suffered from a considerable chip on the shoulder, and were really scared of anyone who came under the categories of 'upper class', 'big business', 'society', etc. In spite of their sense of inferiority, both collectively and as individuals, the Russians had a strong consciousness of Great Power superiority. Khrushchev was suspicious of the bourgeoisie, but liked to talk to people who mattered, whether they were American senators or English lords. Fundamentally, the

Russians were more drawn to Big Powers like themselves and to their representatives than to smaller ones, however loyal they might be to the Soviet regime and however close their relationship with them.

Everyone knows by now that the way to impress the Russians is not to send them someone whose political ideas are close to theirs—a left-wing socialist, for instance—but rather, someone who is of importance in his own country. For this reason, Sir Stafford Cripps, who was a Utopian socialist, was an unsuitable ambassador, while Lord Beaverbrook, capitalist and press lord, impressed the Russians enormously when he was sent on a mission to Moscow during the war. I noticed that the Soviet officials loved to try and win over die-hard Conservative MPs. In Stockholm, the Soviet counsellor, Semyonov, discussing political life in Denmark after the war, asked innocently: 'The Conservative Party is a reliable one, isn't it?' When the Duke of Wellington came to Moscow (not that he was a diehard Conservative MP, but maybe they thought he was) they made a great fuss of him. In the interests of winning the good opinion of western capitalists they were quite able to disown those who believed themselves to be their true friends. Once we had a parliamentary delegation visiting Russia and an entertainment was arranged for them in the reception room. When they had all assembled, there was a pause, then the Dean of Canterbury, the Revd. Hewlett Johnson, was escorted in. To most MPs at that time the 'Red Dean' was anathema and rejected as a fellow-traveller. The deputy leader of the delegation (the leader happened to be away), a Labour MP, went up to the Russians and told them roundly that if the Dean remained there, the delegation would walk out. Shortly afterwards, we witnessed the astonishing spectacle of the Dean being hustled out of the building.

At a National Day reception the Russians and Khrushchev showed no particular desire to talk to, say, the Czechoslovak Ambassador if they could talk to the British or American. After the Soviet Union had opened relations with West Germany, the West German Ambassador was given first-class treatment, while his East German counterpart was often left by himself in a corner. Moreover, the Soviet leaders instinctively felt more western than eastern. Although it fitted into their political scheme to aspire to be on the closest terms with the Chinese, they had a minimum of things in common with them, and it happened sometimes at National Day receptions when toasts were drunk that Bulganin would drink to all the Great Powers and their representatives and forget China. Once a minor official had to pull him by the sleeve and remind him of his omission. As relations subsequently deteriorated between Moscow and Peking, this is not as surprising now as it was when it happened.

This interest in talking to the west, this wish to get together with the great ones, was one of the reasons why Stalin's successors called so insistently for summit talks. The post-Stalin generation of Russians wanted to have contact with the west but not just through Communists and fellow-travellers or representatives of the working class with similar backgrounds to themselves. They wanted to be on terms of equality with the top ones in the capitalistic world. Like Hitler and the Nazis they longed to be treated on an equal footing with the west, as members of their 'club'.

There was perhaps more hope that agreement could be reached between east and west as long as there was someone in control of Russia who was extrovert and pragmatic and was anxious to be accepted in 'high society'. Still, one had to reckon with that stubbornness which was part of Khrushchev's character, and behind which was his well-founded conviction that he was on a good wicket and did not need to make concessions. I am sure that he genuinely believed that time was on his side and that if he waited long enough, all countries would adopt a regime which was sympathetic to the Soviet one. Indeed I think he was so convinced of this at one time, that he thought that if he unscrewed the clamps and let the people free they would all choose Communism without any pressure being applied to them. Probably the enormous success of his visits to India and Burma went to his head somewhat. He was also a human being, in the way that Stalin certainly was not, and he wished to better the lot, if not of humanity at large, at any rate of his own people.

None the less I did not then see any prospect of notable advances being made for many years to come. But I did believe that through more frequent contact between east and west, through the visits of the Soviet leaders abroad and through the first-hand experience they acquired there of how the world actually was, in contrast to what Soviet propaganda depicted it to be, there would be a steady increase in mutual understanding. I never thought there was any likelihood that Soviet leaders would make any concessions as long as they were in a position of strength. They had no serious difficulties which would incline them towards a conciliatory attitude. Externally, their position was very strong. Internally, it was always a question mark, but they continued to represent a formidable military and economic power. Though palace revolution might follow palace revolution, this did not necessarily effect the strength of the Soviet position. Unlike the situation in other countries, where governments are generally dependent upon the parliamentary position and the public will, the Soviet leaders had no need to take popular opinion into account. The Russian people had been so conditioned over centuries that they would accept almost any demand which was made of them, and if public opinion were ever to matter, Khrushchev could always claim that he had made the lot of the Soviet people infinitely happier than it was under Stalin. Around and beneath him, he had an enormous official and semi-official cast who were concerned about keeping the regime going and not reducing the empire which they governed.

But Khrushchev's imagination was easily captured by grand ideas —'hare-brained' his enemies called them. The prospect of achieving understanding with the only other Great Power which could really challenge the Soviet Union, the United States of America, was unquestionably attractive to him and he would probably have been prepared to make some sacrifices to obtain it. He also calculated that if he could come to an agreement with America, the other countries would gradually have to fall in with it and would cease to be a problem to him. But, perhaps most important of all, he was a realist and knew only too well that growing tension and the massing of nuclear armaments on both sides must lead to the destruction of everything—even his own cherished world which he and his generation had fought so hard for—unless some common ground could be reached.

When I came back to England after three years in Russia I was often greeted with the remark: 'Well I don't suppose you're sorry to be finished with that?' My answer was unorthodox. 'On the contrary, I am very sorry it's all over. I have not finished. I have not even begun. I needed to stay another three years at least.'

What was the fascination of Russia? First of all, I found it satisfying from a professional point of view. There was the enormous excitement of watching the Soviet experiment. Would it work? Would the Communist bloc outstrip the capitalist world? What would happen if they did? What would happen if they failed? The competitive co-existence between east and west was a challenge to both systems and could be a healthy and exhilarating process, were it not for the political tension underlying it and the awful nuclear threat in the background. In the Soviet Union, which was developing rapidly and in an orthodox way, life was full of surprises. Each morning's *Pravda* brought us something new and kept us guessing. Next, Russia was a very beautiful country. It was a land where nature was often unspoiled and where even human nature could reveal itself in a new and refreshing light. It had its own enchantment. We travelled a lot and would like to have done more. The theatrical and concert life of Moscow and Leningrad always offered a treat to those who loved the best in Russian literature and music. Finally, there were the opportunities one had to educate oneself about Russia—its history, the national character of the people, their literature, their art. How little we learn about Russia in England at schools, universities and in our daily round. And how important it is to grasp every opportunity we have of learning something about this great and formidable people, the proper understanding of whom is vital now and will be indispensable in the years to come. It is also important to remember that Soviet Russia can still teach us much about the Russia that was, which had so much to offer from Pushkin to Chekhov, from Glinka to Mussorgsky, and from medieval Russian icons and frescoes to nineteenth-century Russian painting.

BOOK III

Czechoslovakia Again 1960-1975

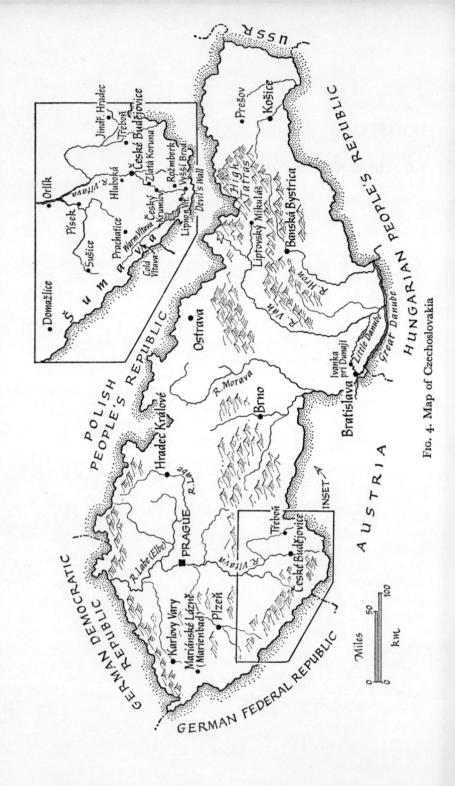

Fig. 4. Map of Czechoslovakia

11. The Native's Return

When I had served my tour in Moscow in 1957 I was appointed Librarian, Director of Research, and Keeper of the Papers at the Foreign Office. This was a grand and imposing title for a very modest and somewhat academic post.

After three years of this glorified 'paper work' (which gave me rich opportunities for reading) I felt that, at the age of fifty-one, it was about time I was appointed head of a mission somewhere. It was the old conflict within me: was I to be a man of action or a back-room boy? 'How happy could I be with either, were t'other dear charmer away,' as MacHeath sings in *The Beggar's Opera*. When one is first tried out in a position of such responsibility, it is generally at unimportant and unrewarding posts, unless one is a 'picked man' who has a reserved seat on the 'inner circuit' of the Foreign Office. I had no wish to go to the minor posts in Africa or South-East Asia, of which there were now so many. As it happened, except for Vienna and Athens, the missions in Central and South-Eastern Europe, which I considered interesting, were not popular with my colleagues.

By chance, the only vacancy likely to come my way at that time was Prague. Twelve years had passed since I had last served there and I had to overcome the latent effects of the trauma of 1948, before I could steel myself to go back. I had in the meantime been far enough away from my beloved city to face a return to it, even if conditions there had drastically changed.

What had become of it since the *coup d'état*? My most poignant memory of my last days in Prague was of filing with the crowd past Jan Masaryk's body and, later, standing in our garden at Smíchov, watching the enormous column of people following the funeral cortège as it threaded its way along the Karmelitská below. On that fatal 10 March when Jan fell or was thrown from the window of his flat in the Černín Palace, a shroud of terror seemed to descend on Prague. It was the first of a long succession of horrors which were to reach their climax in the trials of the fifties. The beautiful, bright and innocent city of Prague was back in the sinister twilight of Meyrinck's *Golem* and Kafka's *Trial*.

The years rolled by. All the horrors of byegone ages were resurrected: incarceration in dank dungeons, fabricated accusations, torture, forced confessions and—antisemitism. It was Thomas Masaryk who, braving the jeers of the ultra-nationalistic Czech students of his time, had stood up for a Jewish victim falsely accused of ritual murder. Now a self-styled 'progressive' government in blind obedience to Stalin did not scruple to send Jews to the scaffold with as little humanity and decency as when they had been driven to the gas chambers some ten years earlier by one of the greatest monsters that has ever lived.

In December 1952, eleven of the fourteen defendants in the Slánský trial were executed, ten of them Jews. They included Rudolf Slánský himself, who had been Secretary General of the Party. The only non-Jew among them was Vlado Clementis, ex-Minister of Foreign Affairs. But many more were implicated in the trials and had to endure terrible torture. Four survivors were to play a role in the process of de-Stalinization in Czechoslovakia in 1967 and 1968—Husák, now President and First Secretary of the Communist Party, and the reformers Smrkovský, Goldstücker and Pavel. On a short visit to the Czechoslovak Embassy in London in 1951 I had been horrified to see truly ghoulish figures standing around, who were as un-Czech as anyone could imagine. They were indeed twentieth-century golems.

On 5 March 1953, Stalin died. Following the precedent of other Communist leaders, Klement Gottwald went to the Soviet Union to attend Stalin's funeral and met his death there nine days after it. Strange how Communist leaders seem to develop a built-in resistance to the otherwise so advanced and successful healing methods of Soviet medicine! He was succeeded as President by Antonín Zápotocký, son of 'the founder of Socialism' and himself a product of 'Bolshevist' Kladno. Antonín Novotný succeeded Gottwald as First Secretary of the Party and on Zápotocký's death, became President of the Republic as well. In Czechoslovakia these three men—at that time still honoured in the Czechoslovak pantheon—bore the prime guilt for the martyrdom of some of their most devoted fellow Communists.

Meanwhile the Czechoslovak People's Republic had become the Soviet Union's most faithful satellite. It was said that when it rained in Moscow umbrellas were put up on the Charles Bridge in Prague. As late as two years after Stalin's death, a monstrous monument was unveiled to him in commemoration of the tenth anniversary of the 'liberation' of Prague by the Soviet army. Popularly known as 'The Bread Queue' it stood there until 1963, ten years after his death, when one night it was covertly—but officially—blown up. Without their Jehovah figure, however, the Communist leaders seemed lost. Who or what could they put in its place?

Between 1953 and my return to Prague in 1960, the harsh, unintelligent, uninspiring and incompetent Novotný had been ruling unchallenged over a drab, grey and spiritless land. And official life remained indescribably dull until I left six years later in 1966. *No, bozhe moi, kakaya skuka,* as Pushkin aptly put it.*

I was curious to know how the Czechoslovak authorities would receive me on my return to Prague in 1960. Members of the Party now monopolized the government and, although I had previously got on satisfactorily with Communist intellectuals, many of them had in the meantime gone through purgatory: the gentle Halas, poet of life and death, had died in grief and pain; the anacreontic Nezval had succumbed to normal biological processes and become canonized. Moreover, when I had been Press Attaché, I had dared publicly to criticize the chief organ of the Party, *Rudé Právo.* I wondered if the leadership would still bear a grudge against me. To my surprise, I was well received—at any rate, outwardly and officially.

During my period of preparation I had been busy brushing up my language with Czech members of the BBC (as I had done in 1945). I was therefore able, when I presented my credentials to the President, to speak to him in Czech, even at this stage, and it was as well that I could do so, because the conversation lasted about an hour. President Novotný was extremely unpopular and I soon sensed that there was not a single person, not even among those in his closest entourage, who was enthusiastic about him. When he smiled, which was rare, his eyes were never in step with that smile. They remained cold, hard and full of a pathological resentment, which was only too evident in his public speeches: it came pouring out during almost any conversation I had with him. It was compounded of implacable hatred for the capitalistic world, loathing

* 'My God, what a bore!' (*Evgenii Onegin*)

of the Germans, an inferiority complex, jealousy and insecurity. He presented the paradoxical image of a dictator who was unsure of himself because he knew he was not his own master. On the occasion of the arrival of a new ambassador, a head of state generally goes out of his way to say something friendly about his government. During all the six years I spent in Czechoslovakia, Novotný never once made a friendly reference to anyone in Her Majesty's Government—Labour or Conservative.

It was an unrewarding interview, though members of his entourage wished me to believe that it was a very successful one, because the President had kept me so long. Looking at my predecessor's report I found that his interview had lasted exactly the same time.

A better opportunity to gauge the official attitude was provided by the visit of a British parliamentary delegation immediately after I arrived. The National Assembly (or Parliament) gave a lunch for them at Barrandov Restaurant, to which I was invited. The host was Zdeněk Fierlinger, who had been Prime Minister when I was in Czechoslovakia before, and was now the equivalent of our Speaker. When Fierlinger rose to speak I was eager to know what he would say. He had been quite friendly to me after the war, helped to get the huge Čedok building for our British Information Services, officially opened them for us, when we had them ready, and made encouraging speeches on that and other occasions. I wondered whether he would now find himself obliged to dissociate himself from all that. On the contrary, he made a most amiable speech, referring in a complimentary way to my earlier activities in Prague. It was helpful that he made his remarks in the presence of leading back-benchers of the House of Commons, including the future Attorney-General. But when I gave a reception in honour of the delegation, of the eighty-two Czech guests invited (mostly officials) only thirty-two appeared, the most senior official being the Deputy Minister of Foreign Affairs.

I was far from dismayed by this result. At Moscow, an attendance of thirty-nine per cent of those invited would have been considered a great success. There, if we asked a hundred guests, we were lucky if some twenty came. In February of the following year I tried something more ambitious. I decided to ask eighty people, most of them musicians, including a member of the Central Committee, but also some writers and theatre and film directors.

In the week before my party there was a disaster. Patrice

Lumumba was murdered in the Congo. There were savage reactions in the press and in the streets. The Belgian Embassy was sacked, the Ambassadress herself being nearly struck as she sat in her room, and many of their beautiful paintings were destroyed in an act of vandalism carried out, not by Czechs, but by students from the underdeveloped countries, of whom there were many in Prague at that time. I told my wife this meant that our reception would be boycotted: no one would come at all. We need have had no fears. On the day, sixty-eight people attended, a 'gate' of eighty-five per cent, which surpassed our most optimistic expectations.

While the whole of the Communist world outside was in the deepest mourning and hoarse with tirades against the western powers, the mood inside the Thun Palace was relaxed. One of the musicians said: 'Why, this is fantastic. I have met some musical colleagues here whom I have not seen for years. The British Embassy seems to be the only place where *all* sections of our much divided confraternity can meet together.'

I managed to persuade a trio of musicians (former friends) to give a concert, after which we all trooped upstairs to see a coloured film of Glyndebourne and its operatic performances, on which I improvised a commentary in Czech. The audience was suitably impressed by the film and amused by the occasional unconscious humour of my Czech explanations. When we came down, they all rushed to the buffet and the noise of 'self-service' and conversation was deafening. The talking continued at a high pitch long after the tables were stripped of everything but the drinks and during the performance of a work of Haydn which the American Ambassadress, Alberta Ravendal, and I gave together on two pianos. She was Viennese born and a pianist of professional calibre.

Although we were facing each other and as close to each other as people playing on two pianos can get, the background noise was so overwhelming that I could hardly hear her playing at all and I doubt whether she could hear a note of mine. It made no difference because nobody was listening. But the idea was a good one. Representatives of two of the powers which the Communist press were describing in the most vituperative terms had met together to entertain some of the music-loving Czech world. And luckily, as evidenced by the good turn-out and the friendly attitude of a member of the Central Committee present, the entertainment was not regarded as a threat to the regime.

The reception set the pattern for our future official entertaining. Unlike in Moscow, ministers hardly ever came. (The difference was understandable. They would probably have liked to come but were afraid of what Moscow might say. They were permitted to imitate the Soviet leaders in other things, but not in this.) Czech unofficial guests—although it was sometimes difficult to know who were official and who unofficial—always came if they possibly could, but, for safety's sake, I used to get my secretary to ring round personally to each of them, in case the written invitation had not reached them. In this way, I generally got a firm answer. They were supposed to get clearance from a superior Party authority but those who thought they would be refused permission either came without asking or stayed away. (Those who thought they would get it either came without it or got it.) It showed that in Prague the attitude of the average Czech towards the authorities was more casual than in Moscow. In fact, in spite of the repression in Czechoslovakia, coming there after Moscow was like coming to a western country.

Alas, the hospitality I offered was ill reciprocated by the official representatives of the Czechoslovak state. At first, we were scarcely ever invited out, and if we were, no one took any notice of us. Nothing seemed more calculated than the ostentatious way we were ignored. At one time a gifted Czech film director, whom I had known from my earlier stay in Prague and who had spent the war years in England, invited me to the première of his latest film. However, as he explained to me when I met him a few days before, he had asked us strictly in our *private* capacity as Mr and Mrs Parrott and not as the British Ambassador and Ambassadress. Many ambassadors would have preferred to stay away on those terms, but we went and felt that we had got something extra, not available to other ambassadors.

I was not the only target of this official discourtesy. The American, Canadian and, at times, French Ambassadors received similar treatment. An exception was the Italian Ambassador who succeeded in getting round the authorities by various gimmicks, one of which was to have special medals made for presentation to Czech journalists for their 'services to Italo-Czechoslovak relations'! Once the Protocol Department arranged a visit for the whole Corps to the Škoda factory at Mladá Boleslav. Just as we went into a hall where we were to be given a technical briefing by one of the engineers, the Cuban Ambassador stood up and asked if he could speak. He thereupon read out a telegram of congratulation he had received from the Communist workers of the factory. The text was a scorching attack on the United States and about as offensive as it could be. It was obviously a put-up job and, to say the least, a serious diplomatic breach. The Canadian Ambassador and I did not know whether to walk out. (I do not think the American Ambassador himself was there.) In any case we both of us complained vehemently to the Head of Protocol and insisted that he should rebuke the Cuban Ambassador, which I believe the good man (because he was a good man) tried to do.

Like all Heads of Missions and their wives, we were invited to the receptions given for the countless visitors the Communist powers were courting—Soekarno, Sihanuk and the rest. On such occasions we had to stand and listen to hostile speeches, always uncertain as to whether we should have to walk out or not. There was a notable difference between the Kremlin parties and those given by Novotný at the Castle. In the Kremlin the members of the Soviet Presidium made themselves as hospitable as they could to their guests, invited them to their table, toasted them and beamed with *bonhomie*. Novotný and the members of his politburo used to monopolize all the chairs and sit huddled in a ring in one corner of the main reception room with their backs turned to us, while we were left standing on our own. Novotný only got up when the time came for him to bid farewell to his guests. Sometimes when this happened, he singled me out for a general tirade directed against the west. As he often detained me for a longish time, my diplomatic colleagues, who were anxious to get home, formed a queue behind me. They probably thought I was basking in the President's favour and ground their teeth; in reality, nearly every conversation I had with him on these occasions was disagreeable.

There was one exception to this coldness, however unimportant it may have been. One day we were asked to attend a series of concerts which were regularly held at Bertramka, the house where Mozart stayed when he was in Prague. It was in its garden that he was supposed to have written the Overture to *Don Giovanni* just in the nick of time: as the pages were finished they were carried straight off to the theatre for the orchestra to play, unrehearsed. We welcomed this invitation and found when we arrived that the tiny hall was completely crowded out. A smiling lady appeared and ushered us to seats in the front row. Then, to our amazement, she

got up on the platform and said how happy they all were to greet
the British Ambassador and Ambassadress and so on, and the whole
audience burst into triumphant applause. Afterwards I was made
an honorary member of the Bertramka circle and presumably still
am because I have not read of any expulsion order. Indeed, I was
even asked to contribute an article to its journal on the vexed
question of where Mozart actually stayed on his first visit to Prague,
which I never did because I was not allowed by the authorities to
see the papers of the Thun family. (A historian prepared them all
for me but never received permission to show them to me!)

It happened from time to time that under the influence, perhaps,
of one or two glasses of wine, and with the natural ebullience which
is common to Czechs and Slovaks, some fairly important official—
a Deputy Minister—would personally ask us to make a visit somewhere, which he would himself arrange. I remember, for instance,
how we were once invited to see a paper factory where the machinery was British. I said we should be delighted to do so and asked
whether we should come in our own car? If so, would our prospective host tell us where the place was? He promised to come and fetch
us himself. A few days before he was scheduled to call, he rang up
to say that the boilers in the factory had gone wrong and therefore
the visit would have to be put off. He was very sorry but they would
soon be put right. About three weeks later he rang up again to say
that everything was ready but would I mind making an application
to the Protocol Department of the Ministry of Foreign Affairs, so
as to obtain the necessary clearance? Here I drew the line. It was
insufferable that a high official, after having asked me to be his
guest, should then ask me to beg permission to come. It would put
an entirely wrong complexion on the episode and make it appear
that it was we who were pressing to see the factory. This could give
a hostile authority the opportunity of claiming that I was trying to
pry into things which were not my concern. However, I did not
want to have a row with our prospective host, because I realized
that it was not his fault, but that of the Party organization, who, on
learning that he had issued an invitation to us, had probably rapped
him over the knuckles for not clearing it with them beforehand. The
'Protocol Department' was, in this case, the Party apparatus, a
representative of whom would always decide whether foreign ambassadors should be allowed to go to this place or that. I took no
further action and our would-be host never spoke about it again.

A similar case occurred when the leader of one of the stooge parties, the former Catholic, now 'Peoples', Party, invited us to go with him to Moravia to attend some of the religious festivals which were still taking place on saints' days. He made it sound so tempting, and I gratefully accepted, but he said no more about it and, naturally, nothing came of it. I was not surprised in this case, because a leader of a stooge party had no authority whatsoever. Still, it was a bit steep when he afterwards blamed me for not having accepted his invitation!

Our general experience was that although the horror of the trials had passed, most people were still very cowed. Many of those we had known in happier days were still afraid to see us. One artist's wife I called on, who lived only a stone's throw from us, turned white as a sheet when I rang her bell and nearly shut the door in my face. At length, she let me in and continued the conversation in whispers. Her husband was in gaol and she feared for her son. At a concert I met a former cultural adviser to President Beneš, a member of the Czech National Socialist Party. He had just been let out of prison after serving twelve years and was now a metal worker. 'I had better not be seen talking to you too long,' he added, 'or I'll be back there again.' Another music lover was the ex-Minister, Drtina, of the same party, who had 'jumped out of the window' of the Ministry of Justice and survived his injuries. He spoke to me briefly in the interval of a concert, although nothing about this event, of course. Another night Dr Vladimír Kučera, the former Czechoslovak Minister in Stockholm, reluctantly accepted my offer to drive him home. When I suggested he might later come and see us, he answered: 'Are you mad? I have succeeded at long last in getting my children into a school. Do you want to see them thrown out?' Some bolder friends, who wanted me to come and see them, begged me not to leave my car outside their flats. Could I not leave it in the next street? The idea of an ambassador, whose movements were closely watched, going through the antics of 'leaving his car in the next street' would have been comic if the situation which gave rise to it had not been so tragic.

During these first years I reckoned that about every six months the STB (the Czechoslovak equivalent of the KGB) approached one of our staff. Their attempts were always directed at the weakest or most vital links in our organization. The Chancery guards were on watch at night, and if one of them had been suborned he could

have let STB agents into the premises. They were a fine and reliable
lot of men, to whom we owe a lot, but there was an occasional
black sheep among them. One was once found locked alone in his
flat and dead to the world with an empty crate of beer beside him
(it had happened to him once before in another post). Another's
wife was picked up in the street by the STB, when she had had (or
had obviously been given) a drop too much. There were other
risks. Contrary to rules another member of staff joined a Prague
bridge club where there was always the risk that he might inadvert-
ently incur debts and lay himself open to blackmail. Some of the
staff were said to have involved themselves in 'illegal' purchases
and sales. It was not that they were guilty of any crimes; it was just
that they were stupidly falling into the traps the STB had laid for
them.

One day our Czech driver, who took a truck to Germany once a
fortnight to fetch provisions for the whole Embassy, defected. He
very considerately deposited with the German police a whole set of
instructions he had received from the Security Service. He was to
'chat up' all the girls who had access to safes, cyphers, keys, etc. If
we had needed any proof now of what the STB was up to, we had
it now served to us on a plate. Both my chauffeurs, one after the
other, were arrested by the police and disqualified from driving—
in one case purely to cause me annoyance, I suspect.

Our servants were regularly questioned—every month, I believe—
about how we felt and what we said to them. It was Moscow all
over again. They were asked to report if they saw me looking de-
pressed. I longed to pretend to beat my wife so that they could
hear and report it, but I knew they would never say anything if I
did! No one could be employed by us or remain employed, unless
they reported monthly to the authorities and we could not engage
anyone who had not previously satisfied them that they would.
What they reported was another matter.

Once at one of our receptions a member of our staff asked a Czech
singing teacher if she could bring her child to her for classes. Later,
the singing teacher let us know by indirect channels that she had at
once received a visit from the STB asking her to accommodate an
agent in the adjoining room. She tried to convey to us that somebody at our party must have been an informer. When we checked
up on who could have overheard the conversation, it came as rather
a shock to us.

I was never made to feel that I was under police surveillance myself although, undoubtedly, I was. For the Service Attachés it was another matter. The escort cars trailed them day and night, camped all night outside their houses, harassed them by flashing past them and suddenly jamming on their brakes, or closed in on their wives at picnics. Our Military Attaché took his mother out on an innocent drive in the country and the poor lady was given a disagreeable shaking. His new young assistant became so outraged by this that he put up huge notices in Czech on his car, which read something like this: 'Boys, they're on my neck. Look behind and you'll see the STB.' We felt great sympathy with him, but advised him to play it cool.

Another time, one of my staff came to report to me that for several evenings a woman in the house opposite had been provocatively undressing in front of the window, presumably in an effort to lure him from his duties! One may laugh at this. It could have been mere exhibitionism on the part of the woman, or even lurid imagination on the part of her target, but, if not, it only served to confirm the lengths to which the STB would go to try and seduce us.

The senior Service Attachés were particularly annoyed when they found themselves in a lane surrounded by a group of STB agents. One of them had a signpost marked 'To the Airport 100 metres' which he stuck in the ground, and the rest had a battery of cameras. The attachés who always travelled in pairs, were photographed with these 'props' and shown up as nicely 'caught' in their 'felonious purposes'. When I was summoned to the Ministry of Foreign Affairs and shown the 'dossier', I exploded. When my anger subsided, I appealed to the official to stop all this childish 'fun and games', otherwise their Service Attachés in England might have some unpleasant experiences in their turn. I warned him that the cumulative result might well be a worsening of our relations, just when I had hopes of improving them. Surprisingly enough all the harassment ceased shortly afterwards.

This subversive activity against our Embassy had been going on for twelve years at least. We had a harrowing dossier of successful and unsuccessful attempts on our staff, which we circulated to new arrivals. Unfortunately, a few years later, such episodes began to appear unreal or exaggerated in the outwardly deceptive atmosphere of Prague in the sixties, when Stalin had been dead for seven years or more. But the danger was ever present.

For the time being political life stagnated and it looked as if the icy grip of Stalinism would never melt. In fact, although I did not realize it, we were on the threshold of great changes. But patience was necessary. For the time being I consoled myself with the beauties of Prague and the country. The more I saw of them, the more conscious I was of the criminal way in which the great patrimony of Bohemia was being squandered and its precious culture stifled. I reflected how fortunate we had been in being able to keep our lovely Embassy intact in spite of six years of German occupation and war and twelve years of Stalinist oppression. Although British property, that too was decidedly part of the Czech patrimony.

12. The Thun Palace

According to Robert Bruce-Lockhart, who spent some dissipated years in it, the British Embassy in Prague, the former Thun-Hohenstein palace, was the most beautiful Ambassadorial residence we had anywhere in the world. It was certainly on the best site, not only by comparison with other embassies, but with all public buildings in Prague, because it bordered on the Hradčany or royal castle—now the President's domain. To the ordinary visitor, who came into the courtyard with its enormous neo-Gothic gateway, it might have appeared a gaunt, if imposing, building, its four storeys crowned by an eighteenth-century pediment and frieze, where the royal coat-of-arms had taken the place of the former Thun-Hohenstein family crest. He could not have suspected that, three flights up, the rooms would open out on to the garden, an enchanting retreat, which enjoyed the most wonderful and certainly the most intimate view both of the castle and the famous Cathedral of St Vitus and which had something of the atmosphere of an English cathedral close.

On the second floor there was a long high terrace where an avenue of trees had once been. Now there is only one very gnarled chestnut, which keeps guard outside the Ambassador's office. This terrace offered a magical view of Prague down to the river Vltava. It used to be the grand climax to a suite of three gorgeous reception rooms. When their chandeliers, some gilt or polychrome wood, and others Venetian or Bohemian glass, were all lit up and reflected in the mirrors on the walls, these three rooms offered a magnificent spectacle. No suite of rooms could have provided a more fitting *décor* for a really sumptuous ball, where the ladies in grand toilette and regalia would be reflected in the mirrors, and couples could go out on to the terrace in the intervals to enjoy the cooler air. I could see such a scene come to life as I studied one of Count Josef Oswald

Thun's invitations from 1836, which the servants of those days had pinned on a door, and was still preserved.

Unhappily, soon after my arrival, the Foreign Office decided to box these rooms up and turn them into offices. The reason was the vulnerability of the Service Attachés who had their offices in the courtyard, the wall of which was exposed to the outside. Someone from outside had managed to make a hole and insert a tube into it, which had presumably been used for photographing or tape-recording. It was this intrusion which persuaded the Foreign Office to move the Service Attachés and some of the outlying departments into the shelter of the main building. I regretted that rooms of unique beauty in the palace and much valuable space for entertaining would be sacrificed just at a time when it was again becoming possible and necessary to make full use of them, but there was no alternative but to submit.

The charm of the Thun Palace lay not only in the beauty and homeliness of the buildings but also in the old butler, Jelínek, who seemed to have become part of them. One Sunday in summer, when we returned early from a drive, we found him in a skull cap, sitting on the stairs and reading the *Guardian*. He chose to sit on the stairs because it was the coolest place on a hot day. The skull cap was to protect his bald head from the draught. Why he read the *Guardian* I cannot exactly say, but he preserved every English newspaper in the house in his room.

I seldom ventured into his sanctuary but managed to have a peep into it now and again. He had several interesting books, mostly antiquarian ones. His window looked down on the garden and the cathedral and he would tempt the squirrels into his room by putting out food for them; the result being that, when he was out of the room, they made hay of it, knocking over his things and scattering food on the floor.

He was a typical Moravian, who could converse with equal fluency in German and Czech. The maids said he was 'noble'. Only our guests could tell how much English he knew. He had served in a great house—at Lancut in Poland for the Potockis, where a footman stood behind every guest at meal times. Later, he worked for Count Doubek, the husband of the famous Czech singer, Jarmila Novotná. He had often been entrusted with his employers' financial dealings. In a Europe torn by faction and dissension it was a blessed relief to find someone so calm, dispassionate and reliable. I once asked him what he thought of the *Good Soldier Švejk*. 'You know, sir,' he said, 'the Austrian officers were not as bad as that. I served under them in the war and some were good people. In any case they were much like the rest of us—good and bad.' Though I knew this of course, it was interesting to hear a Czech confirm it.

Once the decision was taken to rebuild the Embassy we had to face the prospect of a radical transformation of the whole building. This was to be carried out by teams of workmen from England and would take a considerable time, and we ourselves would have to find somewhere else to live. Eventually after much heartsearching we reluctantly requisitioned the flat of our hard-worked lady Commercial Secretary and Consul, occupied today by the representative of the British Council.

When we moved back into the renovated residence I made it my business to learn all I could about the beautiful and historic building. Its first recorded owner was alleged to have built it in the fourteenth century, when it 'shone with the splendour of its tower'. During the installation of a lift in 1947, Gothic foundations were revealed, and some of the older Czech workmen found medieval structures round the original Chapel of the Holy Cross on the third floor (converted by the Thun family into a bathroom and used by us as such) and in the winding stairway which led up to the turret. A second circular staircase had originally run from the old first floor to the second, but had been bricked up in more recent times. Under the pool in the garden, repairs revealed the existence of a subterranean chamber or grotto, which also probably went back to medieval times, when the level of the garden may have been lower and the structure situated at ground level.

The palace appears to have been one of the great houses built during the reign of Emperor Charles IV, when the cathedral was rebuilt, the castle restored, the Charles University founded and a new bridge built across the river Vltava. Could any other of our embassies compare with it in antiquity? From its position on the slopes of the Hradčany hill it dominated all that part of Malá Strana (The Small Quarter) which lay between it and the gate tower of the Charles Bridge 300 yards away. From its windows you could see the dreaming spires and roofs of Prague, from the steeple of St Thomas's to the fine patrician house in the square which I imagined belonged to the Montagues until I realized that it was the property of a family called 'Montag'. During the reconstruction in my time some Renaissance frescoes were uncovered representing biblical scenes, possibly Susanna and the Elders. I was glad to be able to preserve them, although they were in our offices.

In 1630 Walter Leslie, a Scottish soldier of fortune and one of the four British mercenaries (two Irishmen, Butler and Deveroux, and two Scotsmen, Gordon and Leslie) who murdered Wallenstein, came into possession of the house. He may have received it in the general 'carve up' after the defeat of the Czech Rising at the Battle of the White Mountain in 1620 or as a gift from a grateful emperor for having helped rid him of a dangerous traitor. At any rate, he achieved great success in Austrian service, numbering among his posts those of Vice-President of the Council of War, Warden of the Sclavonian Marshes, Field-Marshal and Ambassador to the Ottoman Empire, and being decorated with the Order of the Golden Fleece. A memorial to him still stands in the Embassy garden.

He sold the house in 1656 to Count Guidobald Thun-Hohenstein, Archbishop of Salzburg, who, being childless, made a present of it to his brother, Michal Osvald. The latter was an enthusiastic renovator but it was his nephew who had the house rebuilt by the Italian architect, Giovanni Luragho. When we first arrived there was a big room upstairs, which was being used as a ping-pong room, with a four-poster bed in it. This bed was said to have been the Archbishop's and the room was still called the 'Archbishop's Room'. Since the 1960 reconstruction it too has been split up.

Michal Osvald's descendant, Johann Joseph ('the old Count Thun'), was a friend and patron of Mozart, who was his guest on his first visit to Prague in 1787. The problem which I long tried to solve was where he actually stayed on this occasion. He wrote a letter from the Thun Palace to his friend von Jaquin about the Count and his orchestra, but, unfortunately, said next to nothing about the house. He was not really interested in buildings or beautiful objects, preferring people and society. We cannot be absolutely sure that the Thun Palace from which he wrote the letter was the British Embassy, because, at that time, there were at least five Thun palaces scattered all over Prague and three of them in the Malá Strana itself.

In addition to these palaces there was a house called the 'Thun *House*' in Sněmovní which had once been joined to the present Embassy building. It is possible that guests of Mozart's status were housed in this particular building rather than in the palace itself, which for a 'palace' had rather modest dimensions. If this is true, and it is of course only conjecture, Mozart did not stay in the actual British Embassy building in Thunovská but in an outbuilding in another street.

More interesting than the Old Count Thun who died at the age of seventy-seven, a year after Mozart's visit, were his son and daughter-in-law, Franz Josef and Marie Wilhelmine Thun. Franz Josef was the founder of the Klášterec (Klösterle) branch of the Thuns. He was also a good friend of Mozart's, and his wife an even better one. She (formerly Countess Uhlfeld) did much for the musicians living at the time and is mentioned frequently in Mozart's letters. She had been a pupil of Haydn and 'having by chance discovered that Mozart was the composer of a sonata of great merit, she immediately appointed him her instructor on the pianoforte and in singing, though up to that hour he had been living in a garret and enduring extreme privations.'* She was also a patron of Beethoven who dedicated one of his pianoforte trios to her. As one of the favourites of the Emperor Joseph, she did her best to persuade him that Mozart was a great pianist, and invited the composer to her home, when the Emperor was to be present as her guest. Mozart could not go and was 'half-desperate' because of it. He wrote of her: 'I have already dined twice with the Countess Thun, and go there almost every day . . . she is one of the most charming, lovely women I ever knew in my life—and I am in great esteem with her.'

When Mozart finally played before the Emperor, Countess Thun lent him her Stein piano, which was just as well, as, in Mozart's own words, 'the other piano was out of tune and had three of its keys sticking down'.

Her husband was a friend and disciple of Mesmer and acquired a reputation as a hypnotic healer. He was also a Rosicrucian and a freemason, which is interesting in view of the links between Rosicrucianism and freemasonry. Mozart was a freemason, as is well known from the masonic music he composed and the masonic symbolism of his opera *The Magic Flute*. But what is not so well known, is that the only noblemen on whom he called, when coming to Prague for the first time, were freemasons.

Count and Countess Franz Josef Thun had three daughters of great beauty, who were known as the 'Three Graces' and were also referred to in Mozart's letters. The eldest, Marie Elisabeth, married Count Razumovsky, the Russian Ambassador in Vienna, who com-

* *Life of Mozart* by Edward Homes, 1845.

missioned Beethoven's 'Razumovsky' quartets. The second, Marie
Christine, married Prince Karl Lichnovsky, who was a great friend
of Beethoven and was often host to him in his castle at Hradec
(Gratz) in northern Moravia. Beethoven dedicated his Second
Symphony and Pathétique sonata to him. Lichnovsky was a patron
of Mozart too and accompanied him on his tour of Prussia. The
youngest of the 'Graces', Marie Caroline, married an Englishman—
Richard Meade, Earl of Clanwilliam. Their direct descendant is
Flavia, Lady Ebbisham, whom I had the pleasure of taking round
the Thun Palace, while it was being reconstructed.

The palace we were living in thus held many precious memories—
if no tangible memorials—of the greatest musicians, and I would
imagine them playing in that lovely suite of rooms under the light of
the chandeliers, and reflected in the countless mirrors.

But, back to grim reality! Those beautiful reception rooms were
boxed up into a horrid labyrinth—registry, archives, bag rooms, etc.,
and there was nothing left of the dream that had once been. A beautiful
spiral staircase leading from the corner of the dining room to the
floor above, a speciality of old Prague palaces, was removed so as to
create an 'iron curtain' between the Residence and the working
part of the Embassy. The Residence was in fact moved a floor higher
and reduced from a 'palace' into a 'duplex flat'. Of course, it was
more practical for those trying to run it, but now the Foreign
Secretary, when he comes to stay, has to sleep in rooms made in the
attic alongside the kitchen and the maids' quarters. One Foreign
Secretary and his wife complained that the Foreign Office had
rebuilt the residence for a race of supermen, as they had to stand on
tiptoe to see themselves in the mirrors. On the other hand, the
ceilings on the top floor of the *mansarde* were so low that supermen
would have bumped their heads on it.

Up to Count Oswald's day in the Biedermeier period, the Thun
Palace had a wonderful picture gallery including works by
Rembrandt, Franz Hals, Ostade, Raphael, Rubens, Salvator Rosa,
etc. All the rarities had been disposed of years before we arrived, and
we were left with the paintings which were doubtful or of lesser
value. The Ministry of Works inventory mentioned four Poussins.
The canvases have 'Poussin' on the back but gradually sank in
value in the opinion of experts. First they were said to be the work
of Poussin, then of Dughet, and afterwards joined the ranks of the
unknown and unvalued. They were fine paintings none the less.

The great joy of the palace was its garden which lay on the third floor. It led down steps to the terrace in front of the Ambassador's study. In the far corner was a small grotto containing a finely modelled statue of Diana—a copy of the original in the Papal galleries in Rome. Next to the grotto was the memorial to Leslie.

13. From the Palace Window

In the Thun Palace I used to breakfast every day with my eyes rooted to the spot where the rebel nobles hurled from the castle window the King's governors, Martinic and Slavata and their secretary. It was the famous 'Defenestration of Prague' of 1618, which started the Thirty Years War.

It sounds a grisly experience to be thrown out of a window, and drama and, perhaps, poetic justice demand that the victims should not survive, but in this case, they escaped unhurt because the ground was deep in muck. However, make no mistake, the intention of the rebels was to liquidate them, and it was due to their inefficiency rather than their mercy that their victims escaped scot-free. In view of the enormous significance of this event in Czech, and indeed, European history, the descendants of both families set up small obelisks to mark the spot where their ancestors had fallen.

Martinic, who was the nephew and brother-in-law of Slavata, attributed his rescue to divine intervention. He was a good Catholic, and some of his co-religionists who were in a procession at the time vowed they had seen the Virgin wrap him up in her cloak as he fell, and gently parachute him to the ground. He said afterwards that he had not actually been conscious of this, but, during the fall, the heavens had appeared to open and God to be about to receive him into everlasting joys.

Slavata, who fell next, had the bad luck to strike the stone ledge on the way, and hit another stone when he landed. Martinic wanted to rush to the aid of his older relative, but was afraid that if he showed signs of life they would shoot at him from the windows, which, in fact, they did. He therefore rolled cautiously towards the old man and wiped the blood off his face. Their secretary was quite unhurt and rushed away with all speed to Vienna, where he broke the alarming news to the court. Slavata escaped to the famous spa of Teplice (Teplitz-Schönau) and took a cure lasting several weeks.

In this incident, Czech noble families stood ranged against each other. A Lobkovic and a Kinský were among those who dragged the governors to the window, while another Lobkovic and Kinský remained faithful to the Emperor. Germans, too, joined with Czechs in the effort to unseat the Habsburgs. When Martinic had been thrown out, the rebel leader, Count Thurn, said in German: 'Noble gentlemen, here you have the other,' and pointed to Slavata.

It seemed that not only all Bohemian history, but all European history was present either in or outside the Thun Palace.

Next door to the castle the great Cathedral of St Vitus towered above us. It was one of my favourite haunts, not only when I walked alone but when I took guests with me. Thunovská, where the Embassy lay, ended at the foot of the Castle Steps, which led directly up to the cathedral. It was quite a climb and it used to annoy me that I could not take a short cut to it by climbing over Novotný's wall. Indeed, in the years after the First World War there was a wall ladder which the first President, Thomas Masaryk, used when he wanted to visit Sir George Clarke, the British Minister, incognito. A veteran retainer in the Embassy told me how the Czechoslovak police had once come hotfoot to the Embassy to ask whether anyone had seen the President, because they had lost track of him. In the event, he was sitting in Clarke's study having a chat with him. No doubt Novotný could have used this wall ladder too, if it still existed, but he never attempted to do so while I was there. He might have climbed over the wall for sanctuary, had he feared that he would be removed by a *coup d'état* on the lines of 1948, or defenestrated in the fashion of 1618, instead of retiring by the more human methods of Dubček.

The cathedral was better than a Czech history book. It had taken longer to complete than any other church in the world. Founded in the tenth century by 'Good King Wenceslas' (Svatý Václav to the Czechs; no king, but a prince, and no old man with white hair, but a boy), it later became the shrine for his tomb, and was finally completed in the year 1929, the presumed millenary of his death. One of the last sections of the cathedral to be completed were the enormous bronze doors which carried what amounted to a strip cartoon of the saint's life. Four relief panels in bronze tell his story. In the first he is shown picking grapes in a vineyard, because he was so pious that he prepared the sacramental wine with his own hands. In the next he can be seen uniting and consolidating the Czech tribes into one Czech state, and, then, in the panel below, helping the poor ('Yonder peasant, who is he?'). This brief biography ends with his murder on his birthday by his brother Boleslav, who usurped the throne.

In the centre of the cathedral lie, as though by proprietorial right, the stone effigies of three important members of the Habsburg dynasty. In the middle, Ferdinand I, the ardent Spanish-born Catholic, who was the first Habsburg to rule Bohemia; on his left his wife, the Polish Anna of Jagellon, the daughter of the previous king; and on his right, their son, Maximilian II, on whom the Czech people vainly pinned their hopes because he had favoured Protestantism before his accession.

In the semicircular aisle alongside or behind the choir, more and more of Bohemia's history unfolds. The effigies of the medieval Přemysl rulers lie in the side altars. On the right stands the monumental and elaborate silver tomb of St John of Nepomuk, designed by Fischer von Erlach. Its material strikingly symbolizes Bohemia's wealth and power, which derived from her rich silver mines. As if to confirm this, two figures with miners' lamps peer out eerily from underneath the curious 'baroque' Gothic Royal Oratory of King Vladislav, Ferdinand's father-in-law.

How did St John of Nepomuk come to merit so important a tomb? He was the saint of the Jesuits and the Counter-Reformation, whose cult was imposed on the Czechs in a vain effort to break their allegiance to the reformer, Jan Hus, or even to the non-denominational national saint, St Wenceslas. In this fantastic tomb, which is a marvel of the silversmith's art, two aspects of the legend of the saint are combined. We see him as the queen's confessor, and, later, thrown into the Vltava from the Charles Bridge at the king's orders: another defenestration, or perhaps 'depontition'!

The Nepomuk legend became a live political issue in the nineteenth and twentieth centuries, when it was used by the anticlericals to ridicule the traditional beliefs of the then influential Catholic Party. Jan of Pomuk was a real person. He was the administrator of the church in the reign of King Wenceslas IV, the son of the Emperor Charles. The king, after quarrelling with his bishop, was afraid to punish him and vented his wrath on the administrator instead, whom he ordered to be hanged, drawn and quartered and then thrown into the river. The Jan of the legend was a mystical martyr, a Jan of Nepomuk, who had refused to reveal what the

Queen had confessed to him, when the king ordered him to do so. Hence his martyrdom. St John was elevated into the symbol of the inviolability of the confession and now stands for eternity with his finger on his lip, not only in Prague but all over Central Europe. What is the meaning of the stars round his crown? When his body, or rather bits of it, was being thrown over the bridge, awesome miracles took place, which the stars are supposed to symbolize. The legendary place of his 'depontition' is marked by a seventeenth-century plaque on the Charles Bridge.

More 'strip cartoons', this time panels of carved wood, show the acts of vandalism committed by the unpopular Calvinist chaplain of Frederic, the 'Winter King'. We see him hacking away at everything beautiful—another effective piece of Jesuit propaganda, but true. The companion panel shows the flight of Frederic and Elisabeth Stuart, his English Queen, after their defeat at the Battle of the White Mountain in 1620. There they go, lock, stock and barrel— almost forgetting, in their haste, their Prague-born son, the Cavalier Prince Rupert—and good riddance to them, as the picture clearly conveys.

A distinguishing feature of the cathedral is the St Wenceslas chapel, built by the Luxemburg king and emperor, Charles IV, who introduced the cult of St Wenceslas into Bohemia, having spent his childhood in the French court under the influence of the cult of Saint Louis. The chapel lies directly above the original tomb of the Czech saint and martyr. On its walls are mural paintings depicting further scenes from his life. Particularly interesting is the painting showing him chopping down the gallows and razing the prisons. It was said of him that he could not bear to remain in the council chamber when death sentences were passed, and always hurried out. The beautiful polychrome statue of St Wenceslas from the workshop of Peter Parler, the second builder of the cathedral, is one of the most precious adornments of the cathedral. Although its colours have faded, it shows St Wenceslas as he was seen at the time—possibly Charles's own conception of him—young, gentle and dreamy and, although girt with sword and buckler, yet plainly reluctant to use them.

On leaving this superb building there was always plenty to discuss. Why, if it was the shrine of St Wenceslas, was it called after St Vitus? The cathedral was originally founded by St Wenceslas and could not be dedicated to himself, nor was he a saint at the time.

F

Vitus was a Saxon saint, and Wenceslas was on friendly terms with
the Saxon dynasty. The saint always came late to the Imperial
councils held by Henry, the Saxon king, until in the end the king
was so angry with him that he gave orders that none of the princes
should rise and offer their seat to him when he arrived. To everyone's
surprise, when he finally came, the king suddenly stood up himself
and offered him the place of honour. He explained afterwards that
he had been about to rebuke Wenceslas, when he suddenly saw two
angels beside him and a blazing cross on his forehead. Wenceslas's
helmet, which is kept among the relics of the cathedral museum, has a
crucifix on the protective piece covering the forehead. Wenceslas
was in such high favour with the Saxon kings that he succeeded in
obtaining from them some valuable relics of St Vitus, which he
placed in the church he built. So long as the relics of St Vitus were
in the hands of the Franks, fortune was on their side, but when the
relics were transferred to Saxony, power passed to the Saxon kings.
So the Czechs at that time hoped that St Vitus would be a rein-
forcement for them.

What was once a small round church was rebuilt twice and turned
into a cathedral, before it was finally completed in the twentieth
century. The Emperor Charles created the Wenceslas crown and
decreed that it should be worn at every coronation. The crown
jewels were locked away in the Wenceslas chapel and access to the
casket in which they were kept was by seven keys. Even as late as
under the Nazi occupation during the last war, the Reichsprotektor
received from the President the keys of the crown jewels, kept four
for himself and returned three to him. The ceremony symbolized
the momentary extinction of Czech sovereignty.

During the German occupation the Nazis tried to exploit the
historic friendship between St Wenceslas and the Saxon kings to
show that the Czech national saint was the first 'collaborator'. As
can be imagined this had very little effect on the Czechs. On the
contrary, although they had lost much of their historic religious
fervour, the people still regarded St Wenceslas as their intercessor.
In moments of stress they continued to pray to him and in the words
of the ancient chorale—one of the oldest Czech musical compositions
—begged him not to let them perish. Though the saint is a legendary
figure and not much of his legend has historical foundations, his
first biography was written soon enough after his death for there to
be contemporaries still alive who could attest whether what was

written was true or not. We know from it that he was opposed to capital punishment and prisons, that he helped the poor, that he ransomed slaves from the market place and baptized them and that he was literate (unlike most rulers of his time), reading both Latin and Slav. Is it not a good thing that our Christmas carol, 'Good King Wenceslas', which we have all been taught to sing from our childhood, is about a Czech prince whose ideas were so advanced and humane for his time?

14. The Doomed King Vávra

Like Macbeth, President Novotný was haunted by the guilt he felt for the crimes he had committed or connived at. But, unlike him, he could not pin the blame on his wife. Of the top Communist leaders, he was the most guilty after Gottwald and Široký. Although he was not the main fabricator of the Slánský and ensuing trials, he connived at Slánský's arrest and took an active part in assembling the indictments against him. From the autumn of 1951 onwards, when the machinery of the trials was working at top pressure, he was a secretary of the Party and a member of its highest political organs. In 1953, he became First Secretary and then in 1957 President of the Republic, holding both posts until 1968.

He bore even greater responsibility for the 'cover-up' operations which were planned to conceal the truth and delay the rehabilitation of the victims and was particularly vindictive to those of whom he was jealous and with whom he had had personal differences, like Slánský and Šling.*

He had his knife into the Slovaks especially and, in his persecution of the so-called 'Slovak Bourgeois Nationalists', was aided and abetted by the Slovak Prime Minister, Široký, a Prague 'Centralist', who had personal reasons for wishing to liquidate the Foreign Minister, Clementis,† and those Slovaks who had taken part in the Slovak rising against the Germans.

Novotný had a rival in his Cabinet in the person of the more popular and ambitious Deputy Prime Minister and former Minister of the Interior, Barák, who had in his possession a mass of incrimin-

---

* Both these leaders were executed in 1952. Slánský had been General Secretary of the Party and Šling was Secretary of the Regional Committee in Brno, was a 'London Communist' and had an English wife. Slánský's brother was also in Britain during the war.

† Dr Vlado Clementis, who was a Bratislava lawyer, had also been in Britain during the war, where he had blotted his Party copybook by dissociating himself from the Ribbentrop-Molotov Pact. Husák had his training in his office.

ating material against him and the other Communist leaders. In June 1961 it was announced that Barák had been removed from his post. Novotný mystified the public by appointing him Chairman of a new Government Commission on the National Committees, but eight months later had him arrested, tried *in camera* and sentenced to fifteen years' imprisonment. It was clear from the first announcements that Novotný would have liked to charge him with more serious crimes (he accused him of 'seizing political power') and stage a spectacular trial, but in view of opposition in the top ranks of the Party and a possible Soviet veto he had to compromise. Barák was said to have had close contact with the Russians and to have sent a letter to Khrushchev, criticising Novotný's policy. Probably no one in the Czechoslovak leadership minded seeing Barák out of the way, but, equally, no one wished to have the show trials back.

I wanted to meet Barák, but at those receptions or airport meetings where he was present, he always contrived to avoid me. I once asked the Prime Minister, Široký, if he would introduce me to him. At that moment Barák was talking to someone else and Široký was obviously afraid to disturb him. After a while he said: 'He seems to be rather busy. We had better try another time.' Odd behaviour for a premier, but explicable in the light of subsequent events.

It was the Slovaks who received the worst treatment from Novotný and it was poetic justice that they should emerge in time as the main manipulators of his gradual slide from power. The removal of Široký, Novotný's linch-pin, was their first target.

On 3 June 1963, a Slovak journalist named Hysko attacked Široký at the Slovak Congress of Journalists. In a fury Novotný travelled to the Slovak Iron Works at Košice and hit back at him in a speech there. But by 21 September, not only Široký, but all the old guard of Slovak 'Centralists' were on the way out.

The way Široký was dismissed was typical of the Communist system. A brief announcement appeared in the press that he was relieved of his duties 'for shortcomings in his work, for inadequate implementation of the Party line in directing government activity, for certain mistakes in his past political activity, and in view of bad health'. Široký had been a Secretary of the Central Committee since 1935, and had occupied the important posts of Deputy Premier, Premier, Foreign Minister and member of the Presidium since 1945. Yet there was no word of acknowledgement in the press for his long years of Party service.

I commented on this to the Soviet Ambassador, Zimyanin, at a lunch given by the Indian Ambassador. He appeared to be solidly behind Široký and affected to ignore official criticisms of him, maintaining that western journalists were blowing up a quite normal occurrence into a 'crisis', as usual. Did I not respect Široký's natural wish to retire after his long service? I replied that I did but, as it appeared, the Czechoslovak Communist Party did not. We later turned to a discussion of *Dr Zhivago*. 'It's a thoroughly bad book,' he said. 'I haven't read it, but it's obvious that it is.'

With Široký's fall, the First Secretary of the Slovak Communist Party, Karol Bacílek, a Czech, who in 1968 would publicly admit his guilt in the staging of the trials, was also disgraced, and Alexander Dubček was appointed in his place. That then was the end of the long and vindictive struggle between the Slovak 'Centralists', who wanted to rule Slovakia from Prague, and the Slovak 'Nationalists', who played a leading part in the Slovak rising during the war and wanted to liberate Slovakia from too close control from the centre. The defeat of the 'Centralists' led to great changes in Slovakia, as I shall show in the next chapter.

On 12 November 1964, Novotný was re-elected President. At the very end of the magnificent tudor-style Vladislav Hall, beneath the fifteenth-century coats-of-arms of Bohemia and Hungary (both then ruled by the same king), a wooden dais has been erected and draped in red. On it were chairs for the Chairman of the National Assembly, the three Vice-Chairmen and the President-elect of the Republic. In the well of the hall sat the Deputies of the National Assembly, the Presidium of the Slovak National Council, the Central Committee of the Communist Party, the Diplomatic Corps and last, but not least, the President's wife.

The Chairman of the National Assembly, Laštovička (who had by that time succeeded Fierlinger) rose and said that the merging of the functions of the President of the Republic and First Secretary of the Party had been amply justified in Novotný's tenure of office. He therefore proposed his re-election 'in harmony with the wishes of all of our people'. The meeting then unanimously elected Novotný by a show of hands. Scarcely had Laštovička finished putting the questions 'Anyone against? Any abstentions?' than the guns of the Prague garrison burst out into a salvo of salutes. The state flag was slowly hoisted over the palace building.

Laštovička and the new Prime Minister (Lenárt) then left for the residence of the President who, in accordance with custom, like a bride who must not see the bridegroom before the wedding, was not permitted to be present until the result of the election was known. Their return with Novotný was heralded by the fanfare of trumpets from Smetana's opera *Libuše*.

The fulfilment of 'the wishes of all our people' was received with apathy throughout the country. Even the Guard's Band, which played the Czechoslovak National Anthem in the palace courtyard after the election, appeared to do so with an unprecedented dreariness and hopelessness. There was no press acclamation and the few articles that appeared seemed inspired by the desire to explain away what had come as a bitter pill to the vast majority of the country, officials included. However, as the Czechs are a people who by nature always expect the worst, they had no reason to be surprised by the result.

I received instructions from the Prime Minister (Harold Wilson) to convey the congratulations of HMG to the newly elected President. He gave me the option of calling in person and I decided to do so.

The President's room was magnificently spacious with windows looking down over our Embassy. As I came in, he rose from his desk, which was near the door and I conveyed to him the congratulations of our government. He thanked me and escorted me to a round table where we sat and talked. The only others present were the head of his chancellery and an interpreter. There was no representative from the Ministry of Foreign Affairs and the President gave no signs of having been briefed for my call.

In the course of the interview, which lasted an hour and was conducted in Czech, Novotný surprised me by saying, almost defiantly: 'You see, I have been elected, in spite of everything.' There had been numerous plans for the succession to the Presidency, he went on. Various names had been put forward and various solutions proposed involving the separation of the offices of President of the Republic and First Secretary of the Party. The final decision had been to elect him and to continue the two posts in the person of one office holder. This was a specifically Czechoslovak solution; it differed from the method chosen in other socialist countries. Under the bourgeois regime the President had stood apart from the people: in a Socialist state he was chosen by the people and was their representative(!)

Novotný was not only jubilant at having been re-elected and

proud of having become a more constitutional President in the process (he believed that his new 1960 constitution was more democratic than its predecessors), but also enthusiastic about the new economic system of planning and management which he had now adopted as his own, and rated as more progressive than those of the other socialist countries, Yugoslavia included. (An assessment endorsed by the Yugoslav Embassy in Prague.) 'We considered the Yugoslav system,' he told me, 'and eventually plumped for something more advanced and suited to our conditions.' He added that it was nonsense for the western press to write of high-level opposition to the plan. It had been submitted for discussion to responsible officials and academic bodies, and of course there had been differing opinions. But this was only natural when democratic methods were used.

Thus Novotný was shifting ground, moving from his former reactionary position on the extreme right (or left?) to the middle of the road. But it was too late. His failures were too apparent. Nothing he could do would now redeem him in the eyes of the people.

In the oppressive days of Austrian rule, the Czech writer, Havlíček, wrote a satirical poem called *King Lávra*, which for reasons of censorship, was set in Ireland, but which, in fact, made fun of conditions in Bohemia under Austrian rule. A young Czech writer had now turned this poem into a sketch and called it *King Vávra*. King Vávra had ass's ears and, to conceal them, he wore his hair long —very long—and commanded all his subjects to do the same. The barbers, who on rare occasions cut his hair and discovered the horrible truth, were immediately executed. The sketch was performed in Prague in one of the smaller theatres and everyone at once saw who the king was and understood his secret. There was talk that the play might be withdrawn and I decided to go and see it a second time, in case this should indeed happen. There was one vacant seat next to me in the theatre, and, to my surprise, as the lights went down, who should come in and occupy it, but Koucký, the Party Secretary of the time, who was responsible for questions of culture and ideology. It was probably not my place to say it but in the interval I remarked: 'I've heard that this play has been criticized for attacking the leadership, but if you were to see in London a performance called *Beyond the Fringe* and watch how our Prime Ministers are treated in it, you'd regard what we're seeing tonight as chicken-feed.' 'Perhaps so,' he replied, 'but you must agree that the satire in this piece shoots so wildly beyond the mark as to be palpably absurd.' What could I say? And what could I do when King Vávra came to the front of the footlights and shouted 'Culture! We must control culture, or culture will control us!' and everyone in the theatre cheered and stamped. The sequel to the evening was that the play was not only not taken off but its full text was on sale in Prague a few days later.

The ground was crumbling beneath King Vávra's feet. A month before, he had lost his main supporter. The Czechoslovak Communist Party greeted the news of Khrushchev's fall with 'surprise and emotion' and was the only Party which did not immediately rally to the support of Brezhnev. The result was that Novotný could no longer reckon on Soviet help when the attack on him began from within. The Russians were to let him go in 1967 and not recall him when they invaded the country in 1968.

15. Look upon This Picture and upon That

When I presented my credentials Novotný made a great point of his government's successful industrialization of Slovakia. There had long been friction between the Czechs and the Slovaks, the Slovaks feeling themselves underprivileged compared with the Czechs. The Communists maintained that Slovak discontent could easily be satisfied by the economic rehabilitation of their country, which would bring it nearer to the level of Bohemia and Moravia. I thought this a typical Marxist fallacy. Of course it would be better for the Slovaks if their economy were developed, but that would not of itself solve the problem of their relations with the Czechs, because what the Slovaks wanted more than anything else was—devolution. Unfortunately for the Communists, Slovakia had been strongly anti-Communist up to 1948, and opinion was not likely to have changed much during the Novotný period. Naturally, as an agricultural and largely Catholic region, where the priests had had considerable influence, the Communists had been able to make little headway there, although there was a small and radical Communist movement, some of the leaders of which, like Husák, had at one time advocated Slovakia's incorporation into the Soviet Union.

My friend from my Stockholm days, Willi Böhm, who had been a member of Bela Kun's Communist government in Hungary and knew the first generation of Slovak Communists, dwelt on their foreign origin: many of them, he said, were Hungarians, Czechs or Germans. Gottwald, a Czech, had had much of his early Party experience in Slovakia. He had worked in the Slovak revolutionary gymnastic movement and edited Slovak Communist newspapers. The First Secretary of the Slovak Communist Party when I arrived was the Czech Bacílek, and several Slovaks in the Prague leadership had been born and brought up in Bohemia and Moravia. The younger Communists, on the other hand, were pure Slovak, and it was members of this group who were subsequently to be tried and sentenced for the crime of 'bourgeois nationalism'.

Slovaks obstinately continued to be anti-Communist, and even where they were nominal Party members they sometimes acted in a very unorthodox manner. Communists in a Slovak village were once offered a reward for their good Party work and shocked the leadership by asking if they might have a new church built! Even in the mid-sixties it was by no means easy to drive through Slovak villages on Sundays. Crowds of churchgoers poured out into the streets and made them impassable. You could still see a few of the peasants wearing peasant costume at Sunday services or, more rarely, when working in the fields. The Communists would like to have changed this and created a strong industrial proletariat. So, although no one could find fault with the Communist plan of industrializing Slovakia, which was necessary, it could not be forgotten that one of its objects was to form a stronger Communist nucleus in the country, or at least, to increase the number of Party supporters there. This was undoubtedly one of the reasons for the siting of the massive steelworks at Košice, which was to employ 20,000 workers. Once it was set up (although in my time it employed nowhere near 20,000 people), it was the only place in Slovakia where Novotný could have a safe platform, because he was so bitterly hated everywhere else. Even here, he was not immune. According to the Slovak Communist paper *Pravda*, in 1958 some of the leading personalities at the plant had evinced 'a wrong and negative attitude towards the Czechs. This wrong attitude has led them into the arms of the bourgeois nationalists. They have acquired anti-Party opinions.'

In the light of all this, it seemed useful for me to make a tour of the region to see, as far as my inexpert eye allowed me, how they were getting on with industrialization. I thought that, if I quoted what Novotný had told me and based my request on it, the authorities would find it difficult not to acquiesce. The Protocol Department in Prague responded readily to my proposals and produced a rough programme for me. When I pointed out that only one of the three main industries in Slovakia, the chemical industry, was included in it, and that I was seeing nothing of engineering or metallurgy, modifications were introduced and a visit to the East Slovak Steel Works was included at my special request.

This was the first official visit my wife and I paid to any part of Czechoslovakia and when on 12 October 1961 we arrived in Bratislava I expected that somebody would welcome us or, at any rate, inform us of the details of our programme. When I was Press

Attaché in 1945 and 1946, I was the guest of the Slovak National
Council and everything I wanted had been organized for me. (At
that time the Slovak Democratic Party had the main say.) This
time, when I arrived at the hotel in the afternoon, it was as though
no one had heard of us. They at least knew I had booked a room, but
that was all. Offices in Czechoslovakia close rather early in the afternoon (since they make an early start) and it was therefore not
practical to make any *démarche* at that hour. I accordingly waited
until the next morning, hoping that someone would call on us.

A young Slovak from the 'Protocol Department' turned up, rather
lackadaisically, in mid morning but without a programme. I told
him that I had hoped I would be given full details of the planned
visit with a timetable and the names of the people I should be
contacting. He then disappeared and he came back about an hour
later with a very rough programme containing dates, but no times.
When I demurred once more, he replied that I need only go to the
various plants on my provisional list and ask to see the directors. I
told him I was puzzled no courtesy visit to the Chairman of the
Slovak National Council or his representative had been included.
He explained politely but firmly that my trip was being arranged
from Prague 'on an all-state basis' and it was not the custom for
ambassadors to call on representatives of the Slovak National
Council. When I reminded him that the Soviet Ambassador had
recently been received by the Chairman of the Slovak National
Council, he capitulated and promised to arrange for me to be
received by one of the Deputy Chairmen.

Shortly afterwards we were driven off to the building of the
Slovak National Council and swiftly received by the Slovak commissioner in charge of construction. He had evidently been told of
our arrival only at the last moment and just had time to have a
bouquet of flowers prepared for my wife and a book for me. In the
ensuing discussion he was not very illuminating about the National
Council and had repeatedly to turn to our guide for information as
to how many members it had, and what committees were in it. At
this time such matters were still state secrets.

We were then rushed off to the Bratislava 'Mier' Chemical Works
(G. Dimitrov), the point where the pipeline brings the Soviet oil
into Czechoslovakia for refining. It was an important complex of
chemical works employing 6,000 workers, including (later) British
engineers. As we came in, a line of workers who had gathered in the

corridor burst into loud applause. I smiled at the thought that this claque had been specially assembled to mollify my feelings, in case I should think that I was not being properly received there.

Next on our list was a visit to the Comenius University which was founded as late as 1919, the Hungarians not having thought during their period of rule that the Slovaks deserved a higher seat of learning. I told our guide that I hoped that at least the Dean would be there to meet us. However, in his place I was received by two characters who were most unimpressive from an academic point of view. One said he was 'Deputy Quaestor' but looked as if he had either only just graduated or was a 'failed BA'. The other, a more sinister type, said he was the Secretary of the Law Faculty. They both stared at us in silence with X-ray eyes as though they were a couple of STB men. The atmosphere became so strained that I nearly got up and asked if I was not in the wrong building.

Eventually, at our request, we were taken to the English department which was in another building. On the way to it we passed walls which were covered with the crudest propaganda for Cuba and against the USA, which had little to do with the teaching of English. We were taken into a small room where there was a library not even as good as an English prep school library. I saw some faded volumes, familiar from my childhood days on the shelves, but nothing very new. I was not surprised because I had examined every book in the English section of the Prague City Library and it was not much better, considering its size. Later, a scholar from Brno told me that in the university there it was quite impossible to pursue studies of English literature with the books available.

The only English teacher (the others had allegedly been called up on a 'brigade')* had been spending most of her time on American literature, as was confirmed by her accent. The Deputy Quaestor volunteered that he had been her pupil, which was no great recommendation, since he appeared unable to speak any English at all. By this time we had the impression that we were visiting a morgue, and when, to make it more alive, I unloaded a number of English books provided by the British Council, the teacher—watched by our two escorts, who seemed *lictors* rather than *quaestors*—did not have the courage to pick them up or even thank me. Let it be understood that this is how conditions were in Stalinist Slovakia and did not in

* A 'voluntary' levy on all public offices exacted in hard labour in the sugar-beet fields or elsewhere.

any way resemble the Slovakia I was to visit again in a few years time.

Now a word about the itinerary of the tour of the rest of Slovakia which had been prepared. It certainly took us all over Slovakia and contained a few interesting factories, but the hours of my visits were not recorded, only the days on which I should arrive at places. This left us, surprisingly enough, considerable liberty to drive about in our own car wherever we liked and enabled us to see much of the country without any restrictions. It did not, however, help me much in achieving the purpose of my visit: when we arrived at the factories, we nearly always found that the manager had just gone to Prague. We were told that he had been waiting for us, but because he did not know exactly when we were coming, he had left. It was the same story at almost every point. Was it prearranged?

On our way to Košice in East Slovakia we came to a delightful little town in the midst of the Tatras called Liptovský Mikuláš (once Liptovský Svätý Mikuláš, but the saint (svätý) had now been dropped). Liptovský Mikuláš was famous as the town where the Slovak legendary hero Jánošík had been executed. We were supposed to be received by the Chairman of its National Committee, but when we arrived we had some difficulty in finding where his office was. It proved to be on the fourth floor of an ordinary building. I did not know quite what to do. It seemed slightly *infra dig* for an ambassador to go up several stairs and go on knocking about on doors to find out whether anyone was there to greet him or not, and so I decided to ask my Czech driver, who wore a special 'Crown property' uniform provided by the British Ministry of Works, to go up and explore the terrain. The driver, who had a ghastly cold, stumbled down again, saying, 'Yes, they're waiting for you on the fourth floor.'

He guided us up the stairs and opened the door into a room where five or six people were gathered. They were typically friendly and unconventional Slovaks. After a brief chat their Chairman said, 'Very well, now let's go across the road and have some lunch.' The friendly company swept my chauffeur up too, being certainly under the impression that he was an attaché at the British Embassy. After all, he was wearing the 'Queen's uniform'.

Presently we found ourselves in a small restaurant, squashed together round a table. The first thing that happened was that our glasses were filled with *slivovice* and our healths were drunk. My chauffeur, sitting on my right, looked miserably at me, because he knew he must not drink when driving. I said very loudly in Czech: 'My chauffeur has a terribly bad cold and I think we must allow him this time to break the rules about drinking when driving and take *one* glass of this good drink.' The Slovaks roared with pleasure and the chauffeur, looking like a guilty dog, wolfed it down as readily as they did.

In an expansive moment the Chairman confided in us: 'You see, we didn't know when you were coming. We thought you might come yesterday. We wondered whether you might not be coming tomorrow. But we never figured out that you would be coming today. Had we known, we would have shaved.' He won our hearts with that last remark.

After a good lunch, washed down by plenty of drink (in the course of which I continued to keep a firm eye on my chauffeur), a lunch that was saturated with talk of a fabulous Slovak kind about bears which came down from the mountains, etc., but never so much as touched on Slovak industrialization of the Slovak economy, we took leave of them and set out for Košice, driving past the by now almost unmentionable East Slovak Steel Works on the way.

When we reached the town we were received by a very pleasant young man, who turned out to be the cultural representative of the local National Committee. I explained to him that I had not come to Košice on a cultural errand but to study the industrialization of Slovakia. As the Slovak Steel Works were a key point in this plan, I expressed surprise that no visit to this factory seemed to have been arranged. The young man replied that he had nothing to do with industrial questions and his authority was restricted entirely to culture. He accordingly whisked us off straight away to a Slovak school, where we had the ghastly experience of hearing children recite in Russian and Slovak the most abject Stalinist poems in praise of the Red Flag. It was a torment to see these angelic looking children with their fair hair, blue eyes and innocent looks mouthing those servile hymns. Fortunately, we did not have to spend long there, and were rushed off to a children's model railway, which the cultural representative called the 'Pioneer Railway' and of which he was more proud than of any other 'cultural' achievement. We were forced to ride on it, a tiresome and humiliating experience unlikely to afford me much insight into the country's industrialization. After that our guide proposed a visit to the

Botanical Gardens. Here, and not for the first time, I demurred.
'This is an economic tour,' I said firmly. 'The Botanical Garden
plays its part in the economy of our country,' he countered. I
yielded again and went with him.

Later on, as we went through the city we passed the superb
Cathedral of St Elisabeth, dating from 1382. I asked our cultural
guide something about it and other historic buildings in the town
but he was unable to answer my queries. 'You see,' he apologized,
'in my time all the books about these things were written in
Hungarian and I didn't know the language, but I shall arrange for
an expert to show you round tomorrow.' A few minutes afterwards
we passed a bookshop and saw in the window several books in
Slovak about Košice Cathedral—the most easterly Gothic cathedral
in Europe and the finest church building in old Hungary. When our
guide told his chauffeur to drive there, the latter, who was an
aggressive type, asked with a snort: 'What are we going to do there,
pray?' During the tour of the church he accompanied us round
and adopted ostentatious poses of disapproval. The chauffeurs of
Communist officials often act like this. They have the habit of turning
on the car radio without asking permission and then arguing with
their so-called bosses. As is known, they are instructed by the STB
and almost certainly their 'bosses' are under *their* orders.

Our chief guide informed us that he was in charge of all the
theatres in Košice as well as the schools and enquired what we would
like to see in the evening. Among other things, he mentioned a play
about contemporary life in Slovakia and I jumped at that. 'Could we
see that?' I said. 'Of course,' he replied, 'I shall get the tickets and
come to your hotel just before the performance.'

He was as good as his word and, at my suggestion, brought his
wife, who was a teacher and, or so he claimed, spoke Russian very
well, as she had been a pupil of the Russian school at Prešov, a
centre of the Ukrainian minority. After a pleasant drink together,
we walked across the street to the National Theatre. We were on
the point of going up its steps, when he suddenly said, 'Oh, I am
sorry to have to tell you, but I made a mistake about the programme.
They're not performing the play on contemporary life tonight but
the opera *Carmen*.'

It was too much. I stopped where I was and exploded: 'I am
sorry. I did not come all the way to Eastern Slovakia to hear a
performance of *Carmen*. I must see something else.'

'There isn't anything else,' he said.

'Well, is there a film on?' I asked hopelessly.

He looked down the cultural programme and said, 'Well, yes, there is a film, which might perhaps interest you. It's not a Slovak film but a Czech one, and it's about delinquents. It's called *The Awakening*.'

'Very well, then,' I said. 'Let's go and see that.'

'But it doesn't start for another three quarters of an hour.'

I melted. 'Very well, then, let's see the first act of *Carmen* and go to the film afterwards.' And so we did.

We visited many places in Slovakia including two spas, a penicillin factory, a Youth Dam, and wood fibre and television factories—but I never saw the East Slovak Steel Works or learned much about the Slovak economy!

So much for our first visit to Slovakia while it was still very much under the Prague Communist Stalinist heel. Now, for our second, when the true Slovaks had come into their own. After the events described in the previous section I had formed the opinion that Slovakia was important enough to justify more ambassadorial visits than had been made in previous years. Moreover, the Slovaks proved themselves a most attractive and hospitable people even under the repressive conditions prevailing in 1961 and I longed to go back to their country. I secured Foreign Office agreement to myself and my successors regularly going down to Bratislava for a fairly long stay, where we could 'hold court'—that is, arrange a few parties for the local notables and go round and see everybody, as we would in Prague.

In 1964 I sought and received the permission of the Czechoslovak Ministry of Foreign Affairs to stay ten days in Slovakia and then this time to spend them all in Bratislava. This was an unusual thing to do because normally the Slovaks liked to whisk their guests away to the High Tatras, or even to the vineyards in the surroundings of the capital with the result that, although one enjoyed oneself very much, one found at the end of the tour (if one still remained sober) that one had had little chance of meeting any of the Slovak notables, who mainly worked in the capital. The Slovaks did this at least partly because they were intensely proud of the mountainous part of their country—that was to them the true Slovakia—and much enjoyed having an outing there themselves.

How different this second visit was from the first. The Slovaks had at last won their fight against Novotný and secured a change of regime. Novotný had been forced to dismiss the Stalinist, Široký, and most of the young 'bourgeois nationalists' had been rehabilitated and taken the place of those who had tried to liquidate them. It was no longer necessary to worry about whether I should call on anyone in the Slovak National Council. It was on the programme that I should be received by its Chairman. In actual fact I was received not only by him but by the Vice-Chairman and some of the other Commissioners as well.

Once the programme started, it went with a bang. At nine o'clock on the first day, Monday 27 September, I was received by the Deputy Chairman of the Slovak National Council, who could not have been more approachable and apologized for the Chairman's absence in Prague. At ten o'clock I visited the Union of Slovak Writers, where a large number of leading novelists, poets and critics were gathered. The best-known authors were not present but there were several prominent writers there and the views they expressed were remarkably frank. I was told straight out that the young intelligentsia looked to the west (the most important influences on them were French and American) and that they had scarcely any interest in Soviet writing. The only Russian writer who influenced the young was Dostoyevsky, and reactions even to the younger Soviet poets like Yevtushenko, Voznesensky, Rozhdestvensky, etc. were lukewarm, perhaps because the Soviet authorities discouraged attempts to get into touch with them. Extracts from Solzhenitsyn's *Cancer Ward* were all set to be printed as a *feuilleton* in the Bratislava *Pravda*, but had come under a ban from the Soviet authorities. The writers asked to have copies of English books for reviewing. (I did my best to arrange this but nothing came of it.)

At 11.15 a.m. I was received by the Commissioner for Internal Trade and Tourism, who offered us a glass of *borovička* (the Slovak national gin) claiming that in her 'ministerial' capacity she knew what sort was the finest. On parting from her my wife and I received presents—a superbly bound Slovak translation of Shakespeare's sonnets for myself. In the afternoon I was received by the Commissioner for Education and Culture, by the Rector of the Comenius University (and what a different university now) and by the Union of Slovak Composers. In fact the Slovaks had pulled out all the stops for me, as only Slovaks can.

We later went to the film studios and met film directors and film writers. Then in the evening we were taken to a 'hide-out' in the Carpathians, which was a fashionable mountain inn kept by a partisan hero nicknamed 'The Carpathian Wolf', where we sat and ate *živánka* chickens off the spit (roasted over an enormous open fire like a well) or fish similarly grilled. At the same time we were liberally filled with Slovak white wine and entertained with countless Slovak songs. I am told that I danced the csardas, but cannot remember enough to be able to confirm it.

We wound up our stay with a terrific party of our own to which we invited all the big-wigs of Bratislava. I had been allowed a special sum to cover entertaining and we had also brought with us a considerable amount of duty-free whisky and gin. The waiters made free with the bottles and, instead of pouring out the alcohol in small measures, started rapidly filling the tumblers up to the brim and were already handing them round before we could stop them. The noise of the conversation and laughter rose higher and higher and grew louder and louder until suddenly it reached bursting point, after which the temperature dropped to zero. I looked at the bar and saw twenty bottles of whisky and gin completely empty. I at once ordered fifty bottles of local white wine to restore the conviviality at least to normal cocktail party point. I suddenly realized that by proposing that Her Majesty's Ambassador should visit Bratislava regularly and hold court there, I was going to involve the Exchequer in a substantial outlay!

But it was glorious to see such delightfully uninhibited and warm-hearted people. The Slovaks, who did not live in the shadow of the Hradčany (or should I perhaps say of the Central Committee building in Prague), were for that reason and also by temperament much less inhibited than the Czechs. To top it all, there had been a thorough spring cleaning of their regime. Before we left I was received by the Chairman of the Slovak National Council, who paid homage to British officers who had lost their lives in attempting to bring assistance to the Slovak rising. Nothing so friendly had ever been said to us on this subject before.

16. Southern Bohemia

In bygone ages all Bohemia was covered with an impenetrable forest, which effectively isolated it from civilization. The Romans called it the Hercynian Forest. Moravia and Slovakia developed much earlier, because they were nearer the Danube and the main trade routes.

The Hercynian Forest was the Emperor Charlemagne's favourite hunting-ground, and from surviving place-names we know that bears, wolves, lynxes and wild cats haunted its denser parts. So Shakespeare was not altogether wrong when he set his *Winter's Tale* in Bohemia and ended one scene with the stage direction *Exit pursued by a bear*. (Let us pass over in silence the 'sea coast'.)

Today, Bohemia is no longer so densely forested. But along its south-western borders from Domažlice (Taus) to its southernmost tip near the monastery of Vyšší Brod (Hohenfurth) stretches the Bohemian Forest, known to the Germans as the *Böhmerwald* (or to the more nationalistic as the *Bayerischer Wald*). To the Czechs it is the *Šumava*, a name which suggests either the wailing of the wind in the hills above or the roaring of the waters below. Domažlice was the centre of Chodsko, a small region inhabited by a people who for centuries acted as the 'frontier guards' of Bohemia against Bavaria. It is here that Czech settlements thrust deepest into German territory, since the north-western frontier areas were German-speaking. The emblem of the Chodové, as they were called, was a dog's head, and a famous Czech novel and an opera commemorate their exploits. For reasons which are obscure, the Chodové speak a Czech which is hard to understand, as I experienced myself when one day I went too close to a sealed-up and forbidden frontier crossing in this region and was 'held captive' by a cheerful soldier whose language was quite incomprehensible to me. Luckily his superior came along after about ten minutes and spoke good Czech, with the result that I was speedily released and there was no diplomatic incident.

Parts of the forest still remind one today of a primeval jungle, and Prince Schwarzenberg, in whose extensive domains they once lay, appreciated this and turned some 250 acres of it into a nature reserve. Once treasured by emperors for its rich game, it is now impressive for its lack of it, and of human life as well. The Czech writer, Karel Čapek, wrote:

> You walk over the meadows and they squelch under your feet and sway ominously: you save yourself with powerful jumps on to the soil in the forest and with your first step you sink up to your knees in moss, while your stick plunges up to the hilt into a rotten tree stump, which you had hoped to support yourself on. You can hear the mountains moaning and the subterranean waters murmuring, but not the song of a bird nor the humming of a gnat. Careful, Human Being, you have entered the imperium of vegetation!

Thus Čapek brings the Šumava to life—or rather to death. Other writers have compared it to a wave of the sea which has suddenly frozen in motion.

It is in this exotic, freakish and intimidating area that the river Vltava has its sources. This very Czech river, which flows through the whole of Bohemia from south to north, reaching Prague and beyond, before it issues into the Elbe, is not only the main artery of the Bohemian 'heartland' but has been and still is a link between Germans and Czechs, springing from mountain moorlands on the Bavarian border, and washing banks once peopled by both races.

The so-called Warm Vltava (not really warm), which rises on the Black Mountain, travels quite a way south before being joined by the Cold Vltava (certainly very cold). If you cannot go to the Šumava and see this, you can hear it all in Smetana's beautiful tone-poem, *Vltava* (Moldau)—the welling of the streams until they both unite in that glorious undulating and swelling melody, which no one who has once heard it can forget. To every Czech it brings back the unspeakable loveliness and strife-torn history of his country as vividly as do the nostalgic cello passages in Dvořák's *New World Symphony*. If Smetana's *Vltava* is like the river, the river itself is like music in its shades of tone-colour and tempo. It flows through the lifeless gloom of the Šumava peat forests before emerging into a

blaze of mountain meadows, full of gay flowers and edged with
willows and alders.

Its bed narrows as it flows past high cliffs. The trees grow smaller
and rarer, and the river fights its way through a mass of boulders.
Once it roared like an alpine torrent after a cloudburst, but now it is
tamed because in 1959 a twenty-five mile-long reservoir was built
which has stolen its waters. This is the site of the Devil's Wall, which
owed its name to the old legend that the Devil was furious when the
Abbey of Vyšší Brod was built on the bank opposite and vowed to
drown it with all the monks inside. In a single night he tried to build
up a wall of stones which would cause the waters to flood, but the
cock crew before he could finish. The names 'Devil's Pulpit' and
'Phantom' held no horrors for me, remembering from my childhood
days how the Devil had driven all the saints out of my native
Devonshire into Cornwall and filled it with saints' names. Smetana
was so fascinated by the legend that he not only described the roar
of the waters in his tone-poem but also wrote a whole opera about it,
The Devil's Wall, in which the Devil himself was one of the principal
characters.

The towns in south-west Bohemia lay close to the Golden Road,
the ancient trade route along which pack-horse caravans used to
carry salt from the rich storehouses in Salzkammergut, Salzburg and
Bad Reichenhall to saltless Bohemia, taking back corn, beer, malt,
fat and the schnaps of Prachatice.

Prachatice was the great salt emporium of bygone days. On its
fine town hall in Renaissance style I read an inscription which even
at that date provided a unique encomium of the bourgeoisie. 'In
every district there are three kinds of people: the rich, the middle
classes and the poor. Among these the middle classes are best
because the middle is always the best.' Here too, in the old Latin
School, two great Czechs were educated—Hus, who came from
Husinec about a mile away, and less certainly, Žižka, the one-eyed
Hussite commander born at Trocnov near Budějovice. The Golden
Road served as a channel not only for merchandise but also for
doctrines of a seditious kind. Enthusiastic members of the Waldensian
sect came in with the salt merchants and established their network,
disseminating heresies in the centre of Bohemia and beyond, which
helped to promote Hussite beliefs.

Today's place-names recall that the district was once rich in gold.
Where you find the phrase 'good water', it may mean 'gold-bearing

water' because one of the most important tributaries of the Vltava, the Otava, was a gold-bearing stream. The town of Písek (sand) was once called Bohatý Písek (rich sand), and Sušice, lying near it, is connected with the word 'sušit' to dry.

The fine Cistercian Abbey of Vyšší Brod, which survived the Devil's machinations, was founded by the powerful Vok of Rožmberk in 1259 as a stronghold to protect his powerful clan—the Lords of the Rose—against the Czech King Otakar II, who had recently inherited the Babenberg lands of Austria and was thought to be planning a pincer-movement against them from north and south. Indeed, further down the Vltava to the north the king founded the rival Cistercian abbey at Zlatá Koruna (Goldenkrone) as well as the town of Budějovice, or Budweiss, which was to be a royal city.

There was a solemnity and dignity about Vyšší Brod when we called there. We had to ring the bell and were conscious of the silence and venerable peace of the precincts. A nun-like figure opened the door and ushered us through dark but neatly kept corridors. In the church Cistercian Gothic struggled with baroque. Above, lofty pillars stretched up to the vaulted ceiling. Below were massive baroque confessionals recalling the Jesuits and the Counter Reformation. A unique thirteenth-century chapter house, where the vaulting was supported by only two central half pillars, contrasted with a library of dazzling baroque, like a miniature version of Strahov at Prague. But without its famous Madonna of the Master of the Vyšší Brod, a beautiful painting edged with miniatures of all the Czech saints or its nine paintings of the Passion from the same artist's altar, the monastery can never be the same. Since the Nazis took these treasures away and buried them in salt mines, they have been in the Prague National Gallery for safe-keeping.

As the Vltava makes a sharp and unexpected twist due north, we come to the old castle of Rosenberg which gave the Lords of the Rose their name. (Each branch of the family had a five-petalled rose of different colours—not only red and white.) They had numerous other castles in Southern Bohemia—Krumlov (Krumau), Třeboň (Wittingau), Jindřichův Hradec (Neuhaus) and Telč (Teltsch) in Moravia. And their possessions stretched over the frontiers into Austria. At a critical moment of the fateful battle of Dürnkrut between Rudolf of Habsburg and King Otakar II of Bohemia in 1278, the Rožmberks defected and the Czech royal forces, treacherously weakened in the flank, were routed. This brought about the death of King Otakar and the end of the Czech 'empire' in Central Europe.

The river glides slowly down peaceful valleys to reach Krumlov (Krumau), the majestic main seat of the Lords of the Rose. The German Krumau (and we are in that part of south Bohemia where Germans were settled) means 'curved meadow', and the Vltava is seen here to make a series of loops one after another. Karel Čapek has written:

> I do not know how often the Vltava winds here; before you have gone through the town of Krumlov . . . you will find that you have crossed the river about five times and each time you are amazed that it is so golden brown and that it runs so swiftly. How many inhabitants Krumlov has I cannot say, but it has forty-four inns, three churches, one castle and a large one at that, two gates and a huge quantity of monuments. Actually the whole town is one whole historical monument in itself . . . And so you find here old gables, bay windows, dormer windows, arcades, arches, alleys, pinnacles, sgrafito, frescoes, steps going up and down, balustrades, wells, pillars, kerbstones, old nooks, old timberwork, medieval rooms, passages, historic paving, crooked alleys, Christmas cribs, high roofs, a Gothic church, the Minorites and everywhere the red Rožmberk roses; wherever you turn you only see the picturesque and the ancient, and historic splendour, but in the old suburbs there are only small and low houses where you can touch the roofs with your hand, geraniums in the windows and inscriptions over the doors . . . And everything is dominated by the castle above and especially by the tower, one of the most extraordinary towers which I have seen; I might say that towers are a Czech speciality, because nowhere else do they have such remarkable cupolas, onion domes, poppy-heads, lanterns, turrets, galleries and spires, which seem to have been stuck on to the buildings. Every old town has its special tower by which one knows it.

Čapek is right when he says that Krumlov is 'one whole historical monument in itself'. It is more than that, it is a natural museum of painting, architecture, theatre and music. The castle has an enchanting rococo theatre beautifully preserved with scenery and costumes. The stage, with its illusionist scenery, offers unending vistas. But most brilliant of all is the gay and garish Masquerade Hall, the walls of which are covered with paintings of theatrical boxes and galleries peopled by masked figures from the *Commedia dell'Arte* and French comedy. The Rožmberks and their successors, the Schwarzenbergs, did much for the music as well as for the art of Bohemia. In Krumlov they had their own orchestras and this was a great impulse to the musical life of the country. It was thanks to them and other nobles like them that Charles Burney, when he travelled through Europe and came to Bohemia, could write that the Czechs were the most musical of any people he had met. Many of the old instruments from the Rožmberk orchestras are preserved today in the Music Museum in Prague.

From Krumlov—the Rožmberk bastion—the river flows direct to King Otakar's stronghold, Budějovice, passing the abbey of Zlatá Koruna (Goldenkrone), founded by the king to celebrate his victory over the Hungarians. In its church, the third largest in Bohemia, is his tomb and monument.

The Vltava then flows on to another Rožmberk castle, Hluboká (Frauenberg), which later fell into the hands of the next great feudal family, the Schwarzenbergs. The estate is packed with game of all kinds, including deer, roe deer, mufflon, wild boar and pheasants. The castle is a neo-Gothic monstrosity, born of a caprice of Princess Eleonore Schwarzenberg, who went to England in early Victorian times, and wanted to introduce the English architectural style of the period in her own estates. The beautiful Renaissance palace from the time of the Rožmberks was pulled down and the present anomaly put in its place. Tourist guides tell one that it is a 'must' for every Englishman to see, the 'Czech Windsor Castle'. An ugly mausoleum in very much the same style is to be found near a great lake. Inside is a moving memorial to Eleonore's little boy who died tragically. Some people whispered that he was the fruit of an illicit love affair between her and an Englishman and that this accounted for her passion for all things English.

I had an opportunity of spending a few nights, not actually in the castle itself, but in the annexe originally built for the servants and in my time used by guests, who were continually invited there to take part in diplomatic shoots. The first night we had a very jolly dinner in the castle, where the Czechoslovak Foreign Minister, usually rather a reserved and colourless personality, suddenly showed himself to be a true 'party man'. Gone was the extreme caution with which he had always spoken before. He taught us to drink with our left hand (which was the huntsman's way of drinking in Czechoslovakia) and various other local ways which belong to the Czech *Weidmansheil*.

After dinner I withdrew to my bedroom in the annexe. The stove had been banked up considerably and everything inside was red hot. This seemed comforting at first since the temperature was —20° outside and there was no central heating in the building. But I soon found the atmosphere stifling and was so incautious as to open the window. Then later in the night the personnel who had come from Prague to run the annexe arrived. The disturbance woke me up and I began to feel terribly cold. The stove had practically gone and the window was wide open. It took me about a quarter of an hour to pluck up courage to get out of bed, brave the Arctic temperature and shut the window. Hunters must be a tough breed but I had not brought a gun—only a camera to shoot with.

The castle green in front of Hluboká had been the scene of a real-life drama which recalled a Renaissance tragedy. After the death of King Otakar, his queen, Kunhuta, became the mistress of an ambitious Rožmberk named Záviš of Falkenstein, who later seized the regency as well as the guardianship of Otakar's son, the future King Wenceslas II. He subsequently married the queen. Young Wenceslas, brought up in a Hamlet-like situation, revolted against his step-father, the betrayer of his father and seducer of his mother, and when he came of age, gathered his forces and marched him round all the Rožmberk castles, threatening to murder him if the owner did not capitulate. Only one Rožmberk refused—the owner of Hluboká—whereupon Wenceslas immediately beheaded his stepfather on the castle green. The castle has vanished, but apart from the traditional 'White Lady', which all Czech castles have, the ghosts of two souls must haunt Hluboká, a (possibly) illegitimate child and a queen's paramour.

The 'White Lady' was Perchta (Bertha) of Rožmberk who was forced by her parents to marry a stranger instead of the lover to whom she was secretly pledged. Her final tearful parting from him in her room on the day of her wedding was violently interrupted by the entry of her bridegroom, who in his fury called the wedding ceremonies off. The marriage eventually took place, but Bertha was never forgiven by her husband, who exposed her to every kind of humiliation. She bore him two children, one of which died in

infancy, and only found happiness in widowhood. Her picture is to
be seen in every one of the Rožmberk castles; her apparition in every
castle in the country. She wears a long white dress, a white lace cap
and a golden chain. When I was sleeping alone in the Thun Palace
in Prague I hoped she would appear there. At night there was no
one living in, I was totally alone, but I never saw or heard any
ghost—not even the spectre of St Wenceslas who, against his mother's
orders, was supposed to have secretly met his confessor in one of the
underground vaults allegedly connecting the Thun Palace with the
Prague Castle. She probably did not appear because there was no
forthcoming birth, wedding, or happy occurrence, nor any death or
disaster in store, which she would indicate by wearing white or
black gloves.

Goodbye to the Vltava, which has been our lode-star up to now!
'No one has yet made music of it to the last drop. No one has yet
drawn it or written of it as it really is,' said Čapek.

Now for a few final words about another river—the Lužnice—
which is perhaps today even more beautiful because its course and
surroundings have not been disturbed by hydroelectric constructions.
The continual flooding of this river produced a lot of small lakes,
which the Rožmberks joined together in an ingenious way in the
fifteenth century and converted into a network of commercially
rewarding fishing grounds. 80,000 acres, or forty-five per cent of the
area of these fishponds, are devoted to the breeding and fishing of
carp, the Christmas fare of the Catholics throughout Central
Europe, and in Czechoslovakia as important as our turkey. Vast
fleets of lorries with special tanks carry these carp to Austria and
other neighbouring countries, or up to Prague where they are sold
in barrels on the streets.

The catching of the fish is an event to watch. The fishermen wait
several years and then go out to one of the lakes, trapping the carp
in a huge net. As the water recedes it seems to boil with the lash-
ing tails of these struggling monsters, which are often of huge size,
as I can personally attest. When I was invited with other ambassadors to attend this unique ceremony, I was told by the Czech
fishermen involved that before I could become an honorary member of their guild I must bend down and be clouted across the hind-
quarters three times by the largest carp. I accepted the conditions
and received a blow as from a granite block. They then approached
the Soviet Ambassador. He was somewhat evasive at first but when,

as acting *doyen*, I called him to order he submitted like a man. The fishermen were happy. It is not every day you can beat an ambassador across the backside—especially the Soviet Ambassador—but this at least they could do once every three years.

17. 'The Wind of Change'

When I had first called on the Foreign Office before taking up my post in Prague in 1960, I had asked if any ministerial visits were planned. I was told no, because the state of our political relations did not warrant them. I asked whether it would not be truer to say that the lack of ministerial visits helped our political relations remain as frigid as they were. It was indeed a vicious circle and I was resolved to do my best to break it. I realized I must start cautiously from the bottom—perhaps persuade the Foreign Office to send out a very junior Minister as a dove from the ark, and possibly we could then gradually work our way up to the Foreign Secretary. Everything happened as I planned, although it took me five years to accomplish it.

Among the many ministerial visits I particularly treasure the memory of that of Peter Thomas, then Minister of State in the Foreign Office and a Welshman. In planning the programme I thought it could be enriched by arranging for Slovakia to play a larger part in it. The Slovaks, like the Welsh, had their own language, culture and national aspirations. And they thought themselves to be as much under the heel of the Czechs as the Welsh under the English.

The Slovaks responded well and I received word (from secret channels of course) that they would like to have the words and music of some Welsh national songs, so that they might spring a surprise on their visitor. I obliged. At a delightful dinner with the Slovak government in Bratislava the proceedings were interrupted by the entry of gypsy players carrying double basses and churning out in funereal tempo some almost unrecognizable strains. A diplomat is, or should be, ready for every emergency and I quickly whispered to the Minister that it was 'All through the Night'. He was able to bow in grateful recognition. This was swiftly followed by a jazzed-up version of 'Men of Harlech' *ai Zingari*. Then the incredible thing happened. The whole Slovak government—or rather, its chief representatives round the table—burst into song. It was a real musical experience. But the awful sequel was that they turned to us and invited us to make *our* contribution. One Minister and two civil servants croaked forth the only song which they could all agree to sing: 'There is a tavern in the town'. This performance was followed appropriately by a round of *Yakee dars*.

The president of the Board of Trade, Lord Errol, and his wife were rewarding visitors indeed. Once after they had retired for the night, their secretary came down and confided to me that 'the Minister and Lady Errol sometimes like a glass of whisky in their room.' My old butler, Jelínek, was immediately alerted and the deed was well and truly done. A curious epilogue to this was a remark by Sir Hugh Greene, our next house guest. 'This is a wonderful place,' he said. 'Wherever I go I find that dear old man behind me, silently following me with a tumbler of whisky on a tray.'

Lord Errol got on well with the Czechs because he had decided to liberalize Czech trade with the UK from many frustrating restrictions. Czechoslovakia was the first 'Iron Curtain' country with which we did this. No more did we have to witness the terrible Levantine haggling between our Board of Trade and the Czech ministry: 'You take one hundred and fifty more of our clothes-pegs and we'll agree to buy one hundred of your mouse-traps.' The Errols stood up bravely to aggressive treatment from the Czechs—a three-pronged attack by *knedlíky* (Czech dumplings)! The menu of the official lunch he was offered read: 1. Soup *with dumplings*. 2. Roast duck *with dumplings*. 3. Plum *dumplings*. Let me assure the reader that this was a culinary triumph: Czech dumplings are not like English dumplings and there are many varieties. Whoever has been to Austria and had *Zwetschenknödel* will know what I am talking about.

We did not confine our entertaining to Ministers. We had a visit from the British trade union leader, Sir William Carron, and arranged a lunch party for him in the beautiful gardens of the Thun Palace. It was a memorable occasion.

On the table there were, as usual, tumblers of water next to the wine glasses. My Norwegian mother-in-law was staying with us at the time and my attention was suddenly drawn by my youngest son, Jasper, who whispered: 'Grannie says it's not water, but *gin*.'

It was only too true. When we were in Moscow we did not like drinking the tap water, so we boiled it and put it in the refrigerator.

We found it pure and refreshing and our guests liked it. Sir Adrian Boult, in particular, greatly appreciated it. We adopted the same custom when we came to Prague, although it was unnecessary, as the water supply there was very good.

Our maids in Moscow had used old gin bottles for storing the water and our old butler in Prague had done the same. Now, the dry Martini cocktail had struck me as rather watery and I suspected the worst: the old and new gin bottles had been mixed up. Trade unionists seldom drink water when abroad, however, and our guest had not noticed the lapse.

In 1964 Labour had replaced the Conservatives and in April the next year the Foreign Secretary, Michael Stewart, and his wife visited Prague. The primary intention of the Czechoslovak government in inviting this guest was to persuade him to pronounce the Munich agreements invalid *ab initio*—in other words, to state that we regarded them as never having existed.

Of course we could not do that. A treaty, however bad, cannot be made into a 'un-thing', as Beria in the Soviet Union was made into an 'un-person'. Of the four signatories to the treaty, France and Italy had done what the Czechs demanded. They could easily do this as they had both disavowed their past and did not need to feel bound by anything that prewar French and Fascist Italian governments had appended their names to. But in Britain one government had followed another without a break. The West German government disassociated itself from Hitler's Germany too, but the problem was that if they were totally to disavow the German signature on the treaty, it would imply that the Sudeten-Germans had never been German nationals but citizens of Czechoslovakia, which could expose them to criminal proceedings on grounds of treason for any acts they had committed when they were in fact German subjects. It would not be just for all the Sudeten-Germans *en bloc*, on top of having been expelled, to be made liable to prosecution retroactively even if the vast majority of those who had survived were no longer within reach of Communist justice.

After dinner in the drawing-room of the Thun Palace, the Foreign Secretary, his private secretary (Sir) Nicholas Henderson and I discussed how we could meet the Czech demands without compromising our principles.

The next day Stewart told the Czechoslovak Foreign Minister that the Munich agreement was detestable, unjust and dangerous to the peace of Europe, and that it was completely dead and had been so for many years. The mere historical fact that it had once been made could not justify any future claims against Czechoslovakia. When the time came for a final determination of Germany's frontiers by a peace treaty, discussion would start from the basis that the Czechoslovak frontiers were not in question. He also reminded him that the German government themselves had clearly stated that they had no claim at all to any Czechoslovak territory. He could regard propaganda or arguments from any source whatsoever suggesting that there were any claims against the frontiers of Czechoslovakia as mischievous and dangerous to the security of Europe.

The Foreign Secretary spoke well and the Czechs brightened when they heard his words. He had not gone as far as they hoped, but he had at least succeeded in removing the question from the daily agenda.

Another visiting Minister was John Stonehouse, then Parliamentary Secretary at the Ministry of Aviation, who came in September 1964 to attend the Brno Trade Fair and try to persuade the Czechoslovak government to buy some of our VC10s. He was a persuasive salesman and it was not his fault that none were purchased.

His constituency of Wednesbury had a 'twinning' arrangement with the Czech town of Kladno and I was told by the Foreign Office that he would like to visit it during his stay. Now Kladno had the reputation of being Czechoslovakia's 'reddest' city. It was always called 'the Birthplace of Socialism' and was designed in 1920 as the headquarters of a Communist republic. I had no idea whether Stonehouse was a left or right of centre, but whichever he was, I foresaw some dangers. The Czechs might use the occasion to make some propaganda against West Germany or criticize our policy— or that of our allies in NATO. I therefore telegraphed to suggest that it might be better to leave this town out. Stonehouse sent back a message to say that as MP for Wednesbury he could not possibly come to Czechoslovakia without visiting Kladno, but agreed to make the visit brief.

When we arrived together at Kladno there was no propaganda of any kind. Nothing could have been more respectable. We were ushered into a special chamber in the town hall to be welcomed by the City National Committee. At ceremonies of this kind it is usually the interpreter who plays a role out of all proportion to his position, as he is the only one who can speak the language.

When he rose to greet us, he turned first to me (which was correct since I was the Queen's representative), bowed and began '*Your Majesty* . . .'

I could scarcely keep a straight face. The correct address for an Ambassador is, of course, 'Your Excellency', but in Czechoslovakia I was often addressed by lesser dignitaries as 'Comrade Ambassador'. This seemed to be quite appropriate—after all, Ministers were addressed as 'Comrade Minister' and generals as 'Comrade General'. The only flaw was that they were all members of the Party and foreign ambassadors usually were not. More educated people would call me 'Mr Ambassador', or some even, 'Your Excellency', but 'Your Majesty' was reserved for me exclusively at 'the birthplace of Socialism'. Long live royalist, not red Kladno!

Not long before I left my post, Lord Snowdon came out to open an exhibition of industrial design and made a great success of his visit. I went with him to the exhibition and with the experienced eye of a stage director he at once saw what changes needed to be made in lighting and the positioning of the exhibits. Afterwards I took him on a hurried tour of Czechoslovakia and we rushed from theatre to theatre, seeing the first act of one play and a part of the second of another. His observant eye took in all the comic sides of the trip and afterwards when we got back to Prague he convulsed us with his take-off of some of the scenes we had encountered. He drove some of the Communist high-ups through the chilly autumn air in his (or rather Princess Margaret's) Aston Martin at a great pace. They looked like schoolboys who knew they were doing something naughty but enjoyed it.

Combining first-class technical knowledge with the 'common touch' he made an excellent impression. At the opening of the exhibition, I made a short speech in Czech which I did not bother having translated because Lord Snowdon's speech was the main event. In order to raise a laugh, I deliberately used, in various forms, a Czech verb which was difficult for an Englishman to pronounce. The Czechs roared with laughter at hearing me struggle to get out four times what was to them a quite normal word. Snowdon's speech was of course written by the Ministry and could not be anything else but routine. At the reception afterwards, when we were both standing in line, the Czechs all came up laughing and, if perhaps rather tactlessly, congratulated me on my speech.

However, fortunately the Indian Ambassador, who was a good diplomat, later came up and congratulated Snowdon profusely on

G

his speech. 'As for the Ambassador's,' he said, somewhat slightingly, 'I couldn't understand a word of it.' Snowdon shook him warmly by the hand and said: 'Mr Ambassador, you are my first real friend.'

In addition to these visits we had in one year an exhibition of British painting, an industrial exhibition, *Tools for Tomorrow*, the Royal Shakespeare Company with Paul Scofield in *King Lear* and a British Film week. I suppose that year will long live as a high-water mark in Anglo-Czech relations.

On 25 January 1965 Winston Churchill died. We opened a book in the cinema, which we decorated with flowers, and arranged for members of our staff to be there throughout the day. Many mourners came.

One day, in the lunch-time interval, when the room was not manned, I went along to stand in myself. An elderly lady came in, looking sad and frail, and I recognized her at once as Hana Beneš, the former President's wife, who has since died. Together we looked at the photographs of Churchill on the walls and she cried a little as she spoke of his kindness to her husband and herself when they were in England. It was fortunate I was there because no one else in the Embassy would have known who she was. It was a symbolic confirmation of the end of an epoch. My nine years in Czechoslovakia were nearly at an end as well.

On 11 January 1965 I had written to the Foreign Office on 'the wind of change' which had 'blown through the country from top to bottom.' I told them the story of the Czech woman who had recently told her husband: 'First I had a picture of Our Lord over the fireplace, and you told me to stuff it behind the stove and hang up a picture of Masaryk instead. Then you told me to stuff Masaryk's picture behind the stove and replace it with a picture of Stalin. Now Stalin's gone, and as there's no more room behind the stove, I'm going to put up a picture of myself, and I dare you to tell me to stuff that away.' I said that this expressed very well the refusal of the Czechs to be exploited any more and their determination to live for themselves—a feeling which was gradually permeating the whole of Czechoslovakia from top to bottom. The regime would no doubt do its best to pull the reins tighter from time to time, but I doubted whether it would have the strength or resolution to do it effectively. I said that Czechoslovakia was set on a liberal course and would pursue it unless it was deflected from it by some international calamity. It did pursue it, and was deflected.

18. Stifled at Birth

In October 1966 I gave up my post in Prague and retired from the Diplomatic Service. I had in the meantime accepted the offer of the Chair of Russian at Lancaster University and took up my duties immediately. I enlarged the scope of the department by strengthening the historical and literary side and introducing other Slav languages. In 1970 I was to transfer my Chair to a new Department of Central and South-East European Studies, which combined Czechoslovak and Yugoslav studies with non-language studies of the whole region.

My prophecies about Czechoslovakia had been sceptically, if not sarcastically, received by the Foreign Office. But even I myself had not foreseen that the wind of change would blow so soon or so strongly. In the light of what subsequently happened, I am glad that I left when I did. I should hate to have been at my post in 1968 and 1969.

A combination of economic pressures and discontent on the part of the writers, the intelligentsia and the students was to rock Novotný's position. The doomed King Vávra had said: 'We must control culture or culture will control us.' In December 1966, he reorganized the Ministry of Culture, taking it out of the hands of the more liberal Minister of Education, Jiří Hájek, and entrusting it to a safe Party watch-dog, Karel Hoffman, the former chief of Czechoslovak Radio.

At the same time attempts were being made to harass the various literary periodicals, which were the main vehicles of enlightened ideas. Films, which could compete with the west in excellence, were held up, and the 'rehabilitation' of valuable works of literature was shelved. This led, in its turn, to a counter-attack by the writers and artistic intelligentsia, which contributed significantly towards Novotný's downfall.

In 1967 I had an opportunity of visiting Czechoslovakia again. I was asked by a publisher to write a biography of Wallenstein and in the summer of that year made my first re-entry into Prague as a 'free man' to investigate whether material on Wallenstein was available.

The Czechoslovak government seemed anxious to honour me and I was accommodated in the Charles University hostel, an attractive building near the Old Town Square. My room was a spacious one and had a lovely Renaissance ceiling of painted wooden beams. It did not matter that the hostel lacked hot water and food, or that my bath had to be filled each day with buckets of water, carried up many flights of stairs. I did not even mind that no breakfast was available there, because I liked going out to have it in places I would never have visited as a diplomat.

Just before I arrived, there had been a sensational meeting of the Union of Czechoslovak Writers where the playwright Pavel Kohout had read out Solzhenitsyn's letter to the Soviet Writers' Union condemning censorship, and the Party Secretary in charge of ideology, Jiří Hendrych, had stalked out of the hall. One writer who attended the conferences told me something of the extraordinary atmosphere in which the meeting was held. In spite of courageous statements by Vaculík, Kohout, Klíma and Havel, the 'middle of the roaders' (together with some 'reformers') had moved a milk and water 'loyalist' resolution to satisfy the chair. They had also tamely acquiesced in the exclusion of the 'disobedient' writers from the Union's new Central Committee.

The dissident authors had questioned the unreserved support the regime gave to the Arabs. Some of them suggested that Israel's position was like Czechoslovakia's at the time of Munich. Some of the middle-of-the-roaders, especially those who were Jewish, had been nervous about the possible implications of discussions on the Arab-Israel issue. While agreeing with the dissidents, they were doubtful of the wisdom of bringing questions of foreign policy into the debate, especially when that implied criticism of a policy made in the Soviet Union.

At the same time, the young writer, Jan Beneš, was being tried for having sent material to *Svědectví*, an outstanding emigré journal published in Paris under the editorship of Pavel Tigrid. The outcome was that Tigrid was condemned *in absentia* to fourteen years' imprisonment. I had known him since 1945, when he shared a flat in Prague with Ota Ornest, the actor-director with whom I used to read Čapek's *Adam the Creator* when I was beginning Czech in London. I was amused by the thought that throughout the trial he was living securely in a delightful 'mini-chateau' in the environs of Paris, where I had visited him only a few months earlier. Somehow the whole case reminded me of the trial in *The Hunting of the Snark* where

> . . . the snark, with a glass in its eye,
> Dressed in gown, bands and wig was defending a pig
> On the charge of deserting its stye.
> 'Transportation for life' was the sentence it gave
> And *then* to be fined forty pounds.

But

> Their wild exultation was suddenly checked
> When the gaoler informed them, with tears
> Such a sentence would have not the slightest effect
> As the pig had been dead for some years.

In fact, the accused had not been 'dead for some years', but was very much alive. But he could have been dead, as was proved by his first words to me when, after eighteen years, I crossed the threshold of his house to see him again. He said: 'You saved my life.'

I could not recall having done anything of the kind, and assured him I could never have done so, but he insisted. 'Do you remember,' he asked, 'how in 1948 you invited me to join a delegation of journalists, who were to visit the British zone of Germany? You had asked me twice before to go on some similar trip, and each time I had cried off at the last moment. This time, you said: "You've jolly well got to go, or . . ." Well I went, and do you know what happened while I was away? Why, the Prague *coup d'état*, and they would have murdered me if they had caught me at home.'

Tigrid, who in 1948 was the editor of a very enterprising and daring anti-Communist Prague journal *Vývoj*, would unquestionably have suffered a terrible fate if he had remained in Prague. As things turned out, he was the first journalist to set foot in a free country after the *coup* and, naturally, he was a scoop for the world press.

Jan Beneš was not so lucky. He was still in the country and was sentenced to five years' imprisonment. In March 1968, he was pardoned by Novotný—one of the Czech dictator's last acts—and is now in America making a successful career as a novelist.

I was happy and relaxed during my stay. I had a field-day going

round the booksellers where, by special privilege, I was admitted to
the 'reserved' cellars and managed to lay the foundations of my own
precious library of books of 'Bohemica'. One of my most 'refreshing'
experiences was being detained by the police. On the day of my
departure, I drank two large glasses of the excellent Prague beer
and drove off in the direction of the frontier. As I approached the
hill which leads into Pilsen I coasted down with full acceleration.
(Driving in Czechoslovakia was a fairly frustrating experience. When
the road surface was good, you were held up by traffic or speed
limits. When the road was clear of traffic, the surface could be
horrible.) I was just about to overtake a small, somewhat ante-
diluvian, car ahead of me when a uniformed policeman sprang out of
a hiding place and stopped it. 'Well,' I thought, 'if he's been stopped
for speeding, I must surely be in for it too.'

Sure enough, another policeman followed and motioned me to
the side. On such occasions it is best not to know Czech, so I had
some small amusement watching the policeman thumb through a
phrasebook, which he eventually thrust under my nose. To my
amazement, I read the words: 'Na shledanou. Do vidĕnia. Auf
Wiedersehen. Do svidaniya. Adieu. So long.'

What did this mean? Was it just a grateful government giving me
a polite send-off at Pilsen? No. I was hauled out of the car, taken
behind bushes and stood in front of—horrors!—something that
looked like a medieval theodolite. I stiffened. Could it be a breath-
alyser? If so, things looked bad. Two tankards of Velké Popovice!

Presently, to my relief, he pointed to another page in the much-
thumbed book. I read in various languages: 'You have exceeded
the speed limit and are fined thirty crowns.'

I paid it on the spot with a smile of satisfaction. How grand it was
to be a normal person. This could never have happened to me as a
diplomat.

There had been sporadic student trouble when I had been *en poste*
in Prague, and I realized even then that once the Czech and Slovak
youth found an outlet, it would be difficult to contain them. Student
trouble was one of the symptoms of the general malaise which was to
sweep Novotný from his position. Unresolved complaints about un-
satisfactory conditions in their hostels led to the students' 'candle-
light' procession on 31 October 1967, which was brutally dispersed
by the police. On this occasion some 1,500 students marched to the

castle, crying 'More Light! More Light!' While ostensibly protesting against the poor lighting and heating in the hostels, they were quoting Goethe's alleged 'famous last words'.

The repercussions of the disturbances were felt until December 1967 and beyond. A resolution signed by the students said that the protests were the result of the unhealthy atmosphere in the state and stemmed from the general political and economic situation: 'We insist on our right to react to abnormal political conditions in the form of public demonstrations.'

The first inkling I had that something serious was afoot in Prague came from a Czech professor who visited us in November 1967. 'Novotný has been defeated in the Central Committee and has flown to Moscow,' he told me. 'The question is whether they will support him or not. If they don't, what will happen?'

I followed the events immediately leading to Novotný's over-throw with an excitement which was all the keener because that summer I was to be an official guest at the World Congress of Slavists in Prague. While rejoicing at the turn things had taken I remained apprehensive about Soviet reactions to the abolition of censorship and to liberal reforms. And while I admired Dubček's 'human face', I wondered whether it was wise of him to allow the 'old guard', who had acted as Soviet agents, to enjoy unrestricted liberty. I imagined that they would be in contact with the Soviet Embassy and be doing what they could to discredit him.

In the meantime, an interesting job came my way. Parts of the manuscript of Solzhenitsyn's *Cancer Ward* had reached *The Times Literary Supplement* in a Slovak version. I was asked to pronounce on its merits and translate it. It was not easy to translate a Russian author from Slovak, when one did not know the original. It was like boxing with one hand tied behind one's back. I read bits of it to Vladimir Ashkenazy, the Russian pianist, who happened to be stay-ing with us and helped me to restore something of the Russian flavour of the original. The chief organ of the Slovak Communist Party, the Bratislava *Pravda*, had intended to publish the book as a serial. Solzhenitsyn wrote them a special word of warning, asking them not to translate the title as *The Oncological Institute*. The actual title in Russian was *Rakovy Korpus*, which brought out the symbolism of the book, *korpus* meaning both a 'body' and a 'block of buildings'. The word 'ward' does not convey this.

Towards the end of 1967 the university decided to award an

honorary degree to a distinguished scholar from eastern Europe, and an invitation was sent to Professor Ota Šik. At the time this was thought of, he was known merely as a leading theoretician and economic reformer, and it was only subsequently that he achieved greater fame as one of those who were responsible for the overthrow of Novotný. Before we received a reply he had already joined the new Czechoslovak government as one of the deputy prime ministers. This gave the visit a wider dimension. In these circumstances it understandably took him some time to decide whether he could attend or not. But he very much wanted to come and no doubt succeeeded in overcoming the problems of protocol which still seemed to stand in the way of ministerial visits from Communist countries, even when some of the final vestiges of Stalinism had been shaken off.

During the days the Šiks were staying with us in our house, the Warsaw Pact manoeuvres were taking place on Czechoslovak soil, and the burning question was, would the Russians withdraw their forces once the manoeuvres were finished? It was certainly a protracted process. All this time the Šiks were extremely anxious. I bought a selection of papers for them each day so as to keep them informed and they listened intently to the news on the radio. I remember on one occasion it was reported that General Prchlík had made a statement saying that the statutes of the Warsaw Pact should be revised, to give the non-Russian member-states more say in its direction. 'Bold man!' Dr Šik commented prophetically. The General was in fact later sentenced to three years' imprisonment for that remark. It was probably thanks to him that Novotný had been unable to call on the army to maintain him in power.

Dr and Mrs Šik were excellent guests. She was not only both intelligent and attractive and looked stunning at the banquet held in honour of the graduands, but she was also a first-rate conversationalist and must most certainly have had literary gifts. When the formalities were over and they returned to our old vicarage in the evening, Dr Šik took off his dinner jacket (which he had not been used to wearing in Stalinist Czechoslovakia: the last prominent Communist to wear one was Gottwald in October 1947!) and relaxed before the fire. He had great charm, and we were captivated by his gentleness and modesty. His endearing air of apparent diffidence belied his real character, since he had shown great courage and resource when he spoke out against Novotný in the Central Committee. Their visit was one of the most rewarding events of the period of my retirement.

I do not know whether the Home Office had information that the Šiks might be kidnapped, but security measures were intense and most conspicuous. When they went for a short shopping tour in Lancaster, men in plain clothes seemed to be hanging about in all shop entrances, and at all street corners. Dr Šik was clearly not sure whose interests these mysterious but very concrete individuals were serving, and glanced at them somewhat nervously over his shoulder. No wonder!

Not long after the Šiks left, I made my preparations to go to Czechoslovakia once more. I took with me an ice-cooler, which I wanted to give the Šiks as a present. (There was nothing symbolic about it!) But by the time I arrived in Prague, they had left on a visit to Yugoslavia.

The Soviet troops were still meandering all over the country, and I feared that they might turn and march on Prague. What if the frontier were suddenly closed? I had a vague premonition that all was not going to turn out well, and I advanced the time of my arrival by a few days to make sure that I got in before any such hazard presented itself.

As I drove my car across the frontier of Czechoslovakia, I was aware of a complete change of mood. The customs officers and frontier guards were totally different men. They were courteous and all smiles. I was let through with none of the irritating delays and rudeness to which I had been accustomed during the six years that I was Ambassador. In the streets it was the same; I could see the difference when I walked behind the Praguers. They held their heads up and their gait had acquired an unwonted lilt. Postcards of Masaryk were on sale in the streets for the first time in twenty years. When had the Czechs last had reason to smile? I think it must have been long, long ago when 'Papa' Masaryk was still alive.

So much had changed in Prague that it is difficult to convey it in a short space. Everyone knows how the media liberated themselves and adopted an entirely different tone. I would cite only one episode which for me, at any rate, strikingly illustrated the different atmosphere. When I had arrived in Prague in 1960 concerts in churches were only tolerated if they were not advertised. Notices even of organ recitals were not to be found in the press or outside the churches. One had to go inside the porch of St Jacob's to find the programme pinned up on a modest sheet of paper. Although in the mid-sixties there was some relaxation, even up to the time of my departure, the Easter services were interrupted by hooligans with guitars on their backs, who had been bribed by the STB to burst in and play 'beat' at the high altar.

Now I found myself attending a much publicized concert in St Nicholas' Church, in the Malá Strana, the programme of which was devoted to Jesuit composers. The printed programme contained notes recalling some of the benefits the Jesuits had conferred on Bohemia. Up to 1968 a Jesuit had been nothing less than a bogey man. The only Jesuit one dared to mention was Balbín, who in the seventeenth century had written, but dared not publish, a defence of the Czech language and a condemnation of the effects of Habsburg rule!

I had some reservations about the way Dubček was handling the delicate situation. The period of the negotiations at Čierna nad Tisou at the end of July, where Czechs and Slovaks confronted the Soviet Presidium across a table on the Ukrainian-Slovak frontier, was particularly agonizing for us all. For the past few months the government had informed its people about all its measures, and now everything had to be enshrouded in a veil of secrecy again, because the Russians insisted on it. They even demanded that the place of the negotiations be kept dark, but this was impossible. If the Czechoslovak people had not known this at least, they would have feared the worst—that their leaders had already been carried off to Moscow. When reports of the conference reached Prague the lift man in my hotel said: 'It will never again be as good as it has been.'

I had grave misgivings when I read the text of the communiqué issued after the conference of the Warsaw Pact at Bratislava. First of all, the meeting itself represented a retreat from the Czechoslovak stand, since the government had said that they would only have bilateral meetings with the Warsaw states. Next, the wording of the agreement was so un-Czech: it was anachronistic and archaic in the existing situation in Czechoslovakia. Many Czech patriots thought that the government should have insisted on the inclusion of more of the Czechoslovak reformers' ideas in the communiqué. I shared their opinion that Dubček should not have added his name to such a document. No doubt a Soviet invasion could have followed such a rejection, but Czechoslovakia would not then have been taken by surprise and the government's position would have been a cast-iron one from the point of view of principle.

When the Slav Conference was over, I visited some parts of Bohemia connected with Wallenstein and returned to Prague on 19 August to go out for dinner the next evening with some friends. I left their house about midnight, and a few hours later, the Soviet troops were already in Prague. My hosts' house was in the firing line and I heard afterwards how they had lain down on the floor to escape the bullets and then rushed away, taking their baby with them and leaving the house just as it was when I was there, the plates and glasses still on the table—a reminder of the last hours of liberty.

I first became aware of the invasion after breakfast in my hotel, although the troops had already been in the town for some six hours. The news was broken to me by a representative of the British Aircraft Corporation who was staying at the hotel. I rushed to the nearest kiosk to buy a paper and saw that the news-vendor was in tears. 'See what they've done to us,' he cried.

At first the Soviet tanks were stationed at various points in the centre of the town, where they were the object of continuous protest and reproach by the Prague public. I listened in to some of these dialogues. 'Aren't you our allies?' one man was asking. 'Then why do you invade our country and occupy us? And what a way to do it—not like allies but like gangsters!'

The officers and men sitting on their tanks remained stiff as statues, even when addressed in their own language, which so many of the Czechs had been forced to learn under the Stalinist regime. Few answered back. Most were unsure where they were, or who the enemy was. Some of them imagined they were in Vienna. They had obviously been given the minimum explanation of the need for this campaign. After being exposed to these protesting voices hour after hour and day after day they began to wilt and look uncertain and unhappy. One Russian woman, who could have been the mother of a Soviet tank driver, reproached him volubly in Russian: 'Children, how *could* you do it? How *could* you do it?' The tank driver shuffled uncomfortably and a watery look came into his eyes. It was like a scolding voice from home.

Later the tanks were withdrawn from the town and it was just as well. They could not easily have remained there against the back-cloth of violent anti-Russian slogans with which the Wenceslas Square and the bigger streets were plastered, or in face of the demonstrations in the streets. But wave after wave of new tanks passed through Prague all night. The grinding roar, like factory transmission belts, combined with the sickly smell of naphtha nauseated me.

One of the bizarre features of the invasion was the total failure of the invaders to communicate with the population. I had already experienced one invasion—the German invasion of Norway in 1940. Unlike the situation there, no direct orders were issued over the radio and no newsheets or leaflets were printed by the occupying troops. News of curfew times was announced in the Czechoslovak broadcasts, but merely as news and not as orders. Since the inhabitants ran the risk of being shot if they broke the curfew, exact information was a matter of vital importance for everyone.

And it mattered to me too, because the good Iranian Ambassador, who was an old friend of mine, had kindly arranged a party in my honour in two days' time. If I attended it, I and the other guests might run the risk of breaking the curfew. I rang up to ask whether the party would be cancelled, but was told definitely not. It was a great mark of friendship that many of my former colleagues took the risk of coming. The Norwegian Ambassador, who was short-staffed and had to spend the whole evening manning the Embassy and listening to radio bulletins, sent his English wife instead. I was a little surprised that none of my own numerous Embassy risked it. But I cannot say how deeply moved I was by my Iranian colleague's fidelity.

I parked my car outside the Iranian Ambassador's residence, hoping that it would be safe. Just as it was getting dark and the party was breaking up I heard anxious cries from some of my colleagues outside. An ambassador rushed in and urged me to come quick, as a Soviet tank was behind my car and might easily steamroller it. I dashed out and found that it was caught up in a column of tanks led by an armoured patrol car. I leapt into it and had no alternative but to drive off in the column. It must have been an odd sight for the others to watch me leave in those daunting circumstances.

However, it turned out well. The Iranian Embassy was near the Soviet Embassy, where a lot of Soviet vehicles were congregated. It would anyhow have been difficult for me to get out on my own, caught in a Soviet column which zigzagged its way through the traffic, sometimes going over the pavement, and sometimes on the street. I soon found myself on the main road, where I could disengage and shoot off in the opposite direction. I returned to my hotel safe and sound, a great deal more rapidly than I had thought possible.

I was anxious to get home, and the only things which stopped me were uncertainty as to whether I would be allowed to cross the frontier and lack of petrol. After a few days I managed to collect enough of the latter to drive to Germany. While I was on my way through one of the villages, all the bells started ringing. It was the protest signal for a general strike. I saw no troops during the whole journey except at the frontier, where there were some from the German Democratic Republic, but these stayed at a discreet distance. The frontier was still held by Czechoslovak frontier guards, who stoutly maintained that they were in control and let me through without difficulty. I took out with me a precious cargo, books about Czechoslovakia which would soon be difficult to obtain, works of Masaryk and Beneš and of many of the 'bourgeois' historians, whose works had only become available again since Novotný's fall, but would soon disappear, even from libraries.

Soon after the invasion a news-sheet called *Zprávy* was issued and the radio transmitter, *Radio Vltava*, located in the German Democratic Republic, started to propagate the Soviet line. Some Czechs believed that both were run by East Germans under the direction of Dr Ulbricht, who had been one of those urging on the Russians the need to curb Dubček. The notorious *White Book* was published by 'A Press Group of Soviet Journalists' in Moscow to justify the aggression, and when translated into Czech, and circulated throughout the country, its Soviet origin screamed to high heaven. If no other proof of its authorship were needed, sufficient was the fact that of the countless CIA agents who, it claimed, had appeared disguised as tourists just before 21 August, the only one it could identify by name was 'S. Parrott'. My initials are C. C., and only a Russian reading these letters could see them as SS—Steamship or Storm-Trooper? When I was in Moscow I wore a hat with initials stamped in it and I often thought that, if found, it might be taken for state property, because 'CCP' is very like CCCP, which are the Russian letters for USSR. In this piece of contemptible scribble I was quoted as having written in the *Guardian* that my successors and I in Prague were informed long ago of the future 'changes of regime'. What I actually wrote in the *Guardian* of 12 April 1968 was that my *predecessors* and I in Prague reported as far back as the late fifties and the early sixties that (a) Novotný was to be deprived of the First Secretaryship of the Party, and (b) the functions of President and First Secretary would be split.

From that time on, I was classed as the counter-revolutionary *par excellence*. But what could I possibly have had to do with the so-called 'counter-revolution'? Nothing whatsoever. But the mud was to stick to me for a few years. In company with my successor I found myself cited both in Moscow *Pravda* and the Czechoslovak press as one of the villains of the piece. It did not worry me, because I knew that no true Czech would ever write anything of the kind or believe it. My sympathy for Czechs and Slovaks and my love for their culture was well known and appreciated in the only circles which mattered to me.

To have lived with the Czechs during those days of crisis and shared their spirit of defiance was an experience I shall never forget. It is hard to convey the full horror of that act of aggression: an act of an 'ally' against an ally, a Communist party against a Communist party, of four signatories to an agreement against the fifth, with the ink hardly dry on the documents which enshrined it. What was even more chilling was the way it took place. It made me realize that one day I could wake up myself to find No. 10 Downing Street, the Houses of Parliament or Buckingham Palace all occupied by Soviet parachute troops. I was profoundly impressed by the unity which reigned through the unhappy country. Seldom in history had Czechs and Slovaks been so united. There were, of course, a few traitors, but none of them at this time dared raise their voices publicly, let alone attempt to form a Quisling government. Those of us who always believed in the sterling qualities of the Czechs were amply vindicated during these valiant days.

The much-tried nation continued on its road to Calvary. One of the 'stations of the Cross' was the signing of the Treaty of 16 October (deriving from the Moscow Protocol of August) under which Czechoslovakia bound herself to the '*temporary* stationing' of Soviet troops—in fact a permanent occupation, justified only by the so-called Brezhnev doctrine.

There still seemed to be hope. The press continued to write in the same brave, defiant way. Even the liberal weeklies still appeared, though they were at times suspended. The people—especially the radio commentators and journalists—were much more spirited than their government, whom they accused of unnecessary helplessness in the face of the Russians. 'Which state is most neutral?' they asked and then went on: 'Czechoslovakia. It does not interfere, even in its own affairs.'

But I saw that it was only a matter of months before the Iron Curtain would descend again. I recalled the jokes of some fellow-travelling MPs who came to Prague after Churchill's Fulton speech in 1946. While sitting in the National Theatre, one of them pointed to the safety curtain which descended in the interval. 'At last we've found the Iron Curtain,' they jeered. 'Finally we know what it is.' It was easy to talk like that when one's life was spent in the gentlemanly comfort of the British House of Commons.

I had to go to Prague again in January 1969 to continue my researches on Wallenstein. In the autumn of 1968 the Czechoslovak Ambassador, Růžek, asked me to lunch and I took the opportunity of mentioning that I would soon be approaching him for a visa. To my surprise he said: 'Well, I must consult my government and hear their views first.'

The visa I was asking for was a tourist one, which should have been available on demand at forty-eight hours' notice, and I had only informed him as a courtesy. When he went on to say that perhaps the Czechoslovak government might not welcome my presence in Prague at that time, I thought this was going too far. I told him that what he had just said, was a very serious thing to say to an ex-Ambassador. How would he like to be told by the British Ambassador in Prague that he was not welcome in England? (After he relinquished his post he eventually did come back several times and it was never suggested that he might be unwelcome.) Laying great stress on his words Růžek then went on to claim that the invitation to Šik to come to Lancaster to receive an honorary degree had been a political act. It had made the Russians most suspicious and they had watched his movements closely. He further complained that I had not consulted him before we had issued the invitation. I explained that Šik had not been a member of the government when the university decided to invite him. As far as the university was concerned, he was a distinguished academic from Eastern Europe. When I was Ambassador in Prague, the Czechoslovak government had awarded honorary degrees to various Britons, including some Communists, and I was not only not asked to attend (a courtesy we had naturally extended to him) but only learned of the degrees from the newspapers. Růžek objected that Šik was no academic at all and no economist either. His lectures at Oxford had been laughable. We did not pursue this contentious theme and Růžek undertook to let me know about my visa, when he had had a reply from Prague.

At one moment during the meal I expressed my sympathy with the Ambassador at finding his country occupied by Soviet troops. An occupying army impaired a government's sovereignty. To my astonishment he turned deathly white, stood up stiff as a poker and said or almost shouted hysterically: 'Am I not a sovereign ambassador?' The correct answer was 'No,' but I tried to reassure him. We parted amicably—on the surface.

I suspected the reason for his outburst. In the fifties he had been an *apparatchik* in the security department of the Central Committee and had played a part, it was alleged, in the preparation of the horror trials. This was why he was one of the few ambassadors who supported the Soviet invasion. If the 1968 reforms had succeeded he would have had no future. Today he is Deputy Foreign Minister.

It so happened that I had planned to celebrate my sixtieth birthday in London with my family before leaving for Prague. The dinner was to be held on a Friday, and I had a place reserved on a Czechoslovak plane for the following Monday. By Saturday the visa had still not come.

I therefore went personally to the Embassy and said I had come to see if my visa had arrived. The porter ushered me into a room where various people were sitting, having obviously endured a long wait. I did not wish to share their vigil, so I went back to the door-keeper and said: 'I am not sure if you know who I am. My name is Parrott and I was formerly British Ambassador in Prague. Your Ambassador knows about me.' The door-keeper let me feel that he was impressed neither by my former position in Prague nor by my mention of his Ambassador's name, and motioned me back into the room. Suddenly he paused in reflection, turned on his heel and said: 'Did you say *Parrott*? Are you any relation to Honza Parrott?' 'Yes, he is my son.' 'Well, well, of course, I know him very well. Honza's father! Just think of it.' In a moment he had telephoned upstairs and persuaded the Ambassador himself to come straight down in the lift. It was not as former British Ambassador that I now deserved attention, but simply as the father of my son, who was lucky enough to be a friend of the door-keeper.

The Ambassador smiled sadly and said there was no news, and I went off, *unverrichtete Dinge*, as the Germans say—business unfinished. Now I had to go off on Monday, otherwise my whole programme would be upset, and so I decided to switch planes and leave the same day for Vienna in the hope that it might be easier to get to Prague from that city.

I seemed to have judged the situation correctly, for in a taxi from the airport to my hotel the driver offered to take me to Prague straight away. He had driven there last week, he said, and had been in Brno the day before. He had driven businessmen. 'And what about their visas?' 'They got them on the frontier,' he replied. Any business-man could get to Prague but I, a former British Ambassador, could not.

As it turned out, Tony Rumbold, our Ambassador, was away. I went immediately to the Ballplatz (the Austrian Foreign Ministry) instead and sought out a high official there who had been my good friend and former colleague in Prague. I asked him if he knew of any good reason why the Czechoslovak government should wish to prevent a former Ambassador from visiting Prague. He proceeded to call in the Head of their Eastern European Department to advise me. The latter said that he could think of no reason at all. They had not yet had a case of a former Minister of their own re-visiting Prague, but they could always try and see if my friend would like to undertake the experiment. My friend showed no particular eager-ness to oblige! How strange it was that I who, in my historical studies, had so often espoused the cause of the Czechs against Vienna, should now be seeking the advice of the Ballplatz on how to obtain legal access to Prague.

It all worked out well in the end. Another former colleague from Prague, the Canadian Ambassador, Jack McCordick, soon secured a Czechoslovak visa for me in no time and I left for Prague by the afternoon plane.

The city was bathed in sunshine, but the air was steely with frost. The atmosphere was unlike anything I have experienced before. There was, in reality, no atmosphere at all—only an airlessness and a feeling of suspense, as though the world were standing still. All the people of Prague were together with me in a goldfish bowl.

Four days earlier, the funeral had taken place of Jan Palach, the student who had threatened to set fire to himself unless censorship was abolished and the Soviet newsheet *Zprávy* banned. He had kept his word. Hundreds of thousands of people had lined the streets. It was one of the last silent demonstrations against the official Czech capitulation to Soviet demands. Two ex-government Ministers and the undaunted František Kriegl, who had had the courage to vote

in the National Assembly against the Soviet treaty, attended, and
the Rector of the Charles University delivered the oration. Somehow, with this ceremony the flame of liberty went out in Czechoslovakia. But, never fear, it will be lit again.

I went to the Ministries of Culture and Education. I found
officials there whom I still knew, though I wondered how long they
would remain. I was told that there was someone in London who
did not like me. I went to our Embassy and was at once surrounded
in the courtyard by a group of Czech staff. Having read the press
attacks on me, they never thought they would see me again. Some
took it almost as a sign of a new 'thaw' that I had turned up in
Prague. Alas! I had to disabuse them. It was no thaw. If anything,
it was the lull before the storm which was to blow away Dubček and
the last reformers, and put the clock back to 1960—if not to the years
before.

In London two years later, I was invited to give a talk on a Czech
subject at the Great Britain-East European Centre. I chose a totally
unexceptionable theme—the music of Bedřich Smetana. The
Chairman was my old friend, Sir Arthur Bliss. The Culture and
Educational Attachés from the Czechoslovak Embassy were both
present. Afterwards the latter greeted me warmly and brought me
an invitation to lunch from the Ambassador himself, Mr Žemla.

When I got back to Lancaster the next day I happened to see a
copy of the leading Czech daily *Rudé Právo*. It contained an attack
on the Foreign Office, Chatham House and its director, Sir Kenneth
Younger (who was described as an officer in the intelligence service),
the Central Office of Information, the British Council, the Great
Britain-East European Centre and its director, Sir William Harpham,
the BBC, the universities, and, last but not least, myself.

It was incredible. The article abused most of the people and
institutions—and there were not many of them—which were still
prepared to maintain and encourage relations with Czechoslovakia
under its new regime, including the Ambassador's guest-to-be at
lunch. What interests could it possibly serve?

Before the lunch, I wrote a letter of polite protest to the Ambassador. I posted it in good time so he should get it before I came.
However, when I met him he said he had not received it. I wonder
who opened it, and what happened to it?

In the course of our conversation, Mr Žemla told me that I had made a great mistake in employing emigré lecturers at Lancaster. After five years, they became quite out of touch with events at home. I replied that our lecturers had become emigrés as a result of the actions of his government, not of their own choice. I added that if our universities did not employ emigrés there would be no Czech studies, because there were hardly any suitably qualified Englishmen and his government had not provided us with any lecturers from Prague.

I mentioned our talk to a Czech emigré in London, who commented: 'We may be out of touch with events in Prague, but we know enough to be able to say that Mr Žemla was responsible for purging the Czech foreign ministry of its patriotic elements and now he has got as a reward for it the Ambassadorship in London.'

In 1973, the fiftieth anniversary of the death of Jaroslav Hašek, my translation of *The Good Soldier Švejk* was published. It was the first complete translation of that long work into English. Normally when one devotes oneself to a labour of this kind, one's efforts receive some acknowledgement in the press of the country concerned. My translation was practically ignored in Prague and the book was unobtainable in the bookshops—a subject of regret to many Czechs who love the book and read English. It was only when, a year later, the *International Herald Tribune* in Paris published a big article about it, that a brief report on the *article* (not the book) appeared in the Prague press. Czech journalists had to wait until the American capitalist press took up the book before they were allowed to mention it. Of course there were many instances of private appreciation. I learned that the organizers of an exhibition on Hašek in Prague would be grateful for two copies, so I obliged them and I received a nice bronze medallion of Hašek in return. When the Foreign Office gave an official lunch for the Czechoslovak Cultural delegation, which had come over to sign the cultural convention, I was invited to it and the host and chief guest both spoke appreciatively of the book. However, when, six months later I was in Lipnice—the place where Hašek died, and where his museum is to be found—no English translation of his book was on show. Translations into Chinese, Vietnamese, Arabic, probably even Mongolian, but not into English! I had brought a copy with me but nobody asked for it, so I took it back to Prague. I thought they might at least have put my translation on for my visit, even if they took it away immediately after I had gone. The people in charge of the museum had clearly never heard of it.

It had been an unexpected pleasure when the British Academy asked me in 1975 if I would accept their nomination to go to Czechoslovakia as part of their exchange programme. It meant I had the opportunity of spending three weeks in Prague, working on my biography of Hašek, as guest of the Czechoslovak Academy of Sciences. Some people wondered whether the Czech authorities would accept me, but I had no doubt they would, if only because to refuse a candidate nominated by our Academy might jeopardize their return nomination. The sole thing the authorities did in fact do was to cut down my visit by a week, leaving me only eleven days, but that was quite sufficient. When I arrived, I was given every facility and much enjoyed reading Hašek's letters and those of his wife in the collection housed in the beautiful Strahov monastery. It would have tickled the unmonkish Hašek to see a British ex-Ambassador studying his life in an ex-monastery. For me it was a most successful trip.

It was a superb autumn. Prague was as sun-kissed and warm as a Dalmatian summer. In spite of changes it still remained golden. Now and then I caught a glimpse of the Good Soldier Švejk—in a tram, coming out of a beerhouse, or taking his dog for an airing. There he went, 'the shabbily dressed man, going modestly on his way without bothering anyone'. As the Bible puts it: 'And so was fulfilled the prophecy of Jaroslav. "In Austrian times his name was once on the lips of all the citizens of the Kingdom of Bohemia and in the Republic his glory *will not fade*." '

EPILOGUE, 1977

Epilogue, 1977

The last word has still to be said. In September 1976, I retired from my professorship at Lancaster and devoted myself to the completion of these memoirs and my biography of Hašek. Then in January 1977 on the eve of my birthday, I heard on the BBC that I had been accused in Prague of having been a spy. This was no novelty. I had been accused of this twice already, each time when I had just enjoyed, or was about to enjoy, Czech hospitality. Why should it not occur a third time, after my having been a guest of the Czecho-slovak Academy only a little more than a year previously?

Naturally it was nonsense. Ambassadors do not spy. If they did, it would be because their Foreign Ministers had instructed them to do so. So the charge was more of an insult to Sir Alec Douglas Home, Lord Butler and Michael Stewart than to me. The last person whom an intelligence service would choose for espionage would be the Head of a Mission, because he is always in the glare of publicity and is continually shadowed in posts like Prague. If a government made its ambassador spy, it would soon get known and he would then be quite unusable in any other post. No other country would have him. If I wanted to employ a spy, the last person I would choose would be one of my *chers collègues*. They would be utterly hopeless at it, and so would I.

Later, I read a transcript of the Prague TV programme in question. The attack on my successor and myself was much more extensive and insidious than I had at first supposed. The programme, 'which owing to its topicality we have included as an extra tonight', started by telling how my successor Sir William Barker and I had come to Prague in 1945. It did not say that we had come in the normal way, he as First Secretary in the Chancery and I as Press Attaché, but half-suggested that we were disguised. For some unaccountable reason, a photograph of my wife was shown on the screen and her

Christian and maiden names were given—as if she had been a wanted criminal. Heaven knows what pictures they showed of us! Mention was made of a whole host of Czechs, none of whom I had ever heard of. After a string of innuendos about my activities in Prague from 1945 to 1948 without any facts to support them, the commentators then passed to my return there as Ambassador in 1960. My first visit was 'to Bertramka' (at the Mozart museum). It does not happen to have taken place, but what would have been wrong if it had? On the way back I am supposed to have met Josef Loewenbach, a music critic whose musical knowledge I greatly respected. According to the commentator I had 'been apparently preparing a coup with him in 1948'. With dear angelic old Pepi! Well, if I had wanted to prepare a coup, he would not have been a person I would have turned to—for Mussorgsky, yes, but not for a *putsch*. Most people will be surprised to learn that I was plotting a *coup* in 1948.* It is generally believed that the Communists were responsible. But music *was* important. 'For the time being he has a cover. He is studying the history of Mozart's stay in Prague and Czech literature.' True. I have already told about it in this book. 'He wants to write a book about Mozart's stay in Prague.' Not a book, only an article. In fact Bertramka asked me to write one. Did Bertramka come under the Czech government, or not? 'And to translate *The Good Soldier Švejk*.' Quite untrue. At that time I had never dreamed that I would do so. I only had the idea some ten years later. Then followed various snide remarks about me as 'an artist rather than a diplomat' and as a 'friend of our nation'. I am glad they admit at least that—but they don't. They display my photo and play *Eine kleine Nachtmusik* to show that my love for Mozart was just cover. They play *Auld Lang Syne*, not to show me as a lover of Burns but to symbolize my meeting up with all my old 'contacts' again.

After a description of the 'instructions' I was supposed to receive, a Mrs Semeráková was brought on to the scene—the lady in the Ministry of Culture who dealt with British affairs. During my period as Ambassador she enjoyed our hospitality countless times, as was diplomatically correct, because she was known as a loyal representa-

---

* As I describe in *The Tightrope*, during the war the Nazis accused me of plotting against Prince Paul of Yugoslavia, and the Swedish Quislings accused me of conspiring to remove King Gustav of Sweden. The Czechoslovak regime were following fitting precedents.

tive of the regime. She had made arrangements for me when I came to Prague as guest of the government.

Sometimes the broadcast was quite flattering. 'England is proud. Once again she has a strategic bridge-head in our country, more valuable than Gibraltar.' Was I the bridge-head? It's the first time I've been honoured with that title. Again: 'Parrott knows the score: he has a cheerful word, promises generous scholarships, gives out visas.' Indeed, and whom did I give the visas to? Leading Communists. When I got to Prague I discovered that almost all the leading Communist officials were on the Home Office 'Black List' as Communist agents, even including ministers. Probably that is just where they should have been, but I pointed out to London that if we wanted to increase our trade with Czechoslovakia and have more cultural relations we should have to take the leading ministers and officials off it. And this was eventually done with the result that they no longer had to wait for their visas. Yes, I did give out visas.

But by now we are in 1968. 'Hundreds of suspicious journalists arrived from England followed by the former Ambassador, Cecil Parrott. The reason for his visit? Only to say "hello" to friends.' In fact, I was there as a guest of the Czechoslovak government to attend the World Congress of Slavists, just as lots of other foreigners were there to attend that, the Congress of Geologists and other respectable gatherings.

'In the middle of August Parrott is back again.' I only came at the end of July in the first place. This hardly gives me time to go home and get my orders and 'be back again'. But once more Mrs Semeráková knows all about it, because she wanted to make accommodation arrangements for me. Now I have 'a quiet meeting with Goldstücker, the Chairman of the Writers Union. They talk for four hours. One wonders what about?' One wonders indeed, considering I never saw him then and hardly knew him. But still I have not finished. In 1971 I am organizing an emigré's congress at Reading—this in spite of the fact that, although I was asked to take part in it, I did not.

Why did the regime put on this ridiculous programme which would not take in a single intelligent Czech? Did they really believe I was a spy from 1945 to 1948 and from 1960 to 1966, and again in 1968? Of course not. Would they have accepted me as their guest in 1975 if they did? They could hardly have discovered all this about me since September 1975.

When I was in Prague in 1975, I went off on an excursion and left my camera in a restaurant. Would a spy do that? In Communist countries the way to spoil your photographs is to mislay your camera. The films will be ripped out, exposed and ruined. Not only did I get my camera back but the film in it was unspoilt. It came out well.

There is a simple explanation. The regime wanted to find a stick to beat the intellectuals with, those intellectuals of whom they are so afraid, because as this broadcast shows, their own intelligence is so very limited. I was to be a stick for them to use in belabouring brave people like the signatories to the Charter 77 Manifesto and those who might be following their patriotic example. May these modern-day Bretschneiders, of whom Hašek would have been so contemptuous if he were alive, suffer the fate of their prototype in *The Good Soldier Švejk*, and be devoured by their own police hounds!

And why did they make these derogatory remarks about my love of Czech culture? Because they are not Czech, as Czechs have understood this word throughout the centuries. Like King Vávra they say to themselves: 'We must control culture or culture will control us.' Hence their harassment of those who bravely carry on the national traditions of culture in Czechoslovakia today.

Before concluding I might have been tempted to record my personal reflections on the future of Czechoslovakia. But I shall confine myself to reiterating that the Czechs have a great capacity for survival. They survived three hundred years of 'darkness', and the Slovaks a thousand. On top of this, and more recently, both these peoples have endured another quarter of a century of repression when all hope has seemed lost. And yet they have still survived and will continue to do so. Czech culture is indestructible, and it is getting better and better known, and more highly valued, as part of our European heritage.

Let me end with a repetition of the words of Libuše, the judge, ruler and prophetess of the Czech people:

My Czech nation shall never perish.
They shall gloriously overcome the horrors of hell.

Acknowledgements

I should like to thank the Foreign and Commonwealth Office for granting me the privilege, usually accorded to retired ambassadors, of looking through my dispatches. In fact I had written the book before I saw them, having relied on my memory. Nonetheless I found it a great help to see them, because it prevented me, I hope, from getting the chronology wrong. I should like to record my appreciation of the help provided by the Librarian and his staff.

Where I have exceptionally quoted a political document I have obtained permission to do so.

Memoirs are essentially one's own work and no one else can help one very much, but I should like to pay more than a tribute to my wife, who has supported me in my work just as valiantly as she did throughout the events described in these pages.

Finally, I am deeply indebted to Giles de la Mare of Faber and Faber, who has taken so much trouble with this book as he did with its predecessor *The Tightrope* and on whose wise advice and excellent judgement I depended so much.

Index